DEADLOCK

THE INSIDE STORY OF
AMERICA'S CLOSEST ELECTION

BY THE POLITICAL STAFF OF
The Washington Post

PublicAffairs
New York

Portions of this book were originally published, in different form, in *The Washington Post*.

Book Design by Jenny Dossin.

Library of Congress Card Catalog Number: 00–135482

First PublicAffairs Edition 2001

10 9 8 7 6 5 4 3 2 1

CONTENTS

EDITORS' NOTE

This book is the collaboration of a talented and hard-working group of journalists from all over *The Washington Post* newsroom. It is based on dozens of interviews with participants in the Florida recount, including President George W. Bush, Vice President Richard B. Cheney, Sen. Joseph I. Lieberman and Florida Secretary of State Katherine Harris, lawyers and strategists for the presidential campaigns of Bush and former vice president Al Gore, and state and county officials. The interviews took place during and after the recount.

A shorter version of this narrative was published as an eight-part series in *The Post*. The book is more than twice the length of the series and provides a comprehensive account of the extraordinary events in Florida, Texas and Washington during November and December 2000.

Deadlock was written by David Von Drehle, with a prologue and epilogue by Dan Balz. They drew on their own reporting and the reporting of their colleagues:

Joel Achenbach, Mike Allen, Charles Babington, Jo Becker, David S. Broder, Ceci Connolly, Claudia Deane, Helen Dewar, Thomas B. Edsall, Dan Eggen, Juliet Eilperin, James V. Grimaldi, John F. Harris, Spencer S. Hsu, Robert G. Kaiser, Dan Keating, Serge F. Kovaleski, Howard Kurtz, Charles Lane, George Lardner Jr., Jennifer Lenhart, John Mintz, Dana Milbank, Carol Morello, Ellen Nakashima, Eric Pianin, Robert E. Pierre, Michael Powell, Sue Anne Pressley, Lois Romano, Susan Schmidt, Greg Schneider, Alan Sipress, Peter Slevin, Roberto Suro, Matthew Vita, Edward Walsh and April Witt.

Research and fact-checking were done by Alice Crites, Lynn Davis,

Madonna Lebling, Lucy Shackelford and Margot Williams. Kevin McGowan, Gabby Richards, Vince Rinehart and Tim Warren of *The Post's* National copy desk copy-edited the book. The photographs were chosen by Michel duCille and Mary Lou Foy.

And at PublicAffairs, we'd like to acknowledge the contributions of Peter Osnos, Paul Golob, Robert Kimzey and Melanie Johnstone.

LEONARD DOWNIE JR., *executive editor*
STEVE COLL, *managing editor*
BILL HAMILTON, *assistant managing editor/enterprise*

CHRONOLOGY

TUESDAY, NOVEMBER 7:

7:49–8:00 p.m. (EST) Television networks and the Associated Press declare Vice President Al Gore the winner in Florida based on exit poll projections.

10:13 p.m. Voter News Service retracts call in Florida. Television networks reverse call, saying the state is too close to call.

WEDNESDAY, NOVEMBER 8:

2:16 a.m. Fox News Channel calls Florida for Texas Gov. George W. Bush. The other networks follow.

2:30 a.m. Gore phones Bush to concede. Networks report he is trailing in Florida by 50,000 votes.

3:30 a.m. Gore phones Bush to retract concession.

Florida tally shows Bush with 2,909,135 votes, Gore with 2,907,351. Bush lead is 1,784.

A machine recount, triggered by law by a margin of less than one-half of 1 percent, begins immediately.

THURSDAY, NOVEMBER 9:

Gore campaign chairman William Daley and former secretary of state Warren Christopher hold news conference calling for a hand recount of ballots in four counties—Palm Beach, Broward, Volusia and Miami-Dade.

Palm Beach and Volusia counties agree to Gore team request for hand counts.

Friday, November 10:

The automatic recount is completed, but no official results are released.

Broward County votes to conduct sample manual recount of three precincts on Monday, November 13.

Bush and vice presidential nominee Richard B. Cheney are photographed in Austin discussing transition planning.

Gore is photographed playing touch football with his family at his home in Washington.

Associated Press survey shows Bush leading by 327 votes with all counties reporting.

Florida election officials report Bush leading by 960 votes with 66 of the state's 67 counties reporting.

Saturday, November 11:

Palm Beach County starts sample manual recount of four precincts. Bush team files request in U.S. District Court to stop the hand recounts.

Gore meets with Christopher, Daley, and his running mate, Sen. Joseph I. Lieberman, at his home for five hours.

Sunday, November 12:

Palm Beach County finishes sample manual recount. Gore nets 19 votes. The canvassing board votes to undertake a full manual recount.

Volusia County begins hand count of all 184,019 ballots.

Monday, November 13:

Broward County completes sample manual recount. Gore nets four votes. The board rejects a countywide recount.

Secretary of State Katherine Harris refuses to extend the deadline for delivery of recount results.

U.S. District Judge Donald M. Middlebrooks denies Bush request to end recount in four Florida counties.

Volusia County, joined by the Gore campaign, Palm Beach County and the Florida Democratic Party, asks Leon County Circuit Judge Terry P. Lewis to extend deadline.

TUESDAY, NOVEMBER 14:

Leon County Judge Lewis rules that counties must meet the deadline imposed by Harris, but that she may not arbitrarily rule out late returns.

Palm Beach County votes to suspend hand recount after receiving legal opinion from Florida secretary of state's office declaring that the canvassing board lacks the legal authority to manually recount ballots for the entire county.

Miami-Dade County conducts sample hand recount of three precincts. Gore nets six votes. Canvassing board votes not to proceed with full manual recount.

Harris announces the certified returns from 67 counties, showing Bush with a lead of 300 votes. She sets 2:00 p.m. Wednesday deadline for written explanation for any late returns.

WEDNESDAY, NOVEMBER 15:

Harris says she will deny requests for an extended deadline for four Florida counties and plans to certify final election results on November 18 after overseas absentee ballots are counted. Florida Supreme Court, meanwhile, denies her request to stop the hand counts.

Broward County votes to immediately begin a countywide recount after court decisions allow hand counts to continue.

Bush files appeal in 11th U.S. Circuit Court of Appeals seeking to overturn U.S. District Judge Middlebrooks' decision to continue hand counts.

Gore goes on television to offer Bush a deal: accept manual recounts in the four counties and Gore will drop the legal challenges. Bush immediately refuses, calling for the overseas ballots to be counted and added to the certified results.

THURSDAY, NOVEMBER 16:

Florida Supreme Court rules manual recounts can continue, but does not say whether Harris must include them in certified results.

Broward County continues and Palm Beach County begins full recount.

FRIDAY, NOVEMBER 17:

Leon County Judge Lewis upholds Harris's decision to exclude manually recounted ballots.

Florida Supreme Court orders Harris not to certify election results until it hears arguments in the case.

11th U.S. Circuit Court of Appeals rejects Bush request to end recounts.

Miami-Dade County canvassing board votes to conduct a full recount, reversing Tuesday decision.

SATURDAY, NOVEMBER 18:

Overseas ballots are counted. Bush lead grows to 930 votes. Bush forces accuse Democrats of targeting military votes for disqualification, and they attack manual recounts as arbitrary and without standards.

Palm Beach and Broward counties continue hand recounts, and Miami-Dade County schedules one to begin Monday.

Gore lawyers file briefs urging Florida Supreme Court to allow recounts to proceed and to require that the results be included in the final state tally.

SUNDAY, NOVEMBER 19:

Sen. Lieberman, on morning talk shows, disavows efforts to challenge overseas ballots and urges Florida election officials "to go back and take another look" at disqualified ballots from military personnel.

MONDAY, NOVEMBER 20:

Florida Supreme Court hears arguments from Gore and Bush lawyers on whether manual recounts should be included in final vote totals.

Miami-Dade County begins its recount.

TUESDAY, NOVEMBER 21:

Florida Supreme Court rules unanimously that hand-recounted votes can be accepted by the state for five more days, setting a November 26 deadline.

WEDNESDAY, NOVEMBER 22:

Bush says Florida Supreme Court tried to "usurp" the authority of Florida's election officials, and asks U.S. Supreme Court to review its ruling that hand recounts can go forward.

Miami-Dade County votes to halt the recount, citing tight November 26 deadline.

In Washington, Cheney suffers mild heart attack.

Bush goes to state court seeking recount of overseas ballots in 13 counties.

THURSDAY, NOVEMBER 23:

Florida Supreme Court refuses to order Miami-Dade County to resume hand-counting.

Gore's lawyers urge U.S. Supreme Court not to hear George W. Bush's request to have the recounts declared unconstitutional.

Broward County begins reviewing disputed ballots. GOP objects to the standard used.

Palm Beach County suspends the count for Thanksgiving holiday.

FRIDAY, NOVEMBER 24:

U.S. Supreme Court agrees to hear Bush challenge to the Florida Supreme Court's hand recount decision.

Four counties reconsider absentee ballots. Bush nets 24 votes.

Nassau County decides to use Election Day ballot numbers. Bush nets 52 votes.

SATURDAY, NOVEMBER 25:

Broward finishes recount. Gore nets 567 additional votes.

SUNDAY, NOVEMBER 26:

Palm Beach misses 5 p.m. deadline for completing recount and Harris rejects its request for an extension. She certifies Bush the winner of Florida's 25 electoral votes at 7:30 p.m. Recount shows him leading by 537 votes.

Bush goes on television and claims victory in Florida and in the election.

MONDAY, NOVEMBER 27:

Gore files lawsuit in Leon County Circuit Court contesting results in Florida, alleging thousands of ballots in three counties that were not counted cost him the election. Lawsuit asks Leon Circuit Court Judge N. Sanders Sauls to recount the disputed ballots.

Gore delivers nationally televised speech asking the nation for patience while the courts determine who won the most votes.

TUESDAY, NOVEMBER 28:

Leon County Judge Sauls begins hearing on Gore contest. Sauls rejects request for an immediate count of 14,000 disputed ballots, but orders that they be delivered to the court for examination.

WEDNESDAY, NOVEMBER 29:

Bush transition team opens office in McLean, Va.

Leon County Judge Sauls expands his order for ballots to include the more than one million ballots cast in Palm Beach and Miami-Dade counties.

THURSDAY, NOVEMBER 30:

Florida legislative panel recommends that a special session be called to name presidential electors.

Gore attorneys asks Florida Supreme Court to order an immediate hand count of contested ballots in Palm Beach and Miami-Dade.

Palm Beach County sends half a million ballots to Tallahassee in a Ryder truck, with police escort.

FRIDAY, DECEMBER 1:

U.S. Supreme Court hears arguments on Bush appeal of the Florida Supreme Court ruling authorizing recounts.

Florida Supreme Court rejects Gore request for immediate recount of disputed ballots. The court also rejects request for new election in Palm Beach to remedy use of "butterfly" ballots.

Miami-Dade County sends 650,000 ballots by truck to Tallahassee.

SATURDAY, DECEMBER 2:

Leon County Judge Sauls hears testimony on whether 14,000 disputed ballots from Miami-Dade and Palm Beach counties should be recounted.

Bush meets at Texas ranch with Senate Majority Leader Trent Lott and House Speaker J. Dennis Hastert to discuss the economy.

SUNDAY, DECEMBER 3:

Bush and Gore team lawyers give closing arguments before Leon County Judge Sauls in Gore's contest lawsuit.

MONDAY, DECEMBER 4:

U.S. Supreme Court sets aside the Florida Supreme Court's November 21 decision to extend deadlines and include hand recounts, sending it back to the court for clarification.

Leon County Judge Sauls says there is no "credible" evidence that recounts would change the outcome of the election and refuses to overturn the certification of Bush as winner in Florida. Gore's legal advisers immediately appeal the decision.

TUESDAY, DECEMBER 5:

11th U.S. Circuit Court of Appeals hears oral argument on Bush's effort to have the manual recounts declared unconstitutional.

WEDNESDAY, DECEMBER 6:

11th U.S. Circuit Court of Appeals refuses to throw out manual recounts of ballots completed in three Florida counties.

THURSDAY, DECEMBER 7:

Florida Supreme Court hears Gore's appeal of Leon County Judge Sauls's decision rejecting manual recount and upholding certification of Bush as winner.

FRIDAY, DECEMBER 8:

Leon County Circuit Court Judges Nikki Clark and Terry Lewis refuse to disqualify 25,000 absentee ballots in Seminole and Martin counties.

Florida Supreme Court, in 4 to 3 vote, overrules Leon County Judge Sauls, and orders immediate statewide manual recount. Court also rules that 383 votes tabulated earlier should be added to Gore's total. Bush's lead is reduced to 154.

Bush team immediately appeals Florida Supreme Court decision to the U.S. Supreme Court.

Leon County Circuit Judge Lewis begins overseeing the new recounts. He sets target of 2 p.m. Sunday to finish.

Florida legislature begins special session to appoint 25 Bush electors.

SATURDAY, DECEMBER 9:

Counting begins of 43,000 statewide "undervotes," but stops when U.S. Supreme Court, in 5 to 4 decision, grants Bush request for a stay and schedules hearing for Monday.

SUNDAY, DECEMBER 10:

Attorneys for Gore and Bush file briefs to U.S. Supreme Court.

MONDAY, DECEMBER 11:

Attorneys for Gore and Bush argue their cases before the U.S. Supreme Court.

Two key committees in Florida's Republican-controlled legislature vote to name their own slate of 25 Bush electors.

TUESDAY, DECEMBER 12:

Florida House approves resolution authorizing a slate of Bush electors.

Florida Supreme Court upholds two Leon County Circuit Court rulings rejecting requests to disqualify 25,000 absentee ballots in Seminole and Martin counties.

U.S. Supreme Court, in 5 to 4 decision, overturns the Florida Supreme Court decision allowing continued manual recounts across the state and says there is no time to create a new standard for counting.

WEDNESDAY, DECEMBER 13:

9 p.m. Gore concedes election.

10 p.m. Bush claims victory and calls for national unity.

DEADLOCK

On the campaign trail in Florida: Vice President Al Gore addresses a crowd of supporters in Tampa (above) and Texas Gov. George W. Bush talks to a group of senior citizens in Sun City Center.

(Rich Lipski / The Washington Post; AFP Photo / Tannen Maury)

PROLOGUE

■

The Road to Deadlock

Before dawn on Monday, October 23, William Daley, chairman of Vice President Al Gore's presidential campaign, reached for the phone in his Nashville hotel room to dial Stan Greenberg, one of the campaign's pollsters. Election Day was two weeks away and Daley was worried.

Gore's advisers had expected the polls to move in the vice president's direction after the third presidential debate the previous week. Instead, the polls had not budged. Over the weekend, those in Gore's campaign had worked to tamp down perceptions in the press that the race was slipping away, but privately they were concerned. Like others in the campaign, Daley nervously awaited the results of Greenberg's overnight numbers.

"How does it look?" Daley asked Greenberg, who was bunking in the same hotel.

"No change," Greenberg replied.

The pollster's national numbers still showed the race virtually even. The campaign's state-by-state tracking showed the race just as tight. At Gore headquarters, then, the final two weeks of the campaign began on a hopeful note. Despite all his problems, Gore was still in the hunt.

On that same October morning, the mood was brighter at the Austin headquarters of Texas Gov. George W. Bush. The Bush campaign had just launched new ads in Minneapolis-St. Paul, the last step in a weeks-long stealth campaign to steal traditionally Democratic

Minnesota. Chief strategist Karl Rove was preparing to recommend the expenditure of millions of dollars for ads in two other Democratic strongholds, Illinois and California.

The campaign's internal analysis put the Texas governor up five points nationally and leading in states that added up to 312 electoral votes. The campaign's overnight tracking showed Bush ahead—from a point or two to as many as seven—in the key battlegrounds: Ohio, Pennsylvania, Michigan, Missouri, Wisconsin, Washington and, most important of all, in Florida, where Gore was making a huge push.

Polling director Matthew Dowd wandered into Rove's office that afternoon to report that, despite a big boost in advertising by the opposition, the Republicans were outspending the Democrats in every important market. Rove chortled. "I love it when it's a resource war and we've got more resources," he said.

■

In the year 2000, George W. Bush and Albert Gore Jr. fought the longest and most expensive presidential campaign in the history of the country. In the end, after a 36-day post-election battle in Florida that eclipsed the campaign itself for drama and raw partisanship, the 43rd president of the United States was determined by a bitterly divided U.S. Supreme Court late on a cold December night.

The Florida deadlock capped a decade of neck-and-neck political competition. If the 1990s had proved anything, it was that Democrats and Republicans were at parity in national politics. In 1992, Democrats recaptured the White House after a 12-year absence. Two years later, Republicans took control of the House and Senate, pushing Democrats into the minority in the House for the first time in 40 years. But in 1996 President Clinton easily won reelection, the first Democrat since Franklin D. Roosevelt to win consecutive terms. Then in 1998 came Monica Lewinsky and the partisan upheaval of the first impeachment proceedings in more than a century.

The 2000 campaign offered the possibility of an election that finally would resolve the impasse, an election that might signal clearly which party the voters trusted more and why. It didn't turn out that way.

If not the most charismatic candidates ever to run for president, George W. Bush and Al Gore nonetheless battled over big issues— how to educate America's children, how to ensure retirement security for current and future generations, how to sustain economic prosperity, how to define America's role as the world's lone superpower. They were as well matched politically as they were different personally, and from the beginning of the general election campaign in the spring of 2000 to the campaign's final weeks, neither could gain a significant advantage. Their race sprawled from one coast to the other, and as Election Day neared, states that had not been competitive in recent elections suddenly became crucial to the outcome. What happened in Florida is the focus of this book, but how the two sides ended up there is an important prelude.

■

The two campaigns anticipated a showdown in Florida long before most of the political world awoke to the state's significance.

A prevailing assumption had been that Florida was safe for Bush. Over the previous 10 elections, Florida had backed the Republican nominee seven times. And Bush's brother, Jeb, was the governor, with a proven campaign apparatus ready to try to deliver the state.

Despite those factors, neither side believed Florida was locked up for Bush. When Bush's strategists in Austin first mapped out the race in July 1999, mindful that Clinton had carried the state in 1996, Florida was not among those included in the list of Republican base states. Gore's advisers—with strategists Tad Devine and Michael Whouley the most insistent—circled the state as an opportunity for the Democrats even before the primaries were ending.

Changing demographics—the growing number of non-Cuban Hispanics, for example—made the state more attractive to Democrats.

And feelings about issues at the center of the campaign debate, such as Social Security and prescription drug benefits for seniors, seemed to break in the vice president's favor among the large elderly population. Devine believed Florida's elderly had undergone an important transformation politically in the late 1990s. For years, retirees, drawn by the lack of a state income tax, had powered the Republican gains in state races. But with the GOP takeover of Congress in 1994 and subsequent battles over the future of Social Security and Medicare, those voters began to look to Democrats in Washington to protect their retirement security.

The Gore campaign strategy was anchored on a four-cornered electoral map built around key swing states: Pennsylvania, Michigan, Ohio and Florida. Gore's senior strategists considered Pennsylvania and Michigan must-wins for the vice president. But they also believed that a victory in Ohio or Florida would stop Bush. In the late spring, Gore's campaign began advertising in some of the swing media markets in Florida: Tampa, Orlando and Palm Beach. The move was seen as a huge gamble, a potential waste of precious resources against an opponent with the deepest pockets ever seen in a presidential campaign. But the Gore campaign's internal research showed that the advertising was working. In a sign of the GOP's concern, Bush went up with his own ads statewide just before the Republican convention. The battle was joined.

■

Both were sons of politically powerful fathers. Gore's father was a senator from Tennessee who had raised his son to be president. Bush's father was himself the son of a senator, and George Bush had served in the House, as chairman of the Republican Party, as envoy to China and director of the CIA, as Ronald Reagan's vice president and as the 41st president of the United States.

Both grew up amid privilege. Gore was raised in a hotel near Washington's Embassy Row and spent summers at the family farm in

Tennessee. He attended the prestigious St. Albans School in Washington before heading off to college at Harvard. Bush spent his boyhood in Midland, an oil town in west Texas, but as befits the offspring of a wealthy, establishment Yankee family, attended prep school at Phillips Academy in Andover, Massachusetts, before going to college at Yale and business school at Harvard. Both men were on the front edge of the baby boom generation and attended college during the tumultuous 1960s. Gore participated in anti-war activities and experimented with drugs. Bush was content in the environment of fraternity life.

After college, Gore enlisted in the Army and went to Vietnam as a military journalist. He returned to a brief career in journalism and soon entered politics. He was elected to the House in 1976 and to the Senate in 1984, and sought the presidency in 1988, when he was just 40. He wrote a best-selling book about the environment and chose to sit out the 1992 presidential campaign, but that year he was tapped as Clinton's running mate. Together they formed a national ticket that broke the mold of presidential politics: two men of the same generation, the same region and the same wing of the party who seemed to agree politically on almost everything.

After Yale, Bush joined the Texas Air National Guard, flew jets and remained stateside. He ran unsuccessfully for the House from Midland in 1978, then returned to the oil business. He was not a great success. By the time he reached age 40, the most notable thing about his life seemed to be the decision on that birthday to give up drinking—at the urging of his wife, Laura—and try to turn his life around. In 1988, when Gore was seeking the presidency for himself, Bush was working in his father's campaign.

He developed a reputation for a quick temper and fierce loyalty to the family's honor. No one in those days would have predicted that Bush would blossom into a successful politician. With his father in the White House, Bush helped put together a group of investors to buy the Texas Rangers baseball team, then pushed through (with the help of the state) construction of a new stadium. But he had been

mulling a return to politics for some time, and in 1994 he challenged
the popular incumbent governor, Ann Richards. Against the odds, although aided by the Republican tide running across the country, he
won by a surprisingly comfortable margin.

What made a Bush-Gore race even more intriguing was the under-
current of revenge that came with it, for it was Gore, with Clinton,
who drove the elder Bush from the White House in 1992. The former
president harbored some bitterness after that race and never thought
he got a fair shake from the news media during the campaign. His
supporters were even more embittered. The dream of restoring a Bush
to the White House to compensate for the pain of 1992 animated
these Bush Republicans in the formative months of the 2000 campaign.

In the fall of 1998, as he cruised toward reelection as governor of
Texas, Bush already could feel the currents pulling him into the presidential race. Not that he was reluctant. But he marveled at what was
happening. Over dinner at the governor's mansion in Austin one
night that October, Bush remarked to two visitors, "I feel like a cork
in a raging river." All things being equal, Bush might have preferred
to wait until 2004 to run for president. By then, he would have completed two terms as governor, his daughters would have been finishing college and he would have had more time to broaden his
horizons. But few politicians get to pick their moment, and what
Bush was reflecting that night was his understanding that events were
conspiring to make 2000 his.

That was because the Republican Party began the 2000 cycle without a true national leader and with the congressional wing of the
party—which had dominated the GOP since coming to power in
1994—in disrepute. On the day Bush won reelection in Texas in 1998
with 69 percent of the vote, House Republicans lost seats. Within
days, Newt Gingrich stunned the party by announcing that he would
not seek another term as speaker of the House.

The GOP establishment, concerned that the party was seen as too conservative, too mean-spirited and hostile to minorities, was desperate for a different face to project to the country. They found it in Bush and his brother, Jeb, newly elected as governor of Florida. The Bush brothers were youthful and attractive. They preached the politics of inclusion and the doctrine of compassionate conservatism, and had proven they were capable of winning votes among Latinos and, to a more limited extent, African Americans. George W. Bush was able to consolidate his position so quickly in part because of the early and near unanimous support he received from Republican governors. The governors had rallied behind Robert J. Dole in 1996, but in their minds, Dole never quite understood their point of view about governing.

The Republican field of presidential candidates eventually would include a former vice president, the first serious female candidate for president in the party's history, a former two-term governor who had served as a Republican Cabinet officer and a distinguished senator with a compelling personal story as a former Vietnam POW. Nevertheless, Bush surged to the top of the polls on the strength of his name and the Republican establishment's fear of the future.

Al Gore's loyalty to Bill Clinton during the impeachment year would bring him serious political problems in the general election, but at the start-up phase of the presidential race, it proved a clear blessing. Republican efforts to launch impeachment proceedings against the president rallied Democrats to a show of unity unprecedented during Clinton's presidency. Gore faced a potentially crowded field of opponents in the battle for the Democratic nomination. House Democratic leader Richard A. Gephardt was mulling a race, as was Nebraska Sen. Bob Kerrey.

But Gore's potential opponents could read the polls and run the calculations of what they meant. Clinton was an enormously popular figure within his own party. He had repaid the loyalty from the party's base—which plays a dominant role in the nominating process—with a policy agenda that tilted more to the left than at earlier stages of his presidency. Given the unity within the party at the end of 1998, it would prove impossible to mount a successful challenge to Clinton's vice president.

■

Throughout the 2000 campaign, there was always more optimism in Austin than in Nashville. Internal polls in both camps always pointed to a competitive election, but as the election neared the numbers were consistently stronger for the Republican nominee than were those for Gore.

With less than two weeks to go, the Bush camp aimed to expand the electoral map. It was a strategic gamble designed in part to stretch the Democrats' resources to the limit, but also an expression of confidence that the race could break Bush's way at the end.

By October 25 the Bush team was focused as much on long shots as on the state of Florida. On that day, Rove pulled the trigger on a $1 million-a-week advertising buy in California and a big investment in ads in Illinois. The advertising supplemented about $2 million in ads running weekly, financed by the Republican National Committee. Even the candidate believed he had a shot of winning California if the vote broke his way the final weekend. As for Illinois, the Bush camp had made a strategic decision earlier in the fall to pull down its ads in Chicago after research showed that Bush did better in the crucial suburbs in the absence of an advertising war there. The campaign continued to buy downstate markets that reached into Iowa and Kentucky, and Rove always planned a final-weeks blitz in Chicago, in hopes of catching the Democrats off-guard.

All of this reflected the Bush team's belief that undecided voters could be moved at the end of the campaign by the appearance of momentum—what Rove called "the bandwagon effect." Toward the end of the campaign, the Bush team had added a question to the Battleground 2000 tracking poll: Who do you think will win the election? As of October 25, Bush was ahead of Gore by 13 percentage points.

"Gore was up 12 at the end of September," said Matthew Dowd. "Now we're up 13. It's moved dramatically to us. That question is a very important question."

In late October, Gore strategists Tad Devine, Bob Shrum and Stan Greenberg reviewed their strategy during lunch at one of their favorite Nashville haunts, the Mad Platter restaurant. They worried about the race's overall shape.

Overwhelming numbers of voters "think the country's going in the right direction and it's been rising in the last three, four or five days," Greenberg said. "But we carry a lot of baggage into this stage that is making it hard for us to close the deal, which includes the trust issues that are heavily the result of the Clinton period."

There were other problems but that one loomed largest. "They're trying to goad us into running as 'Clinton-Gore,'" Greenberg said. To which Devine added, "That's not a campaign we think we can win."

On Halloween, Devine was in an ebullient mood. "We're rocking and rolling," he told a caller. The morning had brought good news in the overnight tracking. Minnesota was done and Illinois looked solid, despite the late efforts by Bush. Gore was up four in Michigan, up three in Pennsylvania. At lunch, Devine had told Daley and others that, if the tracking also showed Gore ahead in Florida, he planned to fly home to go trick-or-treating with his kids.

The Bush camp was equally upbeat that day. The Midwest looked increasingly solid, with internal tracking still showing Bush up in Ohio, Michigan, Wisconsin and Missouri. Florida had ticked up. "It's 300-plus [electoral votes] if the election were held today," Dowd said.

In Nashville, members of the Gore team were puzzled by Bush's ad blitz in California. Private polling showed Gore up nine points there, despite not advertising. Bush's decision to devote a day of campaigning in California was even more baffling. "They would have been better to flop their asses in Florida," Daley said.

Most of the battleground states remained close, but the confusing electoral map had begun to clarify itself, which prompted Gore to make some tough decisions. Asked about Gore's home state of Tennessee, Greenberg said, "It's not on my list" of likely wins. West Virginia was another problem. The state had not voted for a Republican nominee since 1984 but early in the fall Gore's tracking showed the vice president in solid shape, prompting a decision to stop advertising there. Now Bush was gaining strength and the state was closer than the Democrats wished. "I'd worry more about West Virginia because so many things are piling up there," Greenberg said. "But it's not that many electoral votes." A week later, the Gore team would have killed to have either state.

That afternoon, Daley related his latest theory of the race. He wasn't buying into the bandwagon theory. "This is not going to break for somebody like we traditionally think it will," he said. "This is going to stay like this. It's never going to get outside the margin of error. The odds are we're going to be sitting here Tuesday [Election Day], saying we feel good about Florida or Pennsylvania."

At 6 p.m., Devine was in a cab heading back to the headquarters from the Nashville airport. The Florida tracking had come in a few hours earlier with Gore ahead. "That's all I needed to know," he said. With the three key states leaning to Gore, Devine had jumped in a car to catch a flight home, only to run into a four-hour delay because of an air traffic control breakdown. Devine was very disappointed. "My daughter carved a pumpkin in the shape of Gore 2000," he reported proudly.

■

In a year in which voters seemed only mildly interested in the presidential race, both campaigns recognized that the key to victory likely would lie in the mobilization of their bases of core, active supporters. Their campaigns and their messages put maximum effort into energizing party loyalists rather than reaching out to swing voters.

Bush started the race determined, as his aides so often put it, to be "a different kind of Republican." That implied that Bush would attempt to do what Clinton had done eight years earlier when he ran for president as a New Democrat who challenged liberal orthodoxy in an attempt to move the Democratic Party toward the center. But Bush's effort to cast himself as a different kind of Republican manifested itself more in style than in substance. He was a leader who reflected the power and sensibilities of the Republican governors, and his ideology was less hard-edged than that of some Washington-based conservatives.

Like other governors, he could be pragmatic and results-oriented. But his strategy was less aimed at moving his party to the center and more at softening the party's sharp conservative edges. Bush shrank from challenging the party's conservative wing. Instead, he carefully hewed to conservative orthodoxy, whether on abortion, school vouchers or across-the-board tax cuts. On a few occasions early in his campaign, he appeared to take shots at the Republican majority in Congress, in one case warning the leadership not to attempt to balance the budget on the backs of the poor. But when questioned about his intentions, he quickly pulled back. While he deftly avoided Democratic efforts to hold him responsible for congressional actions, he was just as artful in remaining quietly supportive of congressional Republicans.

Education was one area in which Bush broke with his own party, as he sketched out a stronger role for the federal government in testing, standards and accountability. That represented a departure from Republican doctrine of a few years earlier that called for the elimination of the Department of Education. But long before Bush entered the presidential campaign, Republicans had abandoned the fight to close down the department. Bush's policy prescriptions reflected an emerging consensus even among many conservatives that the party had to define a federal role in education to remain politically viable. Still, Bush's advisers saw education as their version of Clinton's pledge to "end welfare as we know it" in 1992; it was a way to convey that he was different.

Bush was always mindful not just of protecting his conservative flank but cementing relationships with the right. He built ties with leaders of grassroots conservative groups and embraced a massive tax cut. After Arizona Sen. John McCain soundly defeated him in the

New Hampshire primary, Bush moved even more aggressively to rally support from the conservative wing of the party, from the National Rifle Association to the National Right to Life Committee. Those on the GOP right tolerated his efforts to cast himself as a different, more inclusive kind of Republican, confident that on key issues he agreed with them. His advisers believed that there was perhaps no more important strategic goal than maintaining a united Republican Party, including the avid support of conservatives. During the fall campaign, Bush sounded more and more like a conventional Republican. He adamantly defended his big tax cuts and ripped Gore as an advocate of big government.

Gore's emergence as a populist fighter was equally interesting. Throughout the 1980s, he was one of the "New Democrats," active in the Democratic Leadership Council. With Clinton helping the Democrats redefine their positions on domestic issues, Gore became a leader in helping to redefine the party's stance on defense and foreign policy issues. As a senator, Gore nudged the Democrats to put the Vietnam syndrome behind them, prodding his party to embrace the use of military force abroad when necessary. He helped work out a compromise plan on the MX missile during Reagan's presidency and was one of a handful of Democrats who backed the resolution supporting the war in the Persian Gulf in 1991. When he was tapped as Clinton's vice president, the choice seemed to ratify the takeover of the party by the New Democrats.

Institutionally, the Democrats had competing wings: organized labor and other traditional Democrats on the left, the New Democrats and their business friends on the right. In presidential nomination fights, the left had more resources and more troops. That forced Gore to embrace the left to secure his nomination. Challenged by Bill Bradley in the primaries, Gore built his campaign around support from the party's traditional constituencies, particularly labor and minorities. Those groups were most supportive of Clinton during impeachment and came to Gore's rescue in the early primaries after Bradley's campaign initially gained momentum. Gore struggled

throughout the general election to meld his New Democrat background with his new populist stance. He tried to mix centrist policies
with the rhetoric of class warfare. Bashing big corporations, particularly the oil industry, pharmaceuticals and insurance companies, Gore
said his was a fight for the people against the powerful.

Certainly Gore's message was more nuanced than that of an old-
fashioned liberal. He talked about using the surpluses to pay down
the federal debt. Like Bush and Clinton, he supported the death
penalty. He, too, was a free trader—although with enough qualifica-
tions to satisfy his labor constituency. But if he was the beneficiary of
the party's post-impeachment unity during the primaries, he was a
prisoner of it during the general election. In a contest in which mobilization of the base counted most, Gore tilted his appeal to the left,
leaving himself vulnerable to Bush's contention that he would expand
government far more than Clinton ever tried. Gore's friends in the
New Democrat movement tried to defend his apparent shift to the
left, but privately they just shook their heads in frustration.

During the primaries, McCain—and, to a lesser extent, Bradley—
showed the hunger among many independent or swing voters for a
message that went beyond Republican or Democratic orthodoxy.
Still, neither Bush nor Gore was prepared to risk offending his base to
make a genuine effort to reach out to those voters. The general election became a test of both candidates' ability to mobilize their most
loyal troops, not of their ability to expand the electorate.

■

In both campaigns, strategists fought conflicting emotions as they
measured the daily movements in the polls and reacted, shifting resources by a process that combined careful research with gut instinct.
In Austin, Dowd listened to Christmas music in his office to stay
calm. He kept nearby a line Yeats once wrote about his countrymen:
"The Irishman has an abiding sense of tragedy which sustains him
through temporary periods of joy." Michael Whouley, the Boston pro

who masterminded Gore's ground operation, matched dark humor with absolute conviction that his candidate would win. Gore had always struggled in the campaign, he acknowledged, but had always somehow managed to win when it counted. "We will win," he predicted, "but we'll win ugly."

By the final weekend, the two campaigns were staring at two different races. In state after state, Bush's tracking contradicted Gore's. In Michigan, Bush had it 42–38 Bush, while Gore saw it 47–45 Gore. Bush's team had Washington at 46–42 for the Texas governor; Gore's tracking showed it 43–39 for the vice president. Bush led in New Mexico in his tracking; Gore was ahead there in his. Both campaigns showed Iowa even and both had Bush trailing in Pennsylvania. But in Florida, they were far apart: Bush's polling showed the Texas governor ahead 47–42, while Gore's tracking had the vice president ahead 48–45.

As Devine reviewed the money both campaigns were spending in Florida that week, he marveled, "Money's raining out of the sky. They're [the Bush team] enormously concerned about the outcome." He added, "My view of this race, as it has been for many months, is that Pennsylvania and Michigan are the linchpins for us. Either Ohio or Florida could effectively deny them the election and now Florida is our best bet."

When Devine got the numbers on the Friday before the election, he grew more optimistic. Bush's favorable rating was declining. "It's really improving for us," he said.

In Austin, Dowd remained equally hopeful about Florida. "We'll carry it but it will be close," he said.

The Bush campaign approached Election Day still confident, although there was a late development that caused concern. On the Thursday night before the election, Bush confirmed news reports that he had been convicted of driving under the influence of alcohol 24 years earlier. Both campaigns attempted to measure the impact, and their first impressions were that the episode likely would have little effect on the outcome.

Bush had sensed victory on the campaign trail during the final weeks. He had told Wisconsin Gov. Tommy Thompson earlier in October, "I'll be the most surprised man in America if I don't win." Ten days before the election, heading into Wisconsin for a morning rally, he exuded confidence. He would win Michigan, he believed, and predicted he also would win Tennessee. He was nervous about Pennsylvania—the Philadelphia suburbs were still a problem. And Florida? Bush said he would win there, too.

On the day before the election, strategists in both campaigns focused on how to turn out their supporters. Republicans long had held the advantage in getting their supporters to the polls, in part because better-educated or more affluent Americans vote in greater numbers. But starting in 1996 the Democrats—aided by allies in organized labor and other constituencies—demonstrated that they were equal to, if not better than, the Republicans in the ground war. "I will be very surprised if we don't win this and it will be a reflection of turnout intensity," Dowd said. "For them to win, their turnout intensity has to be higher than our turnout intensity, and I just don't see that."

They wouldn't see it until the next day. Whouley had recruited an all-star cast of Democrats to oversee the ground war in battleground states. "The level of the program is the biggest it's ever been," he said. "I think it's going to pay off tomorrow."

On the night before the election, he shared his predictions with uncanny accuracy. He picked every Gore state correctly with one exception: He predicted a victory in Florida.

On Election Day, Bill Daley was making a round of telephone calls to prominent Democrats across the country. One was to House Democratic leader Gephardt in St. Louis. Among the questions Daley asked was one for advice on how the Gore campaign should handle what he thought might be a possible outcome that night: a victory by Gore in the electoral college coupled with a loss in the popular vote. Gephardt offered a counter scenario: a Gore victory in the popular vote and a Bush victory in the electoral college. What do you do about that, he asked? Daley dismissed it as out of hand. "Never going to happen," he said.

Gov. Bush waits for the results on election night at the governor's mansion in Austin, with his brother, Jeb, the governor of Florida, and his mother, former first lady Barbara Bush.

(Charles Ommanney / SABA)

CHAPTER ONE

■

The Longest Day

George W. Bush awoke on Election Day at 6:30 a.m., padded purposefully around the governor's mansion, putting out pet food as the coffee brewed, then read a bit from his Bible. He'd gotten a good night's sleep in his own cozy bed while his opponent was racing around the country in a last, frantic search for votes. After casting his ballot, and posing for photographs as he made some last-minute phone calls to voters, Bush headed for a workout at the University of Texas gym. It was early afternoon when his phone rang. Karl Rove, his chief election strategist, had the first wave of exit polls in hand. The news, stunningly, was that Bush might lose.

"I got the smell," Bush recalled—the smell of defeat. Rove was full of "all the cautionary notes" about margins of error and possibilities. But Bush knew "it could be trouble." His workout mates—Brad Freeman; Craig Stapleton, a cousin by marriage; and Stapleton's son, Walker—noticed that Bush had become suddenly distracted. He wrapped up the exercise and rode silently back to the mansion. He didn't even bother to ask his friends to stay for lunch. "Thanks for coming" was all he said before retreating upstairs to the private residence.

There he told his wife, Laura, what the exit polls showed. Together, they replayed the race. In Bush's mind, he had done everything he could, given that he was running into the headwinds of a strong economy and contented electorate. He believed he had targeted the right states. He sensed great intensity among his own troops on the cam-

paign trail. Now he realized that Vice President Gore had done perhaps an even better job.

Bush told his twin daughters Jenna and Barbara: "Girls, it could be
a long night. Your dad may lose the presidency and the numbers
don't look so good now."

■

That night, in a seventh-floor suite at the Loew's Hotel in
Nashville, Al Gore decided that *he* had lost. He had watched with his
family and closest aides as his victory in Florida was pulled off the
board by the television networks, which were now calling the state
and the election for Bush, in one of the most stunning turnarounds in
American history.

"No," said his daughter Kristin as Bush was declared the winner.
"That's not right. That's not what happened."

But at 2:30 a.m., Gore's campaign chairman, William Daley, telephoned his counterpart for Bush, Donald L. Evans, to alert him that
the vice president would soon concede. Evans wanted to know how
quickly Gore would make a public statement.

"Don, it's probably going to take half an hour," said Daley. "His
kids are getting dressed, they're all crying."

"A half an hour?" Evans seemed incredulous, as Daley recalled it.

"Yes," Daley replied. "We have to travel up there, but we're getting there as fast as we can."

Gore's decision to end it had been quick and businesslike. He had
retreated with Daley and senior adviser Carter Eskew into an aide's
bedroom, and they had concluded that with the grand prize of Florida now in Bush's column, his lead was insurmountable. It was time
to surrender.

■

The deadlock in Florida was an almost unimaginable fluke, like tossing a quarter and having it come to rest on its edge. The virtual tie in Florida was a once-every-few-centuries proposition, and so was a presidential election that hinged on a single deadlocked state. It was a longshot wrapped in a longer shot. And so it happened that laws and institutions built for the press of the commonplace were called on to face the extraordinary.

The election dispute in Florida went on for 36 days—a whirlwind of more than 50 lawsuits, and appeals to every possible court, news conferences, protests, speeches, public hearings, private strategies and televised ballot-counting sessions. It was an all-out war involving America's canniest political soldiers and some of its best legal minds.

Now, in the aftermath, it's possible to start sorting out the threads and peering behind the scenes. It's possible to see more clearly how the candidates reacted and endured. To see George W. Bush, steeled for a long fight, hunkering down at his ranch with friends, furious when they tuned in *Saturday Night Live* and its savage satires. To see Al Gore, intimately managing his recount effort while seething to friends about the enemies he believed were betraying him. He spent part of one fateful afternoon on the phone trying to find out if the mayor of Miami-Dade County had sold him down the river.

And while Gore remained doggedly optimistic, many of his most experienced advisers, including those with the greatest knowledge of recounts, were clear-eyed realists, knowing just how hard it is for any candidate to reverse the results after Election Day. Nearly four days before Gore decided to surrender, his campaign chairman told him: "Forget it."

It's possible to see the key role Gore played in shaping the perception that he had lost a race that was, in fact, a virtual tie. On election night, after the networks declared Bush the winner, Gore cemented that impression by congratulating his opponent—without ever speaking to his own grassroots operatives, who could have warned him that the race was actually too close to call.

It's possible to trace the long arc of the Bush strategy, which was based on the assumption that Gore's chief weapon was the Florida

Supreme Court. From the first days, the Bush forces began moving to bring the state legislature and the federal courts—especially the U.S. Supreme Court—into position to thwart that advantage. The role of Katherine Harris, Florida's Republican secretary of state—and her key adviser, placed at her side by the Bush team—comes into focus. While Harris brooded over the parallels of her ordeal to that of the biblical Queen Esther, she stalled the ballot-counting so critical to Gore's hopes.

The key contribution of Bush's brother, Florida Gov. Jeb Bush, can also be seen: His legal staff, in the first hours after Election Day, moved to keep the state's biggest law firms off Gore's team.

It's possible to understand the pivotal decisions, on both sides, not to pursue an unprecedented—and legally unfounded—statewide hand count of all ballots. And to realize the importance of the Gore team's mishandling of the issue of overseas absentee ballots—a mistake that was exacerbated when Sen. Joseph I. Lieberman abandoned his ground forces on this issue, without warning, on national television. The resulting disarray allowed the Bush team to demand hurried re-counts, thus padding their lead. They called this the "Thanksgiving Stuffing."

And even as Gore protested on television that his team had nothing to do with lawsuits challenging thousands of ballots in two Florida counties, his forces arranged behind the scenes for organized labor to push the cases. Meanwhile, a major Gore donor—a Silicon Valley billionaire—backed the effort with huge cash donations and a chartered jet.

These are the sort of decisions, alliances, power plays, snap judgments and personality flaws revealed when a flukishly close election is played out for staggeringly high stakes. Both sides were nimble and brilliant and occasionally shady; both sides were also capable of miscalculations, divisions and blame. The best and worst of politics were on display in those 36 days, and both sides trafficked in each. This is how it happened.

■

Election Day broke rainy in Nashville, and 850 miles away, in
Austin, it rained as well. The long and fairly pedestrian campaign between Al Gore and George W. Bush, two sons of power—one dutiful,
one prodigal—seemed headed to a soggy ending.

At 5:30 a.m., Matthew Dowd, the Bush campaign's director of
polling, flicked on the computer at his home. Dowd, a former Democrat, adhered to a strict Election Day ritual. He always played golf in
the morning, rain or shine. But today, he needed to see the last tracking poll results before he left for the links.

The last poll he had commissioned, three days earlier, had shown
Bush ahead by five points in Florida, four in Michigan, four in Washington. History, he knew, showed that when there is no incumbent
president running, the election always breaks in favor of the party out
of power in the last days. Now Dowd saw the opposite thing happening on his screen. The Bush leads had vanished. Voters polled on
the Sunday and Monday before Election Day put Bush dead even in
Washington and Florida, down a point in Michigan.

Dowd hoped he would see something different in the exit polls that
afternoon.

For Ron Klain, the day began with an odd phone call. It was not
yet 8 a.m. in Nashville, and Klain, one of the rapid risers of contem-
porary Democratic politics, was taking his time getting to the office.
For the operatives, Election Day is often the dullest day of the year. So
Lester Hyman found Klain at home—not really home, but the place
where Klain had been sleeping for most of the previous three or four
months, while his wife and three kids lived hundreds of miles away.

Hyman, a veteran Washington attorney, was calling to relay an intriguing story he had just heard from his daughter, Liz, a former colleague of Klain's at the Department of Justice. Liz was volunteering at
a polling station in Palm Beach County, Florida. She said people were
streaming from the booths confused, and a bit panicked that they

might accidentally have voted for Patrick J. Buchanan. That's weird, Klain thought. Palm Beach County is packed with Northeastern retirees—Democrats. It should be the last place Buchanan would do well. He filed the news in a corner of his brain and finished getting ready for his last day on the Gore campaign.

The worst months of his life were about to be over.

In the very, very fortunate life of Ron Klain, this election was supposed to be yet another triumph. Scarcely 40 years old, Klain had already been chief of staff to the attorney general and to the vice president. He had clerked for a U.S. Supreme Court justice, advised a president, counseled the Senate Judiciary Committee. His life felt blessed—always had, really, ever since the day in 1968 when Robert F. Kennedy walked into his father's plumbing supply store in Indianapolis to film a campaign advertisement. It was a fluke. His father wasn't into politics. The picture on Klain's wall captures perfectly the moment when a little apple-cheeked boy looked up at a weary, doomed, spectacular politician and glimpsed an irresistible future.

Politics can be a nasty and capricious business, though. Klain's chance to help steer Gore's presidential campaign evaporated early, in the glare of Gore's weak beginnings. In 1999, the candidate turned to one of the party's trench warriors, Tony Coelho, a former member of Congress, to shape things up. And Coelho pushed Klain out of the picture.

Nothing like that had ever happened to Ron Klain. He wasn't used to getting the short end of any stick—let alone the sharp end of the knife. It was devastating. Months on the outside were an unending agony. The worst moment came on Super Tuesday, early in March 2000, when Gore wrapped up the nomination. Klain felt he had done as much as anyone to help Gore get there, but he wasn't even invited to the victory party.

Then Coelho dropped out of the campaign, citing illness, and William Daley, an equally tough but far less jealous man, took over. Daley brought Klain in from the cold, but by that time—July, with the conventions looming—all the real jobs were taken. Klain moved to Nashville, but he found little there for him to do.

He wouldn't say this to many people, but he was happy to be finished. Nearly finished. One more day—and so he walked through the doors of Gore headquarters shortly after 8 a.m. to get started. Klain stopped by the Boiler Room—so named because it was the sweaty heart of the campaign machinery. Campaigning is not glamorous or chit-chatty in the Boiler Room. It is very simple: the finding and delivering of votes. The chief engineer was Michael Whouley. The night before, he had jazzed up his troops by reciting from Shakespeare's *Henry V*, perhaps the greatest pep talk ever written: "Who sheds his blood with me will be my brother!"

Had a weird call from Florida, Klain told Whouley. People are confused in Palm Beach. Think they may have voted for Buchanan when they meant to vote for us.

It was the first Whouley heard of a problem.

Otherwise, Election Day was "pretty boring," Klain later recalled. At least, it started out that way.

■

Gore ended his race in Florida because a win there would finish the Republicans off—it was that simple, or awfully close. Bush chose to end the campaign precisely the way he began it: at his own steady pace (some in his party called it lackadaisical), to his own muffled drumbeat. His tour of five states in the last two days of the campaign seemed tame compared to the nonstop circumnavigation of the Democrats. Gore's moods, high and low, were always right on the surface, but Bush gave the same speech at the same rate with the same afternoon exercise break no matter what. He traveled with his own down pillow.

The day began, and Bush went dutifully through a few Election Day rituals. He and his wife were photographed voting at the Travis

County Courthouse. Then the cameras were invited to catch Bush placing a couple of get-out-the-vote phone calls, one to a guy in Orlando, the other to a woman, Tina Gerhart, in Detroit. Gerhart asked Bush to say hello to her teenage son. Sure, Bush said agreeably. "Phillip?" Bush said a moment later, "George W. Bush. You may have heard of me. . . . I've now heard of you, 'cause of your good mom."

There was a perfunctory feel to it. His heart was more evident in a call that morning to a former business partner, Tom Schieffer. Schieffer found Bush upbeat, eager to game the race, speculating on which states he would win. The apparatus of his campaign would do what was needed, just as it always had. When Bush needed tens of millions, his campaign raised the money. When he needed to crush the insurgency of Sen. John McCain, McCain was crushed. Now he needed some 51 million votes, and he was confident his campaign would find them. He figured he was good for 300 to 310 electoral votes—and 270 was enough to win.

Early in the afternoon, in Austin, Bush went to the University of Texas gym to work out. Since giving up alcohol more than a decade earlier, Bush had become a fitness fanatic, a regular jogger who saw a political campaign as a sort of marathon. The race would not go to the fastest man, but to the one with the steadiest pace and greatest endurance.

Rove's telephone call, with news of the first wave of exit polls, made clear to the candidate that at best, it was going to be a very long night. At worst, Bush was going to lose.

Key states that he had hoped were in his column were coming up dead-even. His dream of winning California was shot. And the worst news of all, the thing that ruined his mood, was the news from the Deep South. States such as North Carolina, Georgia, Louisiana, which ought to be in the bag, were disconcertingly close.

The afternoon was cold and gloomy as Bush rode in his motorcade down the hill past the Texas capitol dome. Sheets of rain fell on the plaza, where thousands of hearty Bush supporters were gathering for mariachi music and sausage wraps and hot chocolate.

Farther down the hill, in the Congress Avenue headquarters of the Bush campaign, policy guru Josh Bolten suggested a road trip to the bowling alley.

■

Joe Lieberman wanted a nap. During the last days of the campaign, he went flat out; his jet sped in an enormous loop from Florida to Nevada to New Mexico to Oregon to Washington to Wisconsin to Minnesota to New Hampshire to Maine to Pennsylvania and then back to Florida. He loved every grueling minute.

Then the first exit poll results arrived in Whouley's Boiler Room. Whouley had been saying for months that this would be "the closest election since 1960," that Gore would win but "win ugly," and it appeared to be coming true. With key colleagues, Whouley began dissecting the numbers in Iowa, New Mexico, Wisconsin, Pennsylvania—and they concluded almost immediately that they were on the knife's edge of the 270 electoral votes that would deliver the White House. They decided to pour on the steam.

Laura Quinn, a communications staffer from party headquarters, jumped on the telephones and began calling radio and television stations in crucial states, offering last-minute interviews with the Democratic candidates. There would be no naps. The candidates took the news dutifully. For Lieberman, the entire campaign had been a delicious blessing. On the day he was named to run with Gore, Lieberman practically levitated from the stage in Nashville. It was a hot, muggy morning, and the running mates' shirts were soaked through, but neither seemed to care. The choice of Lieberman was daring—he was the first Jewish candidate on a major party ticket—and sent a much-needed jolt through the Gore effort. Lieberman launched that day with a joke, and a prayer of thanksgiving, and he played the whole campaign in that same key.

So he was pleased to sit before a single camera with a wire in his ear and an aide reminding him of the names of the anchors chatting with him by satellite. Then he hit the radio. Lieberman was prospecting for votes one by one—he felt like he was running for the state legislature again.

About 5:30, Lieberman went on the air with a popular liberal talk show host in Palm Beach County, Randi Rhodes. He had scarcely started his get-to-the-polls pitch when Rhodes cut in. "You've got a very confusing ballot in Florida, have you heard? I'm not sure if I voted for you and Al Gore, or Pat Buchanan and Ezola Foster."

"Wow!" Lieberman answered. "Now, there's a big difference. You've got to be careful."

Rhodes mentioned that a major law firm—it was the Florida powerhouse of Holland & Knight—was already collecting reports from voters who had trouble with the ballot, and Lieberman immediately picked up on the idea.

"The affidavit idea is very important. Because if the election is close, there's going to be contests all over America."

Gore, too, was on the phone and in front of the cameras all afternoon, and into the evening, chasing the vote-rich afternoon drive-time audiences westward with the setting sun. His wife, Tipper, and oldest daughter, Karenna, also got on the phones to reach friendly talk show hosts, and in every call the message was the same—this is very close, every vote will count, go to the polls, go to the polls.

Data kept rolling in from the field. When the numbers told them a very late push might capture Missouri, Gore loyalists rushed to court to force the voting booths to stay open in St. Louis. A sympathetic judge agreed to three extra hours in the heavily Democratic city, but a higher court almost immediately reversed the ruling. In New Mexico, Democratic activists driving sport-utility vehicles plowed through a snowstorm to knock on the doors of potential voters and offer them rides to the polls. They called unregistered voters in Michigan, where it's possible to register and vote the same day. Other Gore phone banks aimed thousands of calls to union households in Iowa. The Democrats trolled the street corners of Milwaukee, where, two days earlier, they had been caught in a brief scandal—it was revealed that party activists were offering cigarettes to entice homeless people to vote absentee.

There was a lot of campaign experience in that Nashville headquarters, but no one could remember a day when so many victory scenarios were in play. The race was so tight, in so many places. You could put a winning jigsaw puzzle together a lot of different ways. The simplest, by far, was built around three states: Michigan, Florida and Pennsylvania. Sweep those into Gore's column, then add his huge sure things—California, New York, New Jersey, Illinois, Massachusetts and most of New England—and he would be within a few votes of 270.

Michigan, Pennsylvania, Florida—victory.

■

Murray Edelman looks like a college professor, balding and bespectacled, and he has the credentials to match, starting with a doctorate from the University of Chicago. But his business is television news. He runs a small yet intensely influential information factory in a dingy suite of offices near New York's Penn Station: Voter News Service. VNS spends countless months producing absolutely nothing, just getting ready. Then, when a national election comes around, for a few thrilling hours the service produces the most valuable commodity in the world—inside skinny.

That's the day VNS sends thousands of very temporary employees into precincts across the country. These survey takers wait with clipboards in hot sun or driving rain or swirling snow outside the schools and churches and community centers where the business of democracy gets done. They ask voters as they leave: Which candidate did you choose? What's your age, race, gender, religion, income, past voting habits? Thousands and thousands of surveys are completed in a matter of hours, and then tabulated and tallied and transmitted to New York where, in a mad scramble of data crunching, the numbers are aggregated and stratified and broken into batches, then poured into the waiting computers of news organizations around the country. Moments after these batches land, the switchboards of America's political system light up like Vegas. Reporters and editors begin calling their best sources to share the numbers, and these sources in turn pass the word to their own best sources. Between about 1 p.m. and late afternoon on Election Day, any self-respecting pol in America would dump a call from the pope for some fresh exit poll numbers.

Later, after the polls close, the VNS surveyors wait at scientifically selected precincts for actual results, which they relay as soon as possible to headquarters—which swells temporarily into a vast brokerage of data, with hundreds of operators answering hundreds of phones. Then the data flow into the VNS computers. When enough data reach Edelman's computer, he predicts the winner of the Senate seat or presidential electoral votes in question.

Edelman learned his craft from the dean of exit polls, Warren Mitofsky. Together, they ran the polls for CBS, back when that was the richest and best TV news operation ever. They were in the forefront as the networks gradually consolidated their Election Day numbers harvesting. Exit polling remained a separate enterprise for a long time, however, as the cash-rich networks jealously guarded their claims to be first and best with predictions. It was 1990 before they threw in together on this effort, and formed what would become VNS.

On November 7, Election Day, Edelman's temporary offices were a fifth of a mile above Wall Street, on the 93rd floor of the World Trade Center. More than 200 operators were taking calls and collecting surveys; twice that number, in New York and Cincinnati, tap-tapped at keyboards entering actual results as they came in. There was a data manager for each state, a trouble desk, a legal desk, lots of temporary walls and low dividers and glowing screens—"like something out of *Blade Runner*," one witness reported. Murray Edelman sat surrounded by screens at a long table in the restricted-access Decision Room. Only a close look at his computer displays spoiled the high-tech atmosphere—they looked like something out of the Atari years, ridiculously antique and kludgy, multicolored numbers on dark backgrounds written in the all-but-lost language of Mitofsky's sacred computational texts. The basic models for predicting elections from exit polls have not changed in a generation, and neither have the computers, nor even many of the analysts.

Next to the Decision Room was a row of little offices with killer views northward to the heart of Manhattan and the Empire State Building. In these rooms toiled the network representatives, in constant touch with data analysts at each VNS member outfit. For a few years after the founding of the consortium, the members all deferred to Edelman's decisions about when to call races. In 1994, however, ABC broke ranks and formed its own decision desk, using the VNS data to scoop the others. The next time around every network had its own team of experts to rip through the numbers. This year, the competition was fiercer than ever, with VNS calling races, and also the VNS members—CBS, ABC, NBC, Fox, CNN and the Associated Press—doing the same. Six teams (CBS and CNN shared a team) all racing to make the quickest sense of the same riddles.

Midafternoon—2:09 p.m. Eastern time, to be exact—the first slice of exit poll data was dumped by VNS into the computers of subscribers around the country. (*The Washington Post* was one, paying $15,000 for national exit poll numbers and smaller amounts—ranging from $3,500 to $5,600—for results from selected states.) The election was extremely tight, VNS reported: Bush had 49 percent of the sketchy early survey, Gore 48 percent. In Florida, the numbers said Gore 50, Bush 47.

At the Fox News decision desk on Manhattan's Sixth Avenue, John Ellis, a veteran political analyst who had been hired to run the upstart network's operation, was combing through the survey results. The phone rang on his desk.

"Ellis, Bush here."

It was the Republican nominee for president, who happened to be John Ellis's cousin. Bush was done with his workout and now he wanted to chew over the numbers. "Here we go again," Bush said. "Looks tight, huh?"

"I wouldn't worry about early numbers," Ellis answered reassuringly. "Your dad had bad early numbers in '88 and he wound up winning by seven. So who knows?"

But in fact the data contained some very disturbing news for the Bush team. The campaign's internal polls in the final days of the race showed them leading by five points in Florida—now these numbers suggested they were behind by three. Blacks and Jews, two constituencies energized by Gore's voter turnout effort, were hitting the polls in big numbers. The national data were unsettling, too. Gore was gaining ground. In state after state, the exit polls showed a closer contest than Bush had been led to believe—the projections of a fairly comfortable Republican win were falling to pieces. At one point that day, campaign chairman Don Evans looked up from the poll numbers and said, "Every piece of paper we've had here has turned to crap."

At 5:30, after another wave of exit poll results, Ellis walked outside for a cigarette and called his cousin at Bush's private number in the mansion. "Is it really this close?" Bush asked him.

"Yeah," Ellis answered. "It's really close."

■

As the last voters were flipping levers, coloring dots and punching cards on the East Coast, George W. Bush and family climbed into cars in Austin and rode by motorcade down the hill to the Four Seasons hotel. Without a lot of flash, this family was assembling one of the great political dynasties of American history. The candidate's grandfather, Prescott Bush, was a genteel senator from Connecticut, and Prescott's son, George Herbert Walker Bush, reached the White House. The third generation—the president's sons—included governors of two of the largest states, Texas and Florida; one of them, George Walker, called W., was expecting that evening to become only the second presidential son elected president. In the course of W.'s

campaign, meanwhile, another Bush star was born, George P. Bush—
P. for Prescott—the eldest son of the Florida governor. "P.," as he was
called, had the sex appeal of a rock star and the Hispanic heritage of
America's tomorrow.

Victory, according to a schedule already circulated to the press by
the confident campaign, would be claimed by Bush precisely at 11:39
p.m. Eastern time in a speech to last 12 minutes. That would be followed by 15 minutes of fireworks and triumphant waving.

But for now, dinner was starting and the candidate was antsy. On
the way to the restaurant, Bush had told his parents, "It could be a
long night." He kept wandering over to the single TV set in the corner. At 6:50 p.m. Texas time, the television networks began calling
the race in Florida for Vice President Al Gore. No one remembers
George W. Bush saying much, but his body language was screaming.
Then the TV went on the fritz.

Jeb Bush, the governor of Florida, came over and gave him a big
hug. "I'm sorry, brother," Jeb said. Earlier that autumn, Jeb had
joked about what a tense Thanksgiving dinner it would be if Gore
won Florida.

Suddenly the room felt claustrophobic to Bush. There was no television, not enough phones, too many people. Bush turned to his father and whispered in his ear, "I'm not going to stay around, I want
to go back to the mansion."

Brother Marvin, the family joker, began taking reservations for
Maui on Inauguration Day. Jeb disappeared, a cell phone to his ear.

When campaign communications director Karen P. Hughes joined
Bush at the mansion a half hour later, she found Bush standing in
front of a television, his father seated on a couch nearby. "How are
you, Mr. President?" Hughes asked the elder Bush. Not so good right
now, the former president replied.

"Defeat," George W. Bush recalled, "was settling in."

"You've got to understand my frame of mind at this point," he
said. "You're like, you're spent, you've run the race, it's out of your
hands. It's been in your hands for 18 months, starting [in June 1999]

with getting on the airplane in Austin, Texas, called *Great Expectations*."

In another state capital, Tallahassee, Jeb's senior staff was gathered at the home of Lt. Gov. Frank Brogan to watch the election returns. It did not escape Jeb's loyalists that, but for a twist or two of fate, this might have been the younger brother's day in the sun. His staff was a gathering of bright young conservatives of every hue—acting general counsel Frank Jimenez, the son of Cuban immigrants; deputy general counsel Reginald Brown, an African American; budget director Donna Arduin and others. They nursed dreams of leading the next wave of Republican politics. In 1994, however, George W. won in Texas while Jeb lost in Florida. That turned out to be the crucial bounce of the trampoline. W. rose higher.

But a Bush win was a Bush win, and Jeb's people were eager. The crowd was barely through Brogan's door, however, when the networks went like dominoes, all calling Florida for Gore between 7:49 p.m. and 8 p.m. Eastern time.

Disbelief. A chirping of cell phones. In the westernmost Panhandle, on Central time, the polls weren't even closed! Calls went out in a desperate search for information. Soon, one of the phones rang with a call from Jeb Bush in Austin—he wanted to know what was going on. Gradually, the numbers accumulated. And they told a different story:

It's not true.

■

The decision desks were squirreled away in buildings all across Manhattan, cramped, grim, slapdash—and packed with talent. "Election night is probably the most exciting night to come around every two years. And a good presidential election night—one that's close—that's what I dream of," says the blustery guru, Warren Mitofsky. That's why he was running the CBS desk, as he has done, off and on, for decades. Excitement was the juice that attracted number jockeys from polling companies and consulting combines across the country. Joe Lenski, for example. Normally, he's vice president of Edison Media Research, crafting polls that require weeks of analysis. But when Americans vote, he sits for a day at Mitofsky's right hand. "It's like a video game," he says of calling elections. "You get the same thrill an Air Force pilot must get flying a jet plane."

Early on Election Day, after glancing at the first exit polls, the networks polished off about two-thirds of the races, the easy calls. Incumbency is a staggering advantage in American politics. Very few ins become outs. That left the close Senate contests—and a presidential cliffhanger. But when 7 p.m. reached the East Coast and polls began closing in a large number of states, the race for the White House suddenly appeared quite simple on the ancient screens of the VNS computers. The early numbers were all Al Gore.

As the experts watched the real numbers arrive, they sensed they might be seeing the decisive story of 2000. The screens displayed, to the trained eye, nine different models for analyzing votes—tracking pre-election polls, exit polling, party turnout, geographical influences and so on. One display simply reported the slowly gathering actual results. At 7:50 p.m. the model at the top of the screen—the one marked "composite"—showed Florida at 51.4 percent for Gore and 46.2 percent for Bush. Next to the keyword STATUS on the right hand side of the screen appeared the word CALL.

If anything, the initial reports from key precincts suggested to some analysts that Gore was actually doing even better than the VNS screens projected. John Moody, the Fox vice president in charge of election night coverage, began badgering John Ellis to make the call. NBC, CBS and CNN had all given Florida to Gore, he said. Ellis's team wanted to wait for a few more precincts, but the pressure was piling up furiously.

"Okay, Florida goes Gore," Ellis shouted to Moody. It was 7:52 p.m.

Within minutes, Ellis's phone was ringing. It was cousin Jeb. "Are you sure?" the Florida governor asked.

"Jeb, I'm sorry," Ellis said. "I'm looking at a screenful of Gore."

"But the polls haven't closed in the Panhandle."

"It's not going to help," Ellis answered. "I'm sorry."

The networks' decision made no sense to Bush strategist Karl Rove. As he compared notes with Jeb Bush by phone, each man reinforced the other's skepticism. Rove's office was adjacent to polling director Dowd's at campaign headquarters, and each had a huge glass window on the corridor. A crowd of campaign staffers milled about, peering in at the two strategists as they and other senior staff members groped for hope in the Florida vote counts. Months earlier, the campaign had put together a detailed model of Florida, showing what it would take from each county to carry the state. Comparing the real results to their model, the Bush team quickly concluded that the state was still far too close to call.

But Florida was in the Gore column, and with it came the confident pronouncements from the television pundits that W. was finished. Only one dissenting voice was immediately heard. Mary Matalin, CNN's conservative pundit, was well-versed in grassroots politics, having run the get-out-the-vote effort for three Republican presidential candidates. When she heard Florida called for Gore, she sat down in an empty cubicle at CNN's Washington bureau, and started calling the Republican field commanders in Florida. They assured her there was no way Gore had carried the state.

"I'm going to go out on a limb here," she said when she returned to the air. "We have early data. The spread is 2 percent. The raw total is just 4,000 votes at this point. If it continues at this pace, there are half a million absentee ballots out there."

CNN's veteran election analyst, Bill Schneider, scoffed. "When we call the state," he intoned, "we're pretty sure that state is going to go for the winner."

Weeks later, the VNS experts would conclude that they were victims of a weird confluence: The exit polls overestimated the Gore vote, falling just barely within the margin of error. And they underestimated the Bush vote, by miscalculating the number of absentee ballots. This was the beginning of the worst night ever for the decision desks, and in the aftermath some pollsters would ask if the data crunchers allowed themselves to be swayed by the sexy story glimmering, mirage-like, on their computers. Gore had been the laggard all along in this race—for him to win in the end would make great melodrama. Did Gore's genuinely strong showings in Pennsylvania and Michigan cast a halo over the interpretation of the Florida results?

Not so, Mitofsky said afterward. "It's only the second time in 33 years I've seen a sample on election night give us a wrong winner without serious data errors. The chances are 1 in 200."

■

There were a couple of experts who could have saved the networks from themselves, if anyone had asked. Nick Baldick and Karl Koch were a pair of wisecracking nuts-and-bolts guys, Michael Whouley's Florida field generals. When the networks gave Gore the win, Whouley called his guys to pat them on the back. They were two of his best; they had helped win the state for Bill Clinton and Gore in 1996.

When Whouley and strategist Tad Devine started steering money and resources into the state in early summer, it was partly just to mess with Bush's head. After all, the man's brother was governor; Bush—like everyone else—figured Florida was in the bag. But then the numbers began to move toward Gore, and Whouley urged more and more effort. He encouraged speculation that Sen. Bob Graham, the most popular politician in the state, might be Gore's running mate. He arranged for Florida's convention delegates to cast the votes in Los Angeles that officially gave Gore the nomination. And when money got tight in the last weeks, Whouley pressed Daley to keep pumping millions into Florida. This was the sort of cunning and focus and strategic thinking that left a lot of Gore's people secretly believing that the entire campaign should have been run by Michael

Whouley, a man raised in the tactical heart of Democratic politics: Boston. Whouley was not a Washington guy. He did not court the columnists or chase the cameras. He was about one thing: getting Gore votes. Now he was basking in his vindication.

"He was like, 'Congrats, man,'" Baldick remembered. "'You just go down there, and you won it.' And I'm like, 'I'm a little worried about these numbers, Michael.'"

The Florida guys quite frankly couldn't figure out what the networks were talking about. True, the turnout was huge for Gore in South Florida, the headwaters of all Democratic hopes in that state. But the "little counties," the "Dixies," as Baldick and Koch called them—all the rural counties of northern and central Florida—were bleeding heavily. Everywhere the Democrats had expected to lose by 1,000 votes, they seemed to be losing by 1,500. Instead of 3,000, Bush was winning by 3,500. These little parcels of surplus votes could bury Gore. (In Austin, Bush's people saw precisely the same thing.)

Whouley didn't want to hear it. So the Florida guys toned down their doubts dramatically when, a few minutes later, Lieberman called to praise them. They knew Gore's running mate took special pride in his immense popularity with South Florida voters, and they didn't want to burst his bubble. So Koch said simply: "Thank you. It's still very close. I'll be much happier when all the numbers are in." And Lieberman signed off cheerfully.

■

Back at the Austin mansion, the Bush family hit the phones. The more they talked, the better they felt. But on television, the analysts were growing more and more confident about Gore. The tone of the evening threatened to spin out of Bush's control. A quick decision was made.

Communications czar Karen Hughes arranged for a small pool of reporters to visit the candidate in his living room. Bush said, with apparent calm and certainty, that the voters in Florida had yet to be heard from. Down the street at Rove's office, the round-faced strategist appeared by satellite on several networks to protest the early call in Florida.

This barrage landed squarely on Michael Whouley, whose misgivings after talking to his Florida troops now deepened. "We always thought if we won the troika"—Florida, Michigan and Pennsylvania—"we'd win the election." He understood, as a tactician, how important it was for Bush to extinguish talk of an early Gore victory, because voters were still going to the polls in Western states. Besides the presidential contest, those states included some crucial House and Senate races in which every Republican vote would be needed. But he also grew concerned that the Republicans might know something the TV people didn't.

Those TV people also worried about the warnings from Austin. University of Michigan professor Christopher Achen was working for ABC that night, and he recalled the "well-known and well-established tendency" of exit polls to favor the Democrat. In 1996, VNS subscribers—including *The Washington Post*—had to retract an embarrassing prediction that the Democratic challenger had defeated New Hampshire Sen. Robert C. Smith. Knowing this, and knowing that Florida had been tight all through the autumn, "we were gambling," Achen later said. "Anybody who called it [for Gore] was gambling."

When actual returns cause a change in a VNS prediction, the data erupt in red on one corner of the consortium screens. As 9 p.m. came and went, and more real votes flowed in from Florida, things grew extremely tense. Already, the next day's news cycle was looming, as journalists scrambled to position themselves to unveil the new administration. ABC's *Nightline* anchor, Ted Koppel, in Atlanta, talked to the decision desk, eager to know, "Am I going to Austin or Nashville?" When Koppel called again at about 9:40 to ask if he should head for Gore headquarters, the analysts advised him to wait. "It's a 50–50 chance that Florida is in trouble," said decision desk chief Carolyn Smith.

Minutes later, VNS flashed a bulletin to its members, warning of possible botched data from the Jacksonville area. The screw tight-ened. At 9:50, in a fifth-floor control room at the CNN Center in Atlanta, political director Tom Hannon was discussing his doubts through a headset with his experts in New York. The Florida call, he felt, was creating a sense of inevitability for Gore that did not match reality. Hannon barked a terse instruction into anchor Judy Woodruff's earpiece: "We've got to pull Florida back. New infor-mation." Woodruff was surprised, and unhappy. She craned her long neck to study the competition on a bank of monitors across the newsroom, but it was hard to see without her glasses.

The other networks were following suit. "If you're disgusted with us, frankly, I don't blame you," apologized Dan Rather, who liked to say he'd rather walk through a furnace in a gasoline suit than be wrong. NBC was the last to back off, at 10:15, two minutes after VNS flashed this bulletin: "We're retracting our call in FL because we don't have our previous confidence."

In Austin, Dorothy "Doro" Koch, the youngest Bush sibling, had gone to her room and climbed into bed. "Everyone was numb," re-called Joe O'Neill, George W. Bush's lifelong friend. "It was like be-ing in the middle of a family celebration and learning that your mother had just committed suicide."

Two hours later, Doro's teenagers started screaming in the hallway. She burst into the hallway, hair flying everywhere, "like a crazy lady from an insane asylum," as she remembered. The kids told her that the television had retracted the prediction. Her brother's hopes were still alive. She remembers Jeb a few minutes later, emerging from his own room looking alive again, a cell phone pressed to each ear as he hustled over to the mansion.

"Well," Marvin cracked, "Jeb can come in from the ledge now." Everyone laughed.

■

An internal investigation eventually determined that VNS significantly miscalculated the absentee turnout. Early voting is one of the hottest trends in politics, and the election forecasters have not kept up. Nothing in the exit polling models developed by Mitofsky and Edelman took absentee voting of a significant magnitude into account—a simple, devastating mistake.

That wasn't the only problem. The choice of sample precincts in the Tampa area turned out to be too Democratic. Then the first round of actual vote totals from selected Florida precincts, used to check the exit poll results, didn't include any from Tampa—so the network decision teams couldn't discover the Democratic oversample. In other words, each little mistake compounded the next. One of the unspoken assumptions of a complex model, like the VNS projections, is that an error in one candidate's favor in one factor will probably be shaved down by a skew in the other candidate's favor somewhere else. In Florida, in the first hour, every little botch skewed in Gore's direction.

Perhaps if an astute analyst had only one race to study that night, the huge early advantage projected for Gore in the decisive Tampa precincts would have set off alarm bells. But in the reality of election night—with 51 distinct presidential races to watch, plus Senate and gubernatorial contests—the ambiguities of the Florida data were lost in a sea of flashing numbers, until it was too late.

■

Meanwhile, in a government office in DeLand, Florida . . .

Shortly after 10 p.m., Volusia County elections supervisor Deanie Lowe was monitoring her vote count, watching it accumulate, when the county attorney said something she had never heard before: "I just saw Gore's total go backwards."

"I said, 'You are very tired, and your eyes are strained, and that's impossible. It didn't happen,'" Lowe recalled later.

The phone rang. A staff member was calling from an election night party across the street. "Gore just went backwards, Deanie," she said.

Two people could not make the same weird mistake, Lowe figured. So she ran to the tabulation room and ordered that the computers be stopped. Then she got on the phone to her software vendor. The troubleshooter advised her to print out the numbers, and when she studied the printouts, the error leapt off the page. In Precinct 216, home to a couple of hundred voters, Gore had been credited with minus 16,000 votes. "I have never seen a negative sign," Lowe said. The data card for the precinct gave Bush some 2,800 votes and subtracted about 16,000 from Gore, and also from Green Party candidate Ralph Nader. It assigned nearly 10,000 votes to the Socialist Workers Party candidate. A total kerflooey. Lowe got busy removing the offending information from the county tally, then entered the correct numbers, which were: 193 votes for Gore, 22 for Bush, one for Nader and none for the socialist.

Mistakes happen on election night. But this time, the bad numbers lingered for hours. Among the growing millions of Florida votes, Bush had nearly 20,000 Volusia phantoms.

■

With Florida once again up for grabs, both campaigns began frantically calculating alternative victory strategies. In the Boiler Room, Gore's people played mix-and-match with electoral votes: If Gore swept New England, he might squeak through without Florida . . . but then New Hampshire tipped to Bush. If Gore won Tennessee, his home state, the state he had carried massively as a senator . . . then Tennessee went to Bush. If Gore won Arkansas, birthplace of Clintonism . . . then Arkansas went to Bush. For a moment, Gore looked surprisingly strong in Colorado, but then he faded. Gore was looking good in a number of tight, key states, including Iowa, Wisconsin, New Mexico, Oregon and Washington. But as midnight passed, Gore appeared increasingly likely to top out, without Florida, at 267 votes—one state short.

Bush's poker hand became clear much earlier. Before the polls closed, he could imagine capturing the White House without Florida, if he could manage to win virtually every little state where things were tight. But as soon as Bush lost a few close ones, his strategists realized it was unlikely to happen. Without Florida, he was looking at 246 electoral votes—possibly 251 with New Mexico, maybe 258 with Oregon.

It was all coming down to Florida. Nearing 2 a.m., the network experts were no longer peering into the entrails of the exit polls. They were dealing in simple arithmetic, noodling over a formula they called the "need-get ratio"—asking over and over again, with each new batch of votes: How many ballots had been recorded for each candidate, and how many were left to go? Bush had a small but significant lead—roughly 50,000 votes with 97 percent of the Florida precincts reporting. The need-get asked: Could Gore get the votes he needed to overtake Bush, given the total votes left uncounted?

Fox's Ellis called George W. Bush again and asked what he thought about the Florida situation.

"What do you think?" Bush fired back.

"I think you've got it," Ellis said. The math was simple: Around this time, VNS was showing Bush leading Florida by 51,433 votes, with 179,713 remaining to be counted. Gore would have to win 64 percent of the outstanding votes to pull out a win. (In fact, twice that many votes were still left to be counted.) Ellis's boss, John Moody, paid another visit to the decision desk. The analysts pointed at squiggly lines he could not understand. It was time for a prayer, Moody thought. They were about to take a leap of faith.

Anchor Brit Hume made the declaration at 2:16. "Fox News projects George W. Bush the winner in Florida, and thus, it appears, the winner of the presidency of the United States," he said. Hume added: "I feel a little bit apprehensive about the whole thing. I have no reason to doubt our decision desk, but there it is."

An NBC analyst was on the phone to VNS at that same moment, comparing calculations. Then Fox called it. The NBC man hung up and advised his network to follow suit. At CBS, executive producer

Al Ortiz urged his desk to double-check their numbers: "Don't be stampeded by this," he remembered saying. But his network, and the others, went like a string of firecrackers.

Only VNS and the AP—the two outfits most insulated from competitive pressures, and the only two collecting their own raw data—refused to call the race. It hardly made any difference, though. When the news hit the giant TV screens at the sopping-wet street fair in Austin, hundreds and hundreds of chilled Bush backers started screaming and jumping up and down. Red, white and blue floodlights danced over the capitol dome. Shouts of "We won! We won!" could be heard all over the plaza, then Stevie Wonder's "Signed, Sealed, Delivered" blared from the loudspeakers.

The news landed quite differently in Nashville. In a lifetime of politics, Al Gore had developed a reputation as a savage and often lethal fighter. But he had also spent a lifetime learning how to lose gracefully. One of the things he most valued in himself was his ability to be strong through adversity. Other people cracked, not him. Friends who have weathered many crises with Gore always return to the same word: stoic. No matter how hard the loss, his father taught him, "defeat might serve as well as victory to shape the soul and let the glory out."

And so it was that, as his daughters burst into tears, Gore held and consoled them with dry eyes. He retreated with campaign chairman William Daley and Carter Eskew, his longtime adviser, behind a closed door. They decided very quickly that, well, nearly all the votes were counted and Bush had an insurmountable lead and the newspaper deadlines were sliding past and it was time to surrender.

That is what Gore did.

Neither Gore nor Daley nor any of his inner circle picked up the phone to call the Boiler Room at Gore's campaign headquarters nearby. There, they would have found Michael Whouley shouting urgently across a phone line to his staff in Florida, and none of them had any idea what Fox and the other networks were talking about. The race was too close to call.

After conferring with Daley and deciding to concede, Gore ran into

Eli Attie, the young writer who drafted the candidate's speeches. "Do you have an alternate statement?" Gore asked. Meaning, an alternate to the victory speech.

Attie nodded. He had found some downtime a few days earlier to prepare a concession speech, too. Someone told him once that the way to guarantee victory is to prepare for defeat. The campaign that has a concession speech written will never have to give it.

"Why don't you meet me in my room?" the candidate said, moving toward the elevators.

Attie walked to the speech prep room, where his laptop was humming lightly on a corner table. He noticed Ron Klain slumped in a chair, looking like he was on the verge of tears. Election Day was no longer boring at all. The speechwriter pulled up the concession speech and hit the print button, then collected his papers and went to Gore's room.

Gore had wanted to mention Tennessee in his speech. By then, it was clear he would lose his home state, just as his father—the man who set him on his path toward the presidency—had lost Tennessee in his final Senate race 30 years earlier. Those electoral votes would have put him over the top. Gore wanted to say he still loved the place, it was his home and he would return there. Win or lose, he had wanted a graceful, gracious speech.

"Is this the number?" Gore asked Daley, waving a slip of paper. Attie gathered up his things to join the motorcade to the Gore rally—then he realized: The number! It must have been the direct line to Bush. The number to call to surrender.

■

In the Boiler Room, Whouley realized he had not spoken to the candidate in hours. Gore had phoned earlier, but Whouley never returned the call—the boss wanted hard numbers and Whouley didn't have any.

Baldick and Koch, the Florida guys, remained skeptical. The race was too close to call earlier, and it was still too tight. For one thing, some freaky stuff was going on in Volusia County. Gore had suddenly popped up nearly 20,000 votes there. The margin wasn't 50,000 in favor of Bush—it was more like 30,000. And Palm Beach County was not nearly as close to completing its count as everyone seemed to think. More than 100,000 votes remained to be counted in that Democratic bastion.

Those same doubts infected Murray Edelman in his Manhattan skyscraper. He worried that rampant competition among his members, plus a noose-tight race, was about to tarnish a lifetime's effort. Over at CBS, the dean, Warren Mitofsky, was stunned. Calling the presidency wrong once was "a nightmare," he later said. Getting it wrong twice in the same night—"that's beyond fiction."

These doubts infected Rove and Dowd in Austin. As the Florida secretary of state's Web site recorded new vote totals, the Bush team reworked its projections, and each time Bush's margin slipped. At a minimum, it looked as if Florida was heading toward an automatic recount. Rove visited the big celebration near the Capitol, but quickly returned to his office, full of anxiety.

"I'm not seeing the same thing they're seeing in the numbers," Karen Hughes recalled Jeb Bush saying when the networks projected Bush as the 43rd president.

No Boiler Room staff were allowed to leave Gore headquarters and hit the party circuit until every key state was "released" by Whouley, and he steadfastly refused to release Florida. Jenny Backus, the sunny and ferocious press secretary of the Democratic National Committee, picked up a phone in the Boiler Room and began dialing one network after another, pressing them to retreat. She steered the TV people away from the VNS vote counts toward the Florida secretary of state's Web site, where the Bush lead was rapidly dwindling.

Then, to everyone's surprise, the Boiler Room televisions began reporting that Gore had called Bush to concede. He was, the networks said, on his way to Nashville's War Memorial to give his formal concession speech.

Florida Attorney General Bob Butterworth, who had chaired Gore's campaign in the state, talked to the Gore team in Tallahassee. "What is he doing? He can't concede!" Butterworth fumed. Under Florida law, in a race this close there would be an automatic recount. By now the margin was down to 6,000 votes and falling fast.

Whouley sent an urgent page to Gore aide Michael Feldman in the motorcade. When Feldman called back, he patched in Daley, who crouched low in his seat with his head in his hands, straining to hear. "What's up, Mike?" he asked.

"This thing's going to automatic recount."

"Oh, shit," Daley said. And he listened as Whouley spelled out the situation—the screwed-up numbers, the tight margin, Butterworth's call. The motorcade was now pulling into a basement garage near the rally site. Daley said he would call back from a hard line.

Daley reached the garage a few moments behind Gore, and as soon as he got out of his car he barked at Feldman to make sure Gore stayed put: "Don't let him go out. Grab him!"

Out on the rain-soaked stage stood the twin transparent panels of the TelePrompTer, where Attie's concession speech was already loaded and ready to roll. "Democracy may not always give us the outcome we want. But the United States of America is the best country ever created—still, as ever, the hope of humankind. We all share in the privilege and challenge of building a more perfect union. . . . And I can't promise it won't be a long and winding road. But this I know in my heart"—and here Gore planned to end with his signature campaign line—"you ain't seen nothing yet."

But now in the stark basement holding room, the Gore camp was frantically weighing whether the speech should be delivered at all. As the cars of the motorcade dumped their passengers, the room increasingly buzzed with news from scores of phone calls. Daley called CBS News President Andrew Heyward. Was CBS considering withdrawing its projection? Heyward parried—What was Gore going to do?

Attie found Gore standing, strangely alone, in the center of the room. "We've got to change some of the language in the speech," Attie said, "because with 99.9 percent of the votes in, you're only 600 votes behind." The candidate looked a bit surprised.

Daley conferred by phone with Butterworth, who explained the recount provision. "Are you sure we have an automatic recount?"

"I'm the attorney general," Butterworth answered. "I'm sure."

Daley placed another call to Evans, asking for more time. "Don, we've got a little problem here. Don't let your guy go out." As Daley recalls it, Evans asked, "Well, what's the problem?

"Well, I'm going to get back to you," Daley replied. Then he added, "Where is the governor? Because the vice president may want to talk to him."

"About what?" Evans asked. He knew what the problem was, he just didn't know what Gore intended to do about it.

"Just, I'll get back to you," Daley said.

Decision time. Gore was pulled into a separate room. If Florida was really too close to call, and if state law mandated a recount, Gore's counselors asked, what was the point of giving up? Several of the most experienced hands present—including Daley and, for that moment, at least, Gore himself—knew the answer: Because recounts almost never change the outcome. But it seemed only sensible to wait awhile to let the picture clarify.

What to do? It made no sense, they all agreed, to have Gore give any kind of statement. The risk was too high that he might come off as recalcitrant or desperate. And so Attie quickly drafted brief remarks for Daley to deliver, essentially placing the election on hold.

But before he went out to face the crowd, Daley told Gore he was sorry he hadn't stopped him from conceding to Bush. "I don't think I served you well there," he said.

These things happen, Gore answered. "Don't feel badly about it."

■

Gore picked up the phone for perhaps the strangest call in American political history.

In Austin, Bush had joined his family and friends downstairs at the mansion, waiting for Gore to make his public concession. Then he would walk the few blocks to his victory party. While waiting, Bush walked back upstairs with his father. The once and would-be presidents had lived the night together, side by side. That's where communications director Karen Hughes found him a few minutes later, cell phone to his ear.

"Circumstances have changed dramatically since I first called you," Al Gore told George W. Bush. It was after 3 a.m. Eastern time. "The state of Florida is too close to call."

"Are you saying what I think you're saying?" Bush asked brusquely, disbelievingly. "Let me make sure I understand. You're calling back to retract that concession?"

"Don't get snippy about it," Gore spat back.

"Let me explain," Gore continued, with a hint of the pedantic tone he often—and disastrously—adopted. If the results stood up and Bush prevailed, Gore would step aside gracefully and give Bush his full support. "But I don't think we should be going out making statements with the state of Florida in the balance."

Bush was stunned. Didn't Gore realize that the governor of Florida, his brother, was standing right here? Who knew Florida votes better than Jeb? He'd been on the phone and pecking away at the computer for hours, tracking vote patterns that he knew like the angles of his children's faces. "My little brother says it's over," he told Gore.

"I don't think this is something your little brother gets to decide," the vice president answered icily. (Another aide overhearing the call remembered it this way: "With all due respect to your little brother, he is not the final arbiter of who wins Florida.")

"Do what you have to do," Bush said.

As Bush recounted the call to his family and guests, he grew more amazed. Slowly it sank in. His father and Hughes were with him, as were Laura Bush, Richard and Lynne Cheney, former senator Alan Simpson and his wife Ann, and Jeb. "The vice president's changed," Bush told the group. "He's withdrawn" the concession.

Bush asked his brother Jeb to find out more about what was happening in Florida.

Bush decided that campaign chairman Don Evans should go out and speak to supporters who were still waiting outside. "Well," Bush said finally, "I guess there's nothing else to do at this point. We just ought to go to bed."

■

When Gore hung up, he found himself surrounded by about 30 of his top aides and loyal supporters. But there was one man who didn't make the dramatic trip to the War Memorial. When the others raced to the motorcade, Ron Klain trudged to his own hotel room, where he found his wife and one of his children still awake, watching the news. He got undressed and sat on the bed thinking what a bad campaign it had been, personally and professionally, and—while he hated the result—how glad he was it was over.

Then the phone rang.

CHAPTER TWO

■

The Scramble

Go in. Keep quiet. Don't say who you work for.

It was a reconnaissance operation. As the Spirit Airlines DC–9 charter jet winged its way toward Florida, the Gore operatives on board got a crash course in recount strategy from the masters.

The campaign is over.

This is something else.

Information would win this thing. Data: Names of county election supervisors. Vote totals. Hello, ma'am. Any irregularities you might recall? Anything at all? Type of voting machines. Ballot design. May I have a sample ballot, if it's not too much trouble? Any ballots that the machines couldn't read? Oh, that many? Why?

When the election ended in a deadlock, Donnie Fowler, Al Gore's field director, had two hours to come up with a jet, starting at 4 in the morning. He found this one, 72 seats, beautiful—except for the giant GORE-LIEBERMAN painted on the side. This had been, until 24 hours ago, the plane of vice presidential nominee Joseph I. Lieberman. What it boasted in terms of comfort, it lacked in terms of subterfuge.

Coming into Tallahassee, there was much to feel hopeful about: Gore had won the popular vote. Gore seemed just three little electoral votes away from the White House. Gore was fewer than 2,000 votes behind in Florida. Gore had the guys who wrote the book on recounts—literally: *The Recount Primer*, by Timothy Downs, Chris

On Wednesday, November 8, the Gore team swung into action. Former secretary of state Warren Christopher addressed the media in Nashville as campaign chairman William Daley stood by and listened.

(Robert A. Reeder / The Washington Post)

Sautter and John Hardin "Jack" Young. The authors—veteran Democratic trench fighters—tore pages from their book and copied them using the two airborne fax machines. Over the intercom, they lectured the dozing passengers in the science of election challenges.

Recount One, as the flight attendants referred to the plane, touched down, rolled to a stop—and in came a spiffy private jet 50 feet away. The steps went down on the littler plane. A big man with a boy's head of hair ducked his head as he came blinking into the sunlight.

Jeb Bush.

The Republicans waved at the Democrats: Hi, fellas! So much for low-key, thought Fowler, who pushed at the pad of his cell phone. He reached the voice mail of campaign spokesman Mark Fabiani. "Fabiani? It's Fowler. We've landed in Tallahassee and Jeb Bush has pulled up beside us. Our cover is blown."

That's how the fight for Florida began, November 8, barely 14 hours after the polls closed. The challenge Gore faced was right there in the opening pages of *The Recount Primer*. The maxims of any recount are always the same, Gore's tacticians wrote: "If a candidate is ahead, the scope of the recount should be as narrow as possible, and the rules and procedures . . . should duplicate the procedures of election night." Classic recount theory says: "When you've got a lead, you sit on the ball," Young would explain later. A Virginia lawyer and former crew coach, Young loves sports analogies.

"If a candidate is behind," the *Primer* continues, "the scope should be as broad as possible, and the rules should be different from those used election night." In other words, Young said, "It's the end of the fourth quarter. When you're behind, a recount is a Hail Mary. The one who is behind has to gather votes."

How? Expand the universe of possible votes. Seek to examine all the ballots rejected by the machines because no vote registered—the "undervotes." All the paper ballots rejected because they weren't filled out precisely right—look at those, too. Ballots marked twice because they were confusing to some voters—the "overvotes"—look at those. "You get 2,000 pitches, you get a better chance of having homers," Young explained.

Anyone who read and heeded the booklet could predict how the two sides would play America's closest presidential election—at least in the broad outlines. Gore would gamble; Bush would stall. Gore would preach a doctrine of uncounted ballots; Bush would extol the dependability of machines. Gore needed more: more counting, more examination, more weighing and pondering of more ballots. Bush needed it over while he was still ahead.

Flip a few pages ahead in the *Primer*. The trailing candidate knows where to expand the universe only by learning everything possible about the ballots—number, condition, status. Knowledge is power, especially in the early hours. The county election boards may never have done a recount before. Get there first, and become their friendly experts. Figure out the counting standards that will favor your candidate, then generously apply them to every vote, no matter what.

That's why Gore's team swept down in such force so quickly, and why it hoped no one would notice. In the first hours of the deadlock, while hatching strategy, it concluded that the Florida authorities would take a couple of days to get their automatic recount started, and in that time the Democrats could build an arsenal of information. "The theory is: Don't assume anything. When you're behind, you want to gather as much information as you can because you actually are going to make some decisions that are strategic, based on data." The gospel according to Jack Young.

There was just one problem: The Republicans knew the gospel, too. When the War for Florida began, both sides were masters of the other's strategy, because they had fought this battle before, on opposite sides. Before November 8, 2000, perhaps the toughest recount in recent history was a 1984 deadlock in Indiana's 8th Congressional District. "The Bloody 8th," as it came to be known—a six-month ordeal involving three complete recounts, the Antietam of recounts. The

Democrats—Young and Chris Sautter and others winging their way to Florida that first day—had finished Election Day a fraction ahead in that race. They fought to keep the scope narrow and pushed the case into a friendly federal jurisdiction: Congress, then controlled by the Democrats. And they won.

One of the lawyers who lost that battle was on his way to Florida, with every lesson of the Bloody 8th well-learned. He was Benjamin Ginsberg—George W. Bush's campaign counsel.

■

But that is getting ahead of the story.

Earlier that morning in Nashville, Ron Klain had traveled from his hotel room back to headquarters, to the Boiler Room, where he found the campaign's field marshal, Michael Whouley, with Young, Joe Sandler—the Democratic Party's chief lawyer—and others already huddled around a table mapping out the recount.

Whouley had been saying for months that the election would be extremely close. Based on that forecast, Sandler and Young had formed teams of lawyers in at least 20 key states, ready for any kind of trouble, and they had brushed up a bit on at least 20 sets of election statutes. After the networks called the race for Bush and the numbers got hinky, Sandler was told to draft a quick memo on Florida election law, focusing on the power of state courts to set aside the results.

"What are you talking about?" Sandler asked. "He's conceded." That's when he learned that Gore's concession was going to be retracted.

Now it was 4 a.m. Campaign chairman William Daley and others from the Gore high command had arrived, slightly dazed after their weird experience at the downtown rally. They included Bob Shrum and Carter Eskew, the campaign consultants; Frank Hunger, Gore's brother-in-law and best friend; political strategist Tad Devine; campaign manager Donna Brazile; tactician Monica Dixon. They were all around the table, pressing Sandler and Young to explain what they knew of Florida's law.

Any race that ended closer than one-half of 1 percent required an automatic recount, they explained. In this race, with about six million votes cast, the triggering margin was around 30,000—and Bush was ahead of Gore by far less than that. Young and Sandler said Gore's troops could expect a day or two to canvass the votes—a sort of formal tallying—followed by a couple of days to run the ballots back through the machines. Then, in three or four days, the trailing candidate could protest the vote count. Eventually, the whole thing could end up in front of the Florida Supreme Court, which would have extensive power to decide disputes.

In a room full of pols, no one could out-politic Bill Daley. He was nursed, weaned and raised on the business. His father was Chicago's legendary mayor-for-life, Richard Daley. One thing Bill Daley knew about recounts—they almost never change the outcome. Election night counts are always screwed up. Everyone who knows politics knows that. But they generally turn out to be screwed up equally in all directions. You count the votes again and both candidates will gain some and lose some, and both sides will fight tooth and nail. Ultimately, nothing much will shift. And so Daley was skeptical, and he hammered the lawyers with questions.

"Mr. Daley," Sandler finally said, "the recount procedures in Florida are designed to resolve contests in sheriff races and county commissioner races. They never contemplated something the size of this." In challenging a statewide, presidential count, Gore's team would be traveling through unmapped territory.

Daley considered this for a moment. He was sending a small army into Florida on a vague mission, part political, part legal, and the stakes were the presidency. Gore would need a certain kind of person down there—a lawyer, a tiger, a general, old enough to be seasoned but young enough to care desperately.

Ron Klain.

In the first hour of the new campaign, Klain got his fresh start. All the suspicion and bad blood and sharp knives and petty slights—the vile currency of the Gore campaign—were dumped down the sink. This was, for all its faults, a campaign of professionals, which meant a campaign of few loyalties. Klain was needed, so he was back inside.

The amazing thing was the way adrenaline surged through exhausted bodies and warriors reacted with fevered speed. Field director Fowler moved before anyone knew much more than a name on the map: Florida. "I went to the advance teams—give me your best advance people in Nashville. We got a list of 100 people. We made the calls, got them all back to headquarters." Those and more. By 4:20 a.m., there were perhaps 150 people gathered around as Tad Devine delivered a rousing little speech: "This thing isn't over yet!" Then Fowler climbed onto a table and shouted out the details. "Pack your bags for two or three days—but I can't promise you anything. You may be there for two weeks." The troops scattered to shower and pack. Other staffers hit the phones to arrange vans to the airport and, on the other end, hotel rooms and rental cars. They were building a midsized Florida corporation, with branch offices in nearly every county, before dawn.

Gore's army rallied back at headquarters at 6:30 a.m. There were at least 85 people ready to go, and more who had gathered with nothing but the wrinkled clothes they were wearing and a desperate hunger to be a part of this. The plane had 72 seats. When the vans roared off to the airport, people left behind were in tears—that's how thrilling the cause seemed.

The jet took off without the passengers knowing, exactly, where it was headed.

■

There were dead heats all over the country. No one knew, precisely, what the final vote totals would be, but if the trends continued, George W. Bush would lose the popular vote and carry the electoral college by the smallest margin since the light bulb was cutting edge. That's if he held onto Florida. If Gore pried that one loose, Bush would need to challenge the results in New Mexico, Iowa, Oregon, maybe Wisconsin—and what was the chance of pulling that off?

But he had two things to feel good about. First, he was ahead. In politics, as in war, it is easier to hold ground than to capture it. Second, the fight was going to be concentrated in Florida, where his brother was governor.

Nothing was more valuable to Bush in the key first days of the deadlock than his brother's power and network of resources—especially his staff of politically expert lawyers. Gore's recount specialists were right about the value of early knowledge. And Jeb Bush had, in his general counsel's office, some of the sharpest, freshest lawyer-politicians in Florida. They knew the law, the players, the terrain and where the bodies were buried in a way that the Democrats streaming in from Nashville could never match. "There was never a moment when Jeb said, 'Go do this or that,'" said deputy general counsel Reg Brown. "It was just instinctive—people knew that's what he'd want them to do or that it was the right thing to do from a Republican perspective."

When the networks called the race for W. shortly after 2 a.m. on Wednesday, Jeb's team in Tallahassee was instantly queasy. "I knew that not all the precincts were in," said Frank Jimenez, the governor's acting general counsel. As Bush's lead vanished, Jimenez moved to dial his boss's number in Austin, saying, "I gotta call the governor."

Don't do it, someone warned him. They may decide to shoot the messenger.

Jimenez became a key source of information for the Bush camp about legal and procedural aspects of the recount. Around 3:30 a.m., he made the first of a number of calls to the Florida Division of Elections, asking for the latest numbers. Jimenez realized he didn't know much about recounts. Apparently, a lot of people didn't either. CNN somehow reached a midlevel Division of Elections employee at about 4 a.m. The network triumphantly put the man on live. Jimenez—

watching the network from Lt. Gov. Frank Brogan's house—froze. Somebody had to get the guy off the air: He might say something that would set a bad precedent.

Moments later, anchor Bernard Shaw got a slightly puzzled look on his face. "Did we lose Ed Kast?" he asked.

"We may have," Judy Woodruff answered. They had.

Then state Attorney General Bob Butterworth, chairman of the Gore campaign in Florida, turned up a few minutes later on the same network, offering his interpretation of the recount process. Furious, Jimenez headed over to the Division of Elections. A roomful of reporters dutifully noted the arrival of Jeb's lawyer. He headed straight for Clay Roberts, a Republican, a Bush loyalist, director of the division. Jimenez was asking, he said later, for a crash course in recount procedures. "My purpose in going was to confirm the results and to figure out what was going to happen next," he said later. "That's when I learned the governor had a role in the process."

Recount law placed the power to certify the winner—of Florida, and therefore of the presidency—in the hands of the state election canvassing commission, which had three members. One was Secretary of State Katherine Harris, co-chairman of the Bush campaign in Florida. The other two were elections division head Roberts and Jeb Bush. The issue of a conflict of interest was immediately clear. Indeed, in those early days, the role of Jeb Bush and his general counsel would come under intense inspection. Frank Jimenez, a soft-spoken, handsome young man with dark hair and intense eyes, was politically savvy, but nothing in his background had prepared him for this.

The son of Cubans who fled the Castro regime in 1961, Jimenez was an exile success story. He attended Yale Law School, clerking on the federal appeals court in California, joining the Florida insider firm of Steel Hector & Davis. He took a leave from his practice as a white-collar litigator in 1994 to work for Jeb Bush's first, failed run for governor.

Much would be made of the barrage of calls he placed to the Division of Elections in the early days of the disputed vote count. But in his own mind, he later explained, it was all routine. "There have been stories about how I called the Division eight or nine times in the first 48 hours. I think I only got through to Clay [Roberts] a few times, and I was asking very basic, fundamental questions."

Some of those questions apparently had to do with simple matters of law. In the first hours of deadlock, the Florida governor's staff pondered various moves to short-circuit the recount. It considered arguing that Florida recount laws did not apply to presidential elections. Or that the automatic recount provision applied only to individual counties where the margin was closer than one-half of 1 percent—eliminating all of Gore's strongest counties.

None of these ideas panned out. But what ultimately mattered more than theories or phone calls was the work of Jimenez and his staff in the early hours to wrap up the state's biggest law firms. It began at 6:45 a.m., while Gore's team was mustering in Nashville: Jimenez contacted Barry Richard of Greenberg Traurig, a powerhouse outfit, among the best-wired in Florida. Richard was a Democrat—he even hosted fundraisers for the opposition—but Jeb and his staff all trusted him. Richard had recently defended the governor against a lawsuit challenging the use of state letterhead in an appeal to absentee voters. He won the case. Jimenez didn't even bother checking with Austin before signing him up.

Next, Jeb's team looked at Gray Harris & Robinson. A key aide of Jeb Bush was married to a lawyer there. Locked 'em up. Then it turned to Fowler, White, Gillen, Boggs, Villareal & Banker, a big Tallahassee lobbying firm. The senior Republican strategist in Florida, Mac Stipanovich, worked there. They weren't going to help Gore.

But the big prize—even bigger than Greenberg Traurig—was Holland & Knight, the largest firm in Florida, one of the 20 biggest in the world. The side that could sign that firm would have a huge advantage, not simply in terms of legal talent, but in terms of infrastructure. The recount would be fought in jurisdictions around the state. Holland & Knight had 11 Florida offices, in every region—and in every office it had computers, law books, legal secretaries—not to mention desks, phones, conference rooms and coffee for the hundreds of lawyers soon to descend.

The Bush team didn't have much hope of hiring the behemoth. Holland & Knight's managing partner, Bill McBride, was rumored to have ambitions of running against Jeb Bush in 2002. But maybe it could keep the giant on the sidelines. (The Bush team didn't know that a lawyer in the firm was already fielding calls in Palm Beach County complaining about the confusing ballot.)

Bush deputy counsel Reg Brown talked with Steve Uhlfelder, an influential member of the firm and a big man on the Florida scene—he sat on the powerful Board of Regents, overseeing the Florida university system. Although he was a Democrat, Uhlfelder supported Jeb Bush's proposal to replace the existing affirmative action program with a new system granting automatic admission to all top students regardless of race. Out of loyalty to Jeb, he had supported George W.

Uhlfelder had been pushing Jeb's administration hard for an executive order cracking down on software piracy on behalf of a major client, Microsoft. Now Jeb's man wanted to know what Holland & Knight was planning to do about the recount. Uhlfelder assured him the firm was struggling with the question. His own preference, Uhlfelder added, was for the firm to avoid taking sides, and instead to represent various media companies rushing into Florida to cover the dispute.

That was promising. But the Bush team was taking no chances. A lawyer at Gray Harris & Robinson remembered having traded tons of preelection e-mail from Holland & Knight attorneys as part of the "Lawyers for Bush" campaign. Now he downloaded them all for use as ammunition, if needed, to show that the firm could not possibly represent Gore.

But there were key members of the firm who wanted very much to help the vice president. One of the first things Ron Klain did as head

of Gore's legal team was to place a call to Martha Barnett of Holland
& Knight's Tallahassee office. She was perfect to lead the team—a
Democrat and president of the American Bar Association. She was
traveling, but she reversed field and returned to Florida. By noon,
Klain had what he thought was a binding agreement to retain the firm.

Barnett visited Klain around noon, accompanied by the grand old
man of Holland & Knight, Chesterfield Smith. There may be no
larger figure on the state's legal scene than the 83-year-old Smith. A
former president of the Florida Bar and the ABA, he had chaired the
committee that had written the current state Constitution. The three
arranged to meet again at 5 p.m. to begin hatching a strategy.

Barnett and Smith never showed. At 6:30, Klain was told the firm
would not be taking the case. Each side blames the other. McBride
later said the firm was ready to sign up as Gore's lead counsel; Klain
said the firm turned him down.

The Gore team was convinced Holland & Knight simply was reluctant to cross the governor of Florida. In the coming weeks, Democrats would complain frequently about the hidden hand of Jeb Bush,
but his greatest influence was, quite possibly, right there on the surface: For anyone doing business in Florida, it was unnatural to cross
the governor. "The Republicans didn't have to hire the big firms, or
tie them up," a leading Gore strategist said later. "They scared them
shitless. Jeb Bush didn't need to send a note for them to know."

However it happened, within 24 hours after the polls closed in
Florida, the Gore team was effectively closed out of the state's top law
firms. That didn't mean, though, that it had nothing. It went down
the street in Tallahassee and signed up Dexter Douglass, a drawling,
charming old silver-hair who led a tiny firm there. Douglass had two
things going for him. First, he knew everybody. And second, half the
people he knew—scattered through government agencies and the
Florida courts—thought maybe they owed their jobs to him.

■

The Democrats also had their own man high up in Florida government: Bob Butterworth, the longtime state attorney general, a darkly
handsome man shadowed by tragedy and unrealized hopes. Democrats had, for many years, looked at Butterworth and envisioned a
governor—yet he had never made the run. The moment he burst into
the state's front row were the best hours of his career—and the worst
of his life.

On the eve of his first landslide victory in November 1986, Butterworth's mentally ill ex-wife killed their teenage son, Bobby Butterworth III, and then herself. Even 14 years later, it was hard to look
into the attorney general's sober countenance without imagining a
great sadness there, and a sense of what-if. Perhaps he would never
have gotten his chance—Lawton Chiles, the wildly popular Democratic senator, came out of retirement in 1990 to stroll into the governor's mansion. Perhaps Butterworth's chance was yet to come.

Certainly, he had the stature in his party, second only to Sen. Bob
Graham's—and Butterworth's machinery was closer to the ground.
He had served as Gore's state chairman, a job that gained prestige
and zip with each week, as the vice president poured money and time
into Florida. When Wednesday arrived with the race unresolved, Butterworth began applying his influence to guarantee that Gore would
have the best possible chance of capturing Florida's crucial votes—although he said later that his "number one" concern was "the image
of the state."

Butterworth weighed in first as a fierce advocate for standing and
fighting. When news broke that Gore was planning to concede, Butterworth argued forcefully by phone that the margin was much too
close. His knowledge of Florida law was persuasive in this critical
moment. Then, at the urging of the Gore campaign, he went on television in the predawn hours Wednesday to frame the recount in a
favorable light. He was so aggressive about it Frank Jimenez complained, in earshot of a *Miami Herald* reporter, that Butterworth was
trying to "hijack" the election.

All that was before the first dawn. In the next 48 hours, Butterworth would work the phone—himself and through surrogates—to push a ballot-by-ballot recount in troubled Volusia County, where officials initially believed they were required only to check their computer tapes. At one point, the county's canvassing board chairman, Circuit Judge Michael McDermott, received a call from his boss, Robert K. Rouse Jr., chief judge of the circuit. To McDermott's surprise, Butterworth was quickly patched in.

"Mr. Butterworth, in what capacity are you placing this call?" McDermott demanded.

Butterworth answered that he represented both the attorney general's office and the secretary of state—a rather broad interpretation of his role, and one that glossed over the political differences between Butterworth and Harris on the presidential campaign.

McDermott noted tartly that Butterworth was Gore's state chairman. "With all due respect, I think you should disqualify yourself," the judge said.

"At no time did he indicate why the attorney general might have jurisdiction," McDermott recalled later. "I mean, was something criminal going on?"

McDermott abruptly ended the call.

Butterworth claimed later that he had already resigned from Gore's campaign by the time he called McDermott—but no one had bothered to mention it at the time. In fact, no one bothered to tell the Gore campaign until state Democratic chairman Bob Poe said he passed the word along in early December.

Florida's big dogs were walking a fine line. A few hours into the deadlock, both Jeb Bush and Bob Butterworth realized that they might have conflict-of-interest problems. They would have to lead a deeply divided state long after the would-be presidents had gone home or to Washington. Jeb Bush decided that he should recuse himself from the statewide canvassing commission; he called Austin to explain his view.

There was some dissent on his staff—although when Jeb recused himself, his lawyers immediately took brief leaves of absence so they could continue working on the dispute without drawing a state salary. Some doubted that Harris, the secretary of state, could be trusted to remain engaged through a difficult fight. But everyone felt better knowing that Jeb's place would be taken by Agriculture Commissioner Bob Crawford. He was a Democrat, but a Democrat who strongly supported the Bushes.

Jeb hoped Butterworth would appear at a news conference with him—he wanted to project bipartisan integrity. But would he do it? Bush's people worried that, given the wide circulation of Jimenez's "hijack" quote, Butterworth would stiff them. At the last minute, the attorney general agreed to share the podium with Bush—but then the designated hour passed and there was no sign of him. Finally, the governor walked over personally to escort Butterworth before the cameras.

"Never in my wildest dreams did I ever imagine it would be this close," Jeb Bush told reporters Wednesday evening. "I, along with Attorney General Butterworth, are firmly committed to protecting the integrity of Florida's election process and will seek swift enforcement of Florida's election law," he said. "Both of us have pledged to work together with Secretary of State Katherine Harris in this regard."

The tone of teamwork did not last long.

■

This is what both sides found on the ground: chaos. Which suited the slightly slower start of the Austin forces. The Bush team could simply decry the chaos while it got organized. Americans did not want to see chaos surrounding an election. They wanted to see order. Bush would offer order—in the form of a quick resolution. The Gore people also hoped to gain from early chaos, to master it, tame it to their own advantage. So they went directly to the epicenter of the chaos, and plunged in—Palm Beach County.

In 1998, Florida voters, in a little-noticed referendum, simplified access to the statewide ballot. As a result, in 2000, there were 10 candidates eligible to be listed on the presidential ballot—compared to only three, maybe four, in past years. Across the state, elections officials wrestled with ways to get more names into the available space. The elections supervisor in Palm Beach County, Theresa LePore—a hardworking, soft-spoken lifer in the office—rejected the most popular solution, which was to use teensy type. Tens of thousands of her voters were elderly. Even the highway signs in Palm Beach County use extra-large letters. She also decided not to follow the example of Duval County—the Jacksonville area—where the ballot would be split into two sequential pages. (This apparently was very confusing, with thousands of citizens casting votes for one candidate on each page, thus invalidating their ballots.)

Instead, the design LePore chose placed the names on two facing pages, with the punch holes running down the center. Arrows pointed from the names to the holes—but when the ballot cards were fed into the voting machines, the holes didn't always line up perfectly with the arrows. Not that the arrows were entirely clear, either: The hole for a minor third-party candidate, Patrick J. Buchanan, was higher on the card than the hole for Al Gore.

Thanks to the two wing-like pages, this would come to be known as the "butterfly ballot." LePore considered it a rather lovely solution to a difficult problem. The ballot had been shown to the major party county chairmen and to every candidate on the ballot. No one objected. She was excited to be running her first presidential race after 25 years in training under the previous supervisor.

LePore is a doer, not a theorist. As a high school student, she was the kid who never drew a lot of attention, but always got the homecoming float built or a book club organized. The eldest of eight in a close-knit, hard-working Catholic family, LePore got her first job at the elections supervisor's office when she was 16 through her father, Joe, a former city commissioner. She started working part time, and never left. The job suited LePore, who prided herself on organization and order. Her fellow supervisors around Florida teased her about her attention to detail. "When we'd see her, we'd say, 'Here comes Theresa with her carload of paper'—in a loving, kidding way," Sarasota County supervisor Marilyn Gerkin recalled. Running elections also allowed the amiable, but not terribly outgoing, young woman to feel close to the action—she had information that was crucial to candidates, consultants and reporters.

When her mentor stepped down in 1996 and LePore ran for supervisor herself, she declared as a Democrat because that's where the votes are in Palm Beach County. But "she is not political at all," County Commissioner Mary McCarty, a Republican, later said. "She has no use for the Republican or the Democratic party." LePore just liked the excitement of elections. She viewed her job as a public service, a colleague concluded, but she may have gotten in trouble by trying too hard to serve. To see how, consider the story of two voters, Rachel and Paul Berman.

■

The Bermans are two of the 14,000 retired people who live in Century Village, a sprawling, sun-baked complex, part barracks, part country club—and one of the largest, purest concentrations of Democratic votes on the planet. There are state party chairmen in America who don't have the pull of the party boss at Century Village. A Democrat running statewide in Florida can take an 8,000- or 10,000-vote cushion out of just this complex—and there are others approaching its scale all down the Gold Coast of South Florida. That margin is then whittled away by Republican retirees on the Gulf Coast, by farmers in central Florida and by the Deep South conservatives in northern Florida. This is the basic dynamic of all statewide races—southeast Florida versus the rest of the state, with the central Florida suburbs gaining more power every year.

Rachel Berman awoke at 6 a.m. on Election Day to take her daily two-mile walk. Paul rose an hour and a half later, when he heard his wife's key in the lock. Today would be a good day, they thought. They wanted to vote for Gore—but even more, they wanted to vote for Lieberman, "my *landsman*," as Paul Berman called the first Jew on a major party ticket. He was not alone. The old hands in Palm Beach County would credit Lieberman with catalyzing one of the strongest Democratic turnouts in the county's history.

From their apartment, the Bermans could see the large clubhouse, a two-story brick and stucco building a brisk six-minute walk away, where half of Century Village voted. The clubhouse polling station was in a large room that served as bingo hall, dining room and ball-room, where the Bermans like to do the polka and the Lindy Hop on the parquet dance floor.

That morning the lines to vote were "unbelievable," Paul Berman recalled. "Everybody showed up." After standing in line for 20 minutes, the Bermans reached the registration table, only to be asked for identification, which they didn't have. No matter. They decided to go swimming first—it was not yet 10:30 a.m.

They stood in line again, and this time, they were given cards to insert in the Votomatic machines. "I was voting straight Democratic," Rachel Berman said later. "So I don't know whether there was one hole or two holes. I saw Gore, I punched Gore." On these machines, the pages of the ballot fit like a book over the punch holes, and voters flip page by page through their options, stabbing tiny perforated rectangles from their ballot using a sharp-ended stylus. With each turn of the page, the opening over the ballot shifts slightly, directing the stylus into a new row of holes.

The Votomatic was hailed as a big step forward when it was invented in 1962. The basic technology drew on the punch-card readers that stored data for IBM mainframe computers. The advantage of the machines was the speed with which counting machines could tally the cards. It wasn't long, however, before elections experts realized that Votomatic cards are alarmingly unreliable. The tiny perforated rectangles—called "chads"—don't always fall away from the cards. When they stick, they can obscure the holes, making the votes unreadable by the counting machines. The failure rate for Votomatics is 4 percent or more—but since most elections are not terribly close, and since the failures can affect all candidates, there has never been a groundswell to spend tax dollars to replace the machines. In Florida, roughly 20 percent of the counties, including many of the biggest, voted with punch cards.

Paul Berman did not notice anything odd until he was patting his "I voted" sticker onto his polo shirt. There was a commotion. Gradually, as he sorted out the buzz, Paul realized that he had been so intent on voting for Lieberman that he had voted twice. "I voted for Gore, but I also voted for the vice president. I punched two holes instead of one . . . . I said, 'Oh my God, I think I did it wrong.' All I had to do was just punch Gore. It would have been sufficient. But I saw Lieberman—so I punched it, too."

Democratic officials all over the state were bombarded with complaints, and at 11:24 a.m., an attorney for the party sent a fax to Theresa LePore asking her to order deputy supervisors to put up signs in polling places, and issue instructions, clarifying the butterfly ballot. Three and a half hours later, the party faxed another request to LePore, this time requesting special attention to whether the punch holes lined up properly with the ballot.

"Theresa was in a coma," Gore's Florida strategist, Nick Baldick, said later.

Phone lines to elections headquarters in West Palm Beach rang and rang unanswered. When Lois Frankel, the Democratic leader of the Florida House of Representatives, drove to LePore's office around 2 p.m., she recalled, LePore told her: "There's no way to communicate. We have over 500 precincts and the only way we can communicate is they call us."

"Well, they can't call you because the lines have been jammed all day," Frankel answered. So LePore sat down to draft a memo. "ATTENTION ALL POLLWORKERS," the memo began, in bold, underlined letters. "Please remind ALL voters coming in that they are to vote only for one (1) presidential candidate and that they are to punch the hole next to the arrow next to the number next to the candidate they wish to vote for."

"How are we going to get them out?" Frankel remembered asking.
"I've no way to get them out," LePore answered.

■

Ron Klain's office in the Washington outpost of O'Melveny & Myers, where he is a partner, is six floors up in a glass-and-marble palace.
His office in Tallahassee—where his task was nothing less than winning America's closest election, in a recount, and in the courts if necessary—was a storefront phone bank with the phones unplugged. In
a normal election, this place would have dissolved into the bilge of
low-end retail the day after the voting. The Gore campaign pulled the
lease back at the last minute, recast itself as the Gore Recount Committee and called Southern Bell to get the phones turned back on.

He took stock of the situation the first afternoon: Bush's lead had
grown since dawn from a few hundred to 1,784. That was a tiny fraction of six million votes counted, but the chance that it could be made
up by recounting alone seemed unlikely. That was bad news.

The secretary of state, Harris, had announced that she expected the
automatic recount to be done immediately—not, as the Democrats
had hoped, later in the week. More bad news. Gore's recount experts
told Klain they would do the same thing if they were on the Republican side. Move quickly to ratify the election night result, limit the
scrutiny of ballots, and then look surprised if anyone requests more
counting. We've already had a recount. (Which was exactly what the
Republicans began saying.) Still, the fact that it was predictable did-
n't make it any easier to swallow.

In this sea of bad news, the Palm Beach butterfly ballot was the
bright spot for Klain that first day. When he learned that about
19,000 voters in the county punched more than one hole in the
presidential column, he was appalled. Beyond that, Buchanan—
whose punch hole on the ballot fell between the spots for Bush and
Gore—had received several thousand more votes in Palm Beach
than in any other Florida county. "The level of injustice was over-

whelming," Klain recalled. A close look at Florida election law suggested the ballot might even be illegal on several technical grounds—mainly having to do with which side of the name the arrows and punch holes appear.

The outlines of a strategy emerged: Do the automatic recount and hope to close the gap. Follow up with requests for hand counts in a few jurisdictions to keep the clock running. All the while, work on a killer lawsuit challenging the Palm Beach County ballot. To Klain, the idea of hand-counting ballots was "definitely the B-track strategy." The butterfly was Plan A.

This was the opposite of the way Young and Sautter and Downs and even DNC counsel Sandler wanted to go. They felt the lawsuit was all fine and good, but as recount specialists they believed in counting ballots. The more, the better.

As Klain listened, he grew increasingly sure that Gore had won. He said that to Gore in a phone call the next morning. Gore agreed, and said he was ready to fight. But Klain cautioned that with Bush's brother in control of the machinery of state government, Gore should recognize the obstacles ahead.

"Sir, you have to understand," Klain said. "This is Guatemala."

■

It was about 3 a.m. in Los Angeles when Warren Christopher's phone rang. He had just gone to sleep after watching the election drift down to deadlock. Campaign chairman Daley wanted to know if the former secretary of state could come immediately to Nashville to help plan Gore's next move. After hurrying to catch a 6:30 a.m. flight via Denver, Christopher reached Nashville by early afternoon. He headed straight to the hotel suite, where Gore was talking tactics with his exhausted family and crew. Gore had decided to remain for a day or so to sleep in Nashville—although he soon realized that he would be a virtual prisoner in his hotel suite and headed home.

Earlier in the year, Gore had turned to Christopher to lead his search for a running mate, a process that led to a widely acclaimed result: Lieberman. The choice of the 75-year-old Christopher for this duty was easily understandable—he had led the 1992 process that selected Gore for Bill Clinton's ticket. Gore knew "Chris," as he was widely called, to be a measured, canny and sober voice, and a lot tougher than one might guess from his hand-tailored appearance and slightly distant gaze.

In Nashville, Lieberman—always quick with a smile and a wisecrack—shook Christopher's hand and said, "Look what you got me into now." The diplomat and superlawyer sized up the mood. Everyone was dog-tired, but there was a sense of bleary wonderment, too, that Gore's candidacy had come back to life. Now, if only they could find a way to wring a couple of thousand more votes from Florida.

Christopher, along with Daley, took a charter to Tallahassee.

■

He arrived about the same time as James A. Baker III, the Republican Party's own grand old man. Both Gore and Bush turned to former secretaries of state in part because they wanted to present the image of calm, wisdom and supreme dignity to the public. But they were in fact very different men—Baker a politician with a sideline in the law; Christopher a lawyer with a sideline in politics. Baker was always revealing glimpses of his inner pit bull, while Christopher was eternally prim. Although they had held the same job and knew many of the same people, they were not friends.

Baker, who was on the way to his office at Rice University when he first talked to Bush chairman Don Evans, was his generation's most successful campaign manager, having run five consecutive presidential efforts and won in three. He was rewarded with a string of the most prestigious jobs in the world: White House chief of staff, secretary of treasury and finally, secretary of state, the third-ranking position in the executive branch. There had been a lot of talk during the campaign that Baker had been frozen out of W.'s effort because the Bush family still resented his reluctance to run Dad's doomed 1992 operation. But election night found Baker watching the returns alongside his hunting buddy—and W.'s right hand—running mate Richard B. Cheney.

"There was a sense [during the campaign] that there was an issue between Baker and—not me but the Bush family," Bush said later. "That's not the case." Baker's absence, he explained, was part of an effort to make the campaign forward-looking, not "stuck in the past. . . . He understood."

Bush's team realized it needed not just a few lawyers in Florida but an army on the ground. "We knew that the lawyers would be focused on the legal side of all the various arguments that were on the table," recalls Joe Allbaugh, Bush's campaign manager, a huge and intimidating man with a drawl, a brush cut and a silent demeanor. "But you had a PR war and you had a political war. I mean, we had a logistical nightmare on [our] hands."

As the days turned to weeks, Allbaugh would come to think of himself as akin to a character in the film *Stalag 17*, the dark comedy directed by Billy Wilder about a group of Americans in a German prison camp during World War II. Like those POWs, Allbaugh felt he was undergoing an endurance test, and the other side kept trying to break his will. "The only question unresolved was whether I was going to end up like William Holden, the hero, or shot like Peter Graves."

The arrival in Tallahassee of Baker and Christopher led some witnesses to imagine the candidates were searching for a deal. They weren't. Christopher was there to help Gore win—or, if that wasn't possible, to guide him through the dispute with his reputation and future intact. Baker was there to hold the line. There had been a count, and Bush was ahead. "We were on the side of the angels," he recalled.

Baker and Allbaugh met with Gov. Jeb Bush for 90 minutes. Bush briefed them on the situation. Then, in a meeting with the lawyers in the "bull pit"—as the conference room in the state GOP headquarters came to be known—Baker heard some Republican lawyers weighing the idea of a statewide hand count of the ballots, and he stiffened their spines. The way to prevail, he believed, was to resist.

Christopher, arriving with Daley, met with Ron Klain and some of the other recount lawyers. Then the public relations war began. Baker held a news conference early Thursday afternoon in which he accused the Democrats of trying to "destroy . . . the traditional process for selecting our presidents." Christopher and Daley, furious, appeared 90 minutes later to accuse the Bush team of attempting, as Daley put it, to "presumptively crown themselves the victors."

Baker and Christopher talked formally only once during the entire dispute, that afternoon, in the conference room that the Gore high command had staked out at the cozy Governor's Inn in downtown Tallahassee. Baker showed up with Allbaugh and with his longtime aide-de-camp, Robert Zoellick. Baker had proposed the meeting because he thought it would help his side if it was seen as ready to talk. But when he arrived, there was nothing really to talk about. "We're going to differ, but I thought we should meet," Baker said.

"It was not a memorable meeting," Christopher recalled. "It was quite ordinary and expectable. All of us felt like we were going through the motions. There was no way to settle it. There was no middle ground. There was only winning and losing."

The next morning, the two men and their top colleagues happened to be in the same hotel restaurant at the same time for breakfast. William Daley strolled over to say hello. "Let's just get this over with," he said to Baker. "We'll give you Oregon and Iowa"—two other states still counting votes—"and you give us Florida. Let's just trade."

Baker laughed uncomfortably. As they left the restaurant, Daley turned to Christopher and said, "Chris, I think they're pissed."

■

The Rev. Jesse L. Jackson swept into Palm Beach County, and within a day he had organized a protest march. By the first weekend, he was leading a Miami rally along with Kweisi Mfume, president of the NAACP, and other civil rights leaders. Jackson believed there was a strong racial element to the deadlock. The elderly Jewish retirees of the Gold Coast weren't the only ones whose votes were unread by the machines, he said. "Once again, sons and daughters of slavery and Holocaust survivors are bound together with a shared agenda, bound by their hopes and their fears about national public policy."

Florida's racial politics had a hot recent history. (The longer history was deeply troubled.) A year before the election, Jeb Bush had issued an executive order known as "One Florida," ending state affirmative action programs in contracting and higher education. In their place, Bush substituted a race-neutral policy assuring the top 20 percent of graduating seniors entry into the state university system. Bush also issued a nonbinding pledge to increase the percentage of state contracts going to women and minorities.

Bush believed "One Florida" was a bold move to stem a rising tide of support for a constitutional ban on affirmative action. He thought it could gain support for him—and for his brother—in Florida's black community, support he had worked for years to build. "Jeb Bush . . . actually came into the community. And he embraced himself with black ministers. He was able to get a couple of ministers to endorse him," explained Tony Hill, a state legislator who became a leading foe of "One Florida." "I mean, he was like in Disneyland until he came down with his rude awakening."

The political elite praised the initiative, but opposition grew steadily. Hill and state Sen. Kendrick Meek—the rising son of the trailblazing Florida congresswoman from South Florida, Carrie Meek—demanded a meeting with Bush in January 2000. It did not go well. The two sides dug their trenches deeper and deeper, until Bush finally said, according to Hill: "I'll tell you what—if you think I'm going to change my mind, you might as well get you some blankets."

They did. Meek and Hill spent the rest of that day, the entire night and well into the next day sitting in the governor's office suite. A cause was born. Public hearings across the state brought out huge crowds. As the issue gathered strength, observers agreed that Jeb

Bush had blundered by taking the initiative without extensive discussions with black leaders to pave the way. He seemed to rely on the power of his own strong record on diversity, which surpassed that of his Democratic predecessors. But the elimination of affirmative action rubbed a history of grievance among Florida's African Americans, and it wasn't enough for Bush to say, in essence: Trust us.

A rally on March 7 in Tallahassee drew at least 10,000 protesters. There, a rallying cry was born: "We Will Remember in November."

Meek and Hill began a highly effective campaign to turn out black voters on Election Day. They walked large parts of the state. They held rallies and gave interviews. They devised a slogan—"Arrive With Five"—reminding voters to bring their friends to the polls. Republicans often stoked the movement's embers with ill-advised public complaints. State House Speaker John Thrasher, a Republican from Orange Park, joked at one luncheon that the protests against "One Florida" were the "biggest whine-fest in recent history," and he charged that Meek "would rather sing and obstruct" than attempt to find ways to resolve the dispute.

Bush, in Hill's view, had no sense of the ferment within the black electorate: "He had no inkling of an idea that African Americans would turn out in such large numbers." But they did. On Election Day, African Americans in Florida voted at a record rate—an increase of 60 percent over 1996, about 420,000 votes, with more than 9 of 10 going to Gore.

But in the hours and days after the election ended in deadlock, stories proliferated around the state of newly registered black voters whose registrations could not be found when they arrived to vote. African American precincts in South Florida and in Duval County in North Florida were among the most troubled by double-voting, unpunched ballots and other banes of inexperienced voters. There were even stories of voters turned away from the polls or intimidated by police "roadblocks"—the one that came closest to checking out involved a speed trap in front of a polling place near Tallahassee.

"Some say, 'The votes were not counted; this happens all the time. It has happened before,'" Jackson observed in Miami.

■

The law allowed 72 hours after Election Day to request recounts by hand, which meant they had a day to go. But Friday was Veterans Day, a state holiday, and Gore's legal team worried that county offices might be closed. It couldn't risk missing the deadline on a technicality. So Daley, Christopher and Klain met on Thursday to decide what to do.

Gore's recount guys—Young, Sautter, Sandler and Kendall Coffey from Miami—were worried that people had gotten swept up in the hoopla of Palm Beach. By Thursday there were nearly a dozen citizen lawsuits on file and affidavits were coming in by the thousands. Democratic county commissioners were talking openly about conducting a whole new election. As the recount guys saw it, a grand lawsuit might have made sense early Wednesday, when they were trailing by 1,784 votes. But, to everyone's surprise, the mandatory machine recount was shaving hundreds and hundreds of votes from Bush's lead. Young and Sautter had done recounts in which millions of ballots yielded virtually no change at all. "My experience has been in all recounts, the net gain is not very large," Sautter said later. They were lucky. And now that the machine recount had gotten Gore within striking distance, the best course, they felt, was to look at the ballots by hand—as many as possible.

But the idea of hand-counting six million ballots seemed impossibly extravagant. It had never been done before in a presidential race, and there was no provision for doing so under Florida law. The election statutes allowed candidates and parties to request hand counts on a county-by-county basis. Some lawyers later said Gore should have waited for Bush's victory to be certified—a huge public relations hit for Gore—and then pursued a statewide count in the "contest phase." That strategy was not seriously discussed at the time, because the patience of the public was then being measured in hours—maybe days—but certainly not weeks. Or Gore could conceivably have asked 67 counties for 67 counts. And what would happen then? Klain later theorized that the Republicans would have rushed in to oppose every hand count—except in their own best counties. They would have encouraged the counting in GOP strongholds and resisted everywhere else. Result: For days and days, the public would see Bush getting farther and farther ahead, while the pressure mounted for Gore to drop out.

Daley and Christopher agreed to request hand counts only in Palm Beach and Volusia counties—the two places with the most widely reported problems. The media had prepared the ground for complaints there. Klain, too, saw value in having a recount to keep everyone occupied while he developed the butterfly lawsuit. He had persuaded local Democrats to withdraw all their suits, and by early the next week, he believed, he could file the best possible case for relief from the ballot injustice.

Then Coffey chimed in. Coffey had been one of Klain's first calls—Klain was chief of staff at the Justice Department when Coffey was U.S. attorney in Miami. Coffey said: "If you're going to do those two counties, why not do Broward and Miami-Dade, too?"

Both of these South Florida counties used punch cards, and both were home to hundreds of thousands of Democratic voters. Both had large "undervotes"—the term for ballots that showed no presidential vote when they ran through the counting machines, perhaps because the chads were stuck. "Litigation is about process," Young said. "You can always litigate." What Gore needed was more votes, and the only way to get them was by counting.

Daley and Christopher weren't buying.

But a couple of hours later, Nick Baldick visited Klain's room at the Governor's Inn to press the case. "There's a huge amount of undervotes there," he urged. "You've got to count them. You have to go get them to sign off on this." Klain was moved, and took the message to the bosses, who authorized a request in four counties—even though they worried that the public would not stomach the upheaval.

That afternoon, Gore's chief spokesmen appeared before the cameras. Gore, they said, had no intention of getting out of the race. After 20 hours of learning about the Florida results, the Gore camp was "deeply troubled," Daley said. More than 20,000 voters had been "disenfranchised" in Palm Beach County alone—the Buchanan voters, plus the voters who punched too many holes in the presidential column. Christopher joined the attack, calling the butterfly ballot "confusing and illegal"—strong talk for such a circumspect man.

■

With Evans coordinating by telephone from Austin, George W. Bush began recruiting a Florida legal team. So many lawyers—more than 200—tried to get on a conference call Wednesday afternoon that it collapsed, but by that night an instant law firm had been established.

There was a federal courts division, led by litigator Theodore B. Olson of the Washington office of Gibson, Dunn & Crutcher. Olson was an icon of the conservative legal community—a founder of the influential Federalist Society, veteran of 13 U.S. Supreme Court arguments, an authority on the high court and a friend to several of the justices.

Coordinating the traffic: George J. Terwilliger III, the former number two at the Justice Department, now senior partner at White & Case, aided by colleagues Tim Flanigan and Robert Bittman. Bittman had been a key assistant to independent counsel Kenneth W. Starr in the investigation that led to the impeachment of President Clinton. Together, the White & Case partners managed the endless demands for legal analysis, farming questions out to a network of former Supreme Court clerks scattered across the country, from the K Street corridor to the skyscrapers of Chicago.

The state courts division was led by Barry Richard. Bush also recruited a rumpled and brash lawyer named Michael Carvin, who had wide experience with election cases. Like Ted Olson and a number of other key attorneys for Bush, he was a veteran of the Office of Legal Counsel in the Reagan and Bush Justice departments.

The ringmaster of it all was Ben Ginsberg, Bush's campaign general counsel, an election law expert from the insider Washington firm of Patton Boggs. Ginsberg was a veteran of several recounts, including a brief challenge to the 1988 election of Sen. Connie Mack in Florida. He was an expert on Florida law, recount politics and the attitudes of the Bush operation.

So if there was a pyramid, Baker sat at the top of it, helped by longtime aides Margaret Tutwiler and Robert Zoellick and, from the Bush campaign, Allbaugh and Josh Bolten. Just below that were Terwilliger and Ginsberg, and Olson in his own splendid orbit. "There were a lot of chiefs and not many Indians," one lawyer said. But while there were occasional confrontations and raw feelings, many on the team would come to marvel at the spectacle of legal superstars pulling all-nighters to help check the citations of obscure cases.

Baker was spokesman for the effort, its tough-but-distinguished public face, and he was frequently the one who framed the issues for Bush in daily telephone talks. He was also incisive, several of the lawyers recalled, in his scrutiny of key briefs, often predicting the questions the Supreme Court justices would ask. "I was a Meese person," said one, recalling the grudges of the Reagan years, when Baker competed for influence with Reagan's friend Ed Meese. "We had always resented Baker because he ran rings around us. Now I saw why."

The first key conclusion Bush's lawyers reached was that they did not need to worry much about lawsuits challenging Palm Beach's butterfly ballot. The ballot had been properly reviewed before Election Day, it seemed clearly legal under Florida law, and in any event, they found it inconceivable that a court would sustain an effort by Gore to have voters go back to the polls and use a new ballot. As Terwilliger put it: "There are no do-overs in a presidential election."

But they argued heatedly over whether to go to federal court to block hand-recounting of Florida's votes, a potentially damaging move in the public relations war because it would put Bush, rather than Gore, in the role of litigator.

Election law generally is left to the states, and conservative lawyers usually urge federal courts to stay out of state business. But several of Bush's key lawyers felt from the start that they had to map their strategy in the federal system, onerous as that would be to some of their ideological brethren. They knew that Florida's court system led ultimately to a state Supreme Court that was dominated by Democrats and openly hostile to the state's Republican-controlled legislature. They believed their friends were to be found in the federal courts—especially the U.S. Supreme Court, where conservatives held a narrow majority.

But on what legal grounds could they seek redress in the federal system? Every idea they kicked around seemed unconvincing. "The smart people were telling me, 'There isn't a good way,'" Terwilliger remembered. Carvin and John Manning—a colleague from the Reagan Justice Department, now a professor at Columbia University's law school—worked from midnight to 6 a.m., trading ideas and drafting papers.

Could a recount be a violation of First Amendment rights to expression? Nah.

A violation, perhaps, of the due process rights of voters whose ballots are not hand-counted? Weak.

Terwilliger favored the theory that hand-counting some ballots, but not others—with only a vague sense of which marks on a ballot might constitute a vote—was a violation of the equal protection clause of the U.S. Constitution. His partner, Flanigan, thought the claim was extremely weak, and the two men tangled over it. Carvin found he agreed with Flanigan: It was a fairly lame case. After all, Florida's law provided for all election disputes to be funneled eventually into a single courtroom, where a judge could adjudicate all disputes. What could be more equal than that?

So sensitive was the question of federal intervention among conservative lawyers that when word of the plan for an equal protection claim began to drift up to Washington, angry conservatives started "telling Republican lawyers all over Washington that it was a terrible argument," as one recalled. Bush's lawyers had to call and say cut it out, they were doing the best they could.

On Thursday, Frank Jimenez, acting general counsel for Jeb Bush, reported that the Democrats planned to seek recounts in which dimpled ballots would be accepted as evidence of a voter's intent. That did it—Gore might pull ahead with that method.

"We didn't want to be criticized for going to court, but we felt we had to do something offensively," one Bush lawyer recalled.

What about seeking their own hand recounts in Republican-dominated counties, to try to offset Gore's efforts in Democratic counties? For the Bush team, too, the Friday deadline loomed for seeking such recounts. The legal team had identified Republican-dominated counties in which Bush was most likely to pick up votes. Even though they were opposing Gore's recount efforts on principle, should they now file for their own before it was too late?

With just hours to go before deadline, Bush's lawyers met in the bull pit. Ginsberg was there, along with Olson, Bittman, and others. Jeb Bush turned up in a golf shirt and khaki pants as they moved toward a final decision. Ginsberg laid out the facts for the Florida governor. This was ultimately a political decision that would be made in Austin, with Jeb's advice an important element. What do we do?

The governor said he didn't think it made sense to pursue their own recounts. It makes us look bad and runs counter to our argument, he said, according to people present. Besides, he didn't think his brother would get anything out of it. Who knew what standards would be used in the hand recounts and which candidate would ultimately benefit?

The political team's view was that Bush had already maxed out in key GOP counties. After a conference call with Austin, the decision came down: no Republican requests for recounts, but a green light to go into federal court in Miami the next morning.

CHAPTER THREE

■

Deadline

On Thursday, November 9, Benjamin McKay, the young chief of staff to Florida's secretary of state, received a phone call from Jim McGill, a major supporter of George W. Bush. McGill was a leading Tallahassee lobbyist and partner in the local law firm of Fowler, White.

It was a timely call. McKay had a burgeoning problem. His boss, Katherine Harris, found herself at ground zero of an epic political battle. McGill had a solution—Mac Stipanovich.

Everyone in Florida politics knows Stipanovich. With his graying crew cut and close-cropped goatee, J. M. "Mac" Stipanovich cuts a dashing, faintly dangerous figure on the Florida stage. He's a former Marine who loves obscure books and tough fights. As a younger man, he masterminded the 1986 election of Bob Martinez, the lone Republican wedged among three Democratic two-term governors. He then helped run Jeb Bush's failed 1994 campaign and helped get Harris elected secretary of state in 1998, all the while leading the life of a Tallahassee lobbyist—a rich and rewarding life in which he reveled. In 1999, for example, at the end of Gov. Bush's first legislative session, Mac strolled from the Capitol at Bush's side and effused: "I got everything. I don't know what the poor people got, but the rich people are happy and I'm ready to go home."

It so happened that George W. Bush's team already had assured themselves that Stipanovich would be willing to help Harris before McGill proposed the idea. Mac was on his way to Latin class—part

Florida Secretary of State Katherine Harris was the state official responsible for overseeing the election recount. She had been co-chair of the Bush campaign in Florida,
but she saw herself as an impartial enforcer of state law.

(AP/ Wide World Photos)

of his quest for a master's degree in medieval history in his spare time—when his cell phone vibrated. A Bush campaign official—he won't say who—was seeking his help.

"I was asked whether I was going to sit around and parse verbs or whether I was going to get into this fight," he recalled. "Someone like me, you don't need to be told much what to do. You just ride to the sound of gunfire."

Stipanovich came riding into Harris's inner sanctum, advising her on every crucial decision and putting himself in a position to keep the Bush campaign fully informed of every development. Did he coordinate her moves with Bush? Mac demurred: "It's a small town. I know a lot of people and I talk to them all the time," he said afterward. "I don't want to be more specific—did you talk to the Bush campaign, did you talk to the governor's office—I don't want to get into that."

From the beginning, the Gore camp feared that the Bush team and Harris were coordinating their efforts. On election night, a call had been placed from Harris's cell phone to the Texas governor's mansion. Harris later said that she lent the phone to state GOP chairman Al Cardenas.

Harris's closest advisers, in interviews after the election was decided, insisted that Harris acted independently—indeed, that some of her actions were not precisely what the Bush team wanted. For example, Harris declined to speed up one key ruling that would have aided a GOP lawsuit, and she pushed to expedite the entry of the Florida Supreme Court when the Bush team preferred to go slow. Attorneys representing George W. Bush insist they were specifically forbidden to talk strategy with Harris's attorneys during the period when Harris was taking actions to influence the result.

But in almost every instance, Harris's key interpretations of Florida law were pro-Bush. And throughout the crisis, at the side of the relatively inexperienced Harris stood one of Florida's toughest, most seasoned Republican strategists. Stipanovich helped steer Harris through an extraordinary period in which—under ferocious pressure from all sides—she steadily narrowed the options of Al Gore, until at last he ran out of time.

Harris's decisions would make her one of the most polarizing figures of an extremely polarizing episode—loved by those who believed that she was bravely applying the law; reviled by those who, in the words of Gore press secretary Chris Lehane, saw her as a nakedly partisan hack sent to steal an election, "Commissar Harris," he derisively called her.

■

The automatic recount ended on Friday, November 10. Through a series of glitches, corrections and rediscovered ballots, George W. Bush's lead was cut from nearly 1,800 to barely 300. The next day, the War for Florida went from skirmish to siege. Gore had requested hand counts in Volusia, Miami-Dade, Broward and Palm Beach counties—nearly one-third of the total ballots statewide—and in Palm Beach, bright and early this day, they were going to begin a sample count.

Gore's effort to count was launched down a dim and rarely traveled trail. In a fundamental way, the counting-room battle boiled down to a fight over the standards by which the ballots would be counted—and also whether there was time to recount them at all. These were subjective judgments, to be made by little-known members of county canvassing boards, up to their necks in meddlers and pressure groups—and there was no telling how they would come out.

Saturday, 9 a.m., the first test began. Observers for Gore and Bush arrived at the Palm Beach County government building, a modern edifice across the Intercoastal Waterway from the fabled gilt island known as Palm Beach. No doubt many Americans were confused when they first learned that the presidency was hinging on the Palm Beach vote. They didn't realize that the county is one tiny fraction filthy rich, and otherwise Middle America. One part Trump, 99 parts Krump.

The test count was a study of ballots from four precincts—1 percent of the total vote—chosen by the protesting side, the Democrats. If the sample indicated a problem in the overall "vote tabulation," the county canvassing board was instructed by law to count all the ballots.

The punch cards were brought to a small glass-walled room next to Theresa LePore's office. As elections supervisor, she was one of three members of the canvassing board; she was also, by now, the world-renowned author of the "butterfly ballot." Lawyers from each party watched volunteers examine the ballots, and raised protests whenever they disagreed with a decision. Disputed cards were presented to the board for a verdict.

To prevail, Gore needed the "right" standard, but at this point the Democrats couldn't define what that was. They felt confident that if tears, bulges and dents on the pre-perforated rectangles were judged to be votes, Gore could pull ahead in Florida. When Democrats push hard to raise their turnout at the polls, as they did in 2000, they tend to bring out more inexperienced, occasional voters than Republicans do. The rarely spoken secret on both sides in Florida was a belief that, as one Democratic recount expert put it, "Democrats make more mistakes than Republicans."

The canvassing board began with a meeting. Circuit Judge Charles Burton, the board chairman, and Carol Roberts, a Democratic member of the county commission, listened as LePore discussed past practices in Palm Beach. In 1990, she said, the county deemed that a vote should be registered whenever the voter followed the instructions to "punch down through the card" next to the candidate's name. Therefore, "a chad that is hanging or partially punched may be counted as a vote," since it is possible to punch through the card and still not totally dislodge the chad. "But a chad that is fully attached, bearing only an indentation, should not be counted," LePore continued.

That seemed clear enough. But LePore immediately hedged. Other Palm Beach recounts, she said, had applied a "three-corner" rule, which gave credit if three of a chad's four corners were detached. Yet another standard was the "sunshine rule," which tallied a vote if light passed through the ballot in the proper place. The board agreed to use the sunshine rule.

Gore's lead lawyer on the scene, Benedict P. Kuehne of Miami, pushed the board to expand its standard to include all impressions on a punch card—"dimples" or "pregnant" chads—as evidence of voter intent. The board agreed to set such ballots aside and consider them later. Mark Wallace, the Republican counsel, held fast to the sunshine rule.

When the test count began, it became clear to Wallace that light was being seen through way too many ballots. "Objection! Objection!" he blurted again and again. "They were finding light and glimmers of hope, in my opinion," he later explained—although his opponents suspected that he was mostly trying to slow things down.

And indeed, the counting proceeded at a glacial pace, with piles of ballots growing micron by micron: the undervote pile, the overvote pile, a vote for Gore here, a vote for Bush there.

Kuehne decided that Wallace was not the only one stalling. He felt Judge Burton was dragging his heels. Burton was a bit of an enigma to both parties, and would become more mysterious as the ordeal dragged on. He was a Democrat, a one-time intern for Sen. Edward M. Kennedy, a former prosecutor of crimes against children—all of which made liberals think he might be one of them. But he had been appointed to the court by Jeb Bush. No one was quite clear where his heart—or interests—lay. When Kuehne urged the board to move more quickly, "Burton wouldn't listen," the lawyer recalled. "I kept telling them, 'I've been through this before. This is how you need to organize it.'"

Halfway through the first precinct—lunch break. Burton disappeared. "Nobody knew where he went," Kuehne said later. When the judge returned, some 45 minutes later, he announced that the sunlight standard was inappropriate given the 1990 guideline. Two corners of a chad should be detached to count.

Had Burton talked to anyone? Kuehne was suspicious. The way he saw it, if Burton had simply found merit in the pleas of Republicans on the scene, "Fine—we were all lobbying." But if someone in power, someone in Tallahassee, say, had weighed in, that was different. In fact, Burton had gone to speak with Kerey Carpenter, a lawyer in Katherine Harris's office, and two lawyers from the county. He wanted to talk about the standard.

The counting resumed. Now it was Kuehne's turn to protest as potential Gore votes were set on the undervote pile. Twelve hours later, around 2 a.m., an exhausted board emerged into the tiled foyer. Despite the hour, a crowd was waiting. Television lights added to the already heated atmosphere.

Burton read the results: 33 additional votes for Gore, 14 for Bush. Net gain of 19 for Gore.

That was enough for Roberts. "I move that this board conduct a manual recount of all the ballots for the presidential election for the year 2000," she said triumphantly. Cheers erupted among the watching Democrats. Republicans jeered and booed.

Before he would agree to count ballots, Burton wanted an advisory opinion from the secretary of state's office. Harris's lawyer, Kerey Carpenter, was still at the meeting. She advised the board that only evidence of machine malfunction or a natural disaster would justify a hand count. Voter error would not trigger one.

"The vote difference . . . was not due to machine error," LePore said defensively.

Burton said they had better hold off until they got more guidance from Tallahassee.

"Call the vote!" Roberts shouted. "Call the vote! Call the vote!"

Roberts and LePore voted to proceed. Burton voted no. Again there were cheers and jeers. "You'll never be elected in this county again," Monte Friedkin, chairman of the county Democratic committee, shouted at the judge.

■

As the test count was proceeding in Palm Beach, Gore's high command met in Washington at the vice president's residence on the grounds of the Naval Observatory. This would be Gore's command post, a secluded Victorian mansion behind a high fence at the top of Embassy Row. He had a little study in the back of the house, but most of the time he would watch the news reports, read legal briefs, call supporters and hatch strategy from the formal dining room, which he transformed into a Cabinet room. He visited his vice presidential office suite very rarely during the dispute—mindful, no doubt, that he had gotten in hot water after the 1996 campaign for using his official space to do partisan business.

The vice president's lawyers were urging him to narrow the focus of their complaint. Some of the leading newspapers and television pundits who drive Beltway opinion had begun to worry about the length of time and spreading confusion involved in this fight. Some senior Democrats—mostly former office-holders—were quoted measuring the patience of the public in days, not weeks. And everywhere in Washington there was talk of "statesmanship," which, the Gore people mused sourly, always seemed to mean a Gore surrender. Those on the vice president's team worried that support for their effort was about to collapse under their feet. It was time, most of them felt, to consolidate the fight on their best ground—counting ballots—and to kill the other issues, including the butterfly ballot suit.

It was a difficult moment because in their hearts, Gore's advisers had come in those first days to a concrete conviction that their man was the rightful winner. The butterfly ballot and a similarly confusing ballot design in Jacksonville called the "caterpillar"—these had thwarted thousands of voters who wanted to elect Gore. Tens of thousands of ballots across Florida had registered no vote on the counting machines, and they were overwhelmingly concentrated in Democratic precincts. Could anyone truly believe that all those people turned out to vote but then skipped the biggest race on the ballot? The law in Florida seemed clear—a vote was not a matter of technical compliance with instructions. Election officials had an obligation to try to discern the voter's intent. There was case after case in Florida law centering on voters who put their X in the wrong place or colored the wrong dot, and every time the courts said: If, by looking at the ballot, you can tell what the voter meant, it's a vote.

By that standard, Gore had more votes—his aides fervently believed this, from the youngest field worker to the sober lawyer-diplomat Warren Christopher. The decision of the Bush team not to seek any hand counts was proof, to Gore supporters, that they were afraid to see the ballots. In this climate of righteous indignation, it wasn't easy to take issues off the table—but the time, they felt, had come to do just that.

William Daley, Gore's campaign chairman, called Tom Nides that morning and asked him to fetch Gore's running mate, Joe Lieberman, to a meeting. Nides had run Lieberman's end of the presidential campaign, and the two men had a trusting bond. Daley told Nides this: We need to focus the effort. We're getting everyone around the table to make some decisions, and Lieberman is going to be one of the hardest to sell on this. The chairman wanted Nides to talk Joe into this.

Nides agreed to try, and he set off in search of the Connecticut senator. It was Saturday, the Jewish Sabbath, which meant the highly observant Lieberman could not be reached by phone or fax or e-mail. Orthodox Jews do not work on Shabbat, a stricture they honor by not operating machinery or other devices. Lieberman had consulted his rabbi, who advised him that he could take part in political meetings on Shabbat if they were of vital national interest.

Nides found the senator eating lunch at a neighbor's house. Lieberman excused himself from lunch and the two men went to the basement. "Sorry," Nides said, "but we're having a very important meeting over at Gore's house."

"Okay," Lieberman answered. "If it's that important, I'll go." But driving was out of the question on Shabbat. Instead, the two men hiked up the long Wisconsin Avenue hill, trailed by the Secret Service,

and while they walked, Nides explained what was up. "There is consensus," he said, "a general consensus, I believe, along the notion of
narrowing the focus."

"That's great," Lieberman answered. They trudged some more.
Then the senator added: "But I'm not sure I agree with that."

Lieberman's public face was soft and reflective—on the floor of the
Senate he often spoke with brow furrowed thoughtfully, while on the
campaign trail he was genial and playful and funny. But under that,
he was a fighter, and the strange turn of events in Florida had his
dukes up. He felt South Florida was his baby—during the campaign,
reporters joked that he spent so much time there he was probably eligible to cast a ballot himself. He had pushed the butterfly ballot issue
from the moment he first learned of it, in a phone call to a Florida
talk show host on election afternoon. And then there was Lieberman's legal background. That had taught him never to give ground
without getting something in return.

All the way up the hill, a 40-minute walk, Nides tried to convince
the running mate that public relations concerns, if nothing else, dic-
tated this decision. No luck. When they arrived, Nides took Daley
aside and said, "Listen, I have not convinced him. So, good luck."

Gore's wife, Tipper, was there snapping pictures, making the right
joke at the right moment, offering food and sizing people up without
them knowing it. Gore occupied a central chair, beside two easels
held giant pads of paper. Like a New Age consultant, Gore drew dia-
grams and jotted key words. At one point, he drew a series of con-
centric circles to remind everyone of his circles of responsibility. At his
innermost circle, he had responsibilities to himself and to Lieberman
at the center, then moved outward through his closest supporters,
Democrats as a whole and, in the largest circle, the country. He could
not make critical decisions, he explained, without considering the
larger context.

The group talked for five hours—the Gores (including his daughters Karenna and Kristin), Daley, Christopher, Lieberman, Nides,
campaign consultant Carter Eskew and Gore's brother-in-law Frank

Hunger. Participants came and went during the marathon session. Daley and Christopher made the case for dropping the butterfly ballot issue: It was a long shot, at best; pushing a losing case, with the whole world watching, could set them up for a fatal defeat in court. By dumping the threat of a lawsuit, they believed, Gore could seize the high ground politically on the issue of counting ballots.

According to one account, Daley argued that there was no question Gore got hurt by the design of the ballot. But "people get screwed every day," he said. "They don't have a remedy. Ask black people. They get screwed every day. They don't have a remedy. There's no way to solve this problem."

Some concerns were philosophical, others were practical. Gore and his lieutenants realized as they looked at the clock that it wasn't good enough to feel righteous. They needed solutions that could work quickly. As Christopher saw it, Gore's best move was to direct all energy toward the four-county recount. He supported having Gore go before the cameras that weekend and announce that he would drop all other challenges and seek simply a fair count in the four counties.

Every time Gore leaned in that direction, however, Lieberman waved him back. His views, he said, were shaped by the fact that he was once a state attorney general, and he had experienced a super-close election once before. If there was one thing he knew, it was never to close a door. "The American people are patient people," he said. And the public could understand injustice.

Lieberman could not—or would not—see Daley's concern about a remedy. There was simply no way to fix what happened with the ballot, Daley argued. True, the airwaves and op-ed pages were full of suggestions: a new election in Palm Beach . . . or maybe a statistical adjustment that would redistribute most of the Buchanan votes . . . or maybe a mass swearing of affidavits, in which county voters would declare which candidate they really meant to vote for. But seriously: a new presidential election—in one county? Federal law specifically set the date for presidential voting. There was no way. And who was to say the Republicans, infuriated by Gore, would not come out in swamping numbers? As for letting some statistician decide—c'mon. This wasn't a county sheriff's race.

Gore accepted the weakness of the revote argument. The country probably wouldn't accept it, even if a judge allowed it. But with the presidency hanging in the balance, he wasn't prepared to close the door at that moment. He felt he owed the voters in Palm Beach who were angry over the ballot a little more time.

When the meeting broke up, Lieberman asked Gore what he had planned for the evening. Shabbat was over at sundown: How about a movie?

A double-date sounded good. They dug up a copy of *The Washington Post*, scanned the movie listings and picked one. *Men of Honor*.

They liked the sound of that.

∎

It was at this point—as the butterfly lost altitude and the recount became the key battlefield—that the massive advantage of George W. Bush began to come into stark relief. It was not apparent yet in Austin. There, the Bush advisers still felt they were on the defensive. That Saturday night, the communications staff held an aimless meeting that was finally galvanized when Mindy Tucker, the press secretary, said, "Okay, we're in a battle here, and five senior people are sitting here stepping on each other's toes!" Her outburst sent her staff members—and Tucker herself—heading to the airport and to Florida.

Although they may not have realized it at the time, Bush in fact had the high ground. Not necessarily the moral high ground—on that, the public was almost evenly divided, largely depending on how they had voted. Democrats believed that the Bush family machine was stifling the will of the voters through haste and technicalities. Republicans believed Gore was scheming to steal the election by having suspect ballots counted in his favor in Democratic counties.

No, the high ground for Bush was his infinitesimally larger pile of known, counted, recorded votes in Florida. Gore's only hope of changing this all-important fact was to count more ballots in his favor—and counting required many things to happen in precise concert. The county canvassing boards had to agree to count. They had to count expeditiously. They had to count by a broader standard than the machines applied. They had to find hundreds of county employees to staff counting tables. They had to work long hours to meet deadlines. They had to contend with the noise of protesters, the pleadings of friends and patrons and people in high places. They had—more than anything, perhaps—to accomplish a vast and tedious task under the glare of the world's scrutiny. A task that, no matter how well it was done, never could please everyone.

Bush, on the other hand, had only to disrupt the counting from any of these directions, and he was one disruption closer to the moment when time would run out. This was the difference that the initial margin of 1,784 little votes created: Gore needed everything to go right, or nearly everything. Bush only needed one thing after another to go wrong in Gore's path.

At this point, the thing that went wrong for Gore was Katherine Harris.

■

Harris was an easy target—an appearance-conscious woman of inherited wealth and high station who spoke openly around Tallahassee of her hope that co-chairing George W. Bush's Florida campaign might land her a nice presidential appointment. Instead, she sometimes felt, it had landed her in hell. Within a few days after the election ended in deadlock, Harris had become a virtual prisoner, eating most meals in her office because she was afraid to venture into public, and when she did she was shadowed by state bodyguards summoned because of death threats from across the country. She slept fitfully, laying awake most nights to watch television comedians make fun of her appearance. Propped before a flickering set in the wee hours, she rooted for conservative commentator Tucker Carlson on CNN's *The Spin Room*.

Harris was the state's chief elections official. Florida's election had ended in a virtual tie. How the tie was broken would determine the presidency. In a way, then, Katherine Harris was the official in charge of choosing the president. The pressure was incredible. As her chief of staff put it: "We knew early on that the attack was going to come our way. Katherine is going to be the big target. Might as well paint a bull's-eye on her because it's coming our way, boys," said Ben McKay.

For consolation, Harris turned anew to the biblical story of Queen Esther, one of her role models. Esther—the stunningly beautiful Jewish maiden who won the heart of a king and risked her life to save her people. Harris believed that, like Esther, she was endangering herself and her reputation in a good cause. "If I perish, I perish," Harris would tell her staff, until finally they revolted. "No more Esther stories!" they pleaded.

She had a perfect pedigree for Florida politics. Before there was Walt Disney, there was Ben Hill Griffin, Jr., citrus king of central Florida and Harris's grandfather. In all the focus on tourism and retirees and strip malls, it is often forgotten that Florida is one of America's most prosperous agricultural states. Griffin was a super-farmer, baron of endless orange groves and cattle ranches, a millionaire 300 times over. And he was more than that—state legislator, candidate for governor, chairman of the powerful Board of Regents, a counselor to senators and governors and college presidents. How large a figure was he? A case could be made that, in football-mad Florida, the state's spiritual epicenter is the stadium at the University of Florida.

Ben Hill Griffin Stadium.

His granddaughter grew up with a taste for the finer things, for four-star hotels, designer clothing, important friends, stature. Katherine Harris impressed the serious Republicans of her home base, Sarasota, with her ambition, her integrity—but not necessarily her intelligence. In 1994, after working as a real estate broker and serving on various important charitable boards, she won a seat in the state senate. Four impatient years later, at 41, she challenged the Republican incumbent secretary of state to win an office that was about to be phased out of existence. She tried to get the party's blessing to run for the U.S. Senate in 2000, but was passed over.

Then the recount hit. Harris figured the Gore people would make her a target—the Clinton-Gore administration specialized in that sort of thing, she said. It only strengthened her resolve. "I thought it was bizarre that they thought that character assassination would in any way deter me from following the law," she recalled.

McKay, her chief of staff, immediately realized he was outgunned. He hadn't gotten around to hiring a press secretary. His "copy, dump and run" mode of media relations—copy the paper, dump it in the press center and dash out the door before anyone could ask a question—wasn't going to cut it. So he summoned the pros who had worked on Harris's campaign two years earlier, Adam Goodman and Marc Reichelderfer. "Fly your butt up here," he said.

Then he went looking for lawyers.

It was the constant refrain of Florida: More lawyers! They poured in daily from every corner of the country—fuzzy-cheeked associates and senior partners, pols with bar licenses and superlawyers who just liked politics, former clerks to federal judges, appellate judges, justices of the Supreme Court. McKay got lucky in the lawyer sweepstakes. Not only did he get Stipanovich, he also signed up Steel Hector & Davis, a well-connected firm that once had strong Democratic leanings (it has been home to such Florida luminaries as the young Janet Reno). As the state became more Republican, however, so did Steel Hector, whose insider ties to both parties make it the Rose Law Firm of Tallahassee. Jeb Bush's acting general counsel, Frank Jimenez, was a firm alumnus.

Managing partner Joseph Klock simply scoffed at the idea of a pro-Bush slant. "This is not a hotbed of conservative ideology," he said later of Steel Hector. Klock himself was a mixed political bag, an anti-abortion, anti–death penalty Democrat who voted for Bush. But among the other lawyers who did work for Harris—and eventually there would be more than 20 in the firm—"some of the best contributions came from Democrats who voted for Gore," he said. Indeed, one of the attractions of Steel Hector, he theorized, was that a historically Democratic firm would make it harder to accuse Harris of partisanship.

The firm gave the glamour appearances to Klock, a diligent, hardworking attorney, while the daily grind of defending Harris was given a ferocious team of litigators—mostly women, many of them Democrats. Now that he had some troops, McKay established a war room in two offices adjacent to Harris's, hauling in extra computers, white boards, televisions, blank videotapes, coffee and soda for all the sleepless nights ahead.

One of Harris's in-house lawyers, Kerey Carpenter, had urged Judge Burton in Palm Beach to ask for guidance. Watching the exchange on television at home, Jimenez was elated. He thought a favorable opinion from Harris would help the Bush team in federal court the next day. But Sunday, November 12, came and went without a move by the county canvassing board to seek an opinion. About 6 p.m., Jimenez got tired of waiting. He called Clay Roberts to discuss the matter. The head of the elections division told Jimenez that an advisory opinion did not have to be requested by the board—a political party could ask. So Florida GOP chairman Al Cardenas was enlisted to sign the paper and fax it to Roberts.

The wily Stipanovich advised Harris to send her staff home for the night. It would not look good for the secretary of state to issue an opinion on a Sunday night, at the request of the Republican Party, to help George W. Bush. They had enough problems with appearances already.

So it was Monday, only after Burton persuaded his board to ask for advice, that Harris and Roberts were able to put their opinions in writing. Harris reiterated that the statutes required that election results be certified within seven days—by tomorrow. She would not extend the deadline. After that, Harris believed, she had very limited discretion to accept late returns. Only overseas absentee ballots would be counted after the deadline, she declared. For those, the deadline was Friday, November 17. Roberts, meanwhile, on advice from the Steel Hector lawyers, construed the recount law as narrowly as possible. Mere voter error was no justification for looking at ballots in search of dimples, stab marks or hanging chads. Only if the canvassing boards believed their machines had malfunctioned were they to count by hand.

Mac was proud: "Katherine kept turning the screw to bring this election in for a landing," Stipanovich later explained.

■

Week Two of the deadlock had arrived, though to the frantic and harried and exhausted troops on both sides—and the army of reporters covering them—it seemed more like a year. On Tuesday morning, November 14, the Palm Beach canvassing board discovered the opinion faxed from the division of elections the night before, saying they were not justified in hand-counting ballots.

And later that day, they received an opinion saying exactly the opposite from Florida Attorney General Bob Butterworth.

According to the attorney general's Web site, he is not ordinarily in the business of advising people about election law. "Questions arising under the Florida Election Code should be directed to the Division of Elections in the Department of State," the page advises. His policy also is to defer to state agencies: "Attorney General Opinions are not a substitute for the advice and counsel of the attorneys who represent governmental agencies and officials on a day to day basis," the Web site says.

Still, Butterworth was eager to render an opinion this time. He later recalled that he had talked on the phone with an unnamed member of the Gore campaign, who told him the Palm Beach board was getting advice from Harris and was going to be requesting his advice, too. Butterworth had kept in touch with the vice president's team throughout the dispute—he remembered chatting once with Daley, a couple of times with Gore attorneys Mitchell Berger and Kendall Coffey, and several times with officials of the state Democratic Party, about various matters that he said he could not recall. According to Butterworth, his staff began calling Palm Beach, prodding the canvassing board to fax a request.

In his opinion, Butterworth argued that Palm Beach County could keep counting. He hinted strongly that he felt the opinion from Roberts and Harris was a pure political power play, and suggested he had no choice but to respond. "Because the Division of Elections opinion is so clearly at variance with the existing Florida statutes and case law, and because of the immediate impact this erroneous opinion could have on the ongoing recount process, I am issuing this advisory opinion," Butterworth wrote. He maintained that Florida was in danger of creating "a two-tier system" in which Volusia County voters could have their ballots counted because the board there managed to beat the deadline, but South Florida voters could not. It was an analysis that came back to haunt Gore.

But for now, Burton and his board had two opinions—one saying stop and one saying go. The outside counsel to the board, civil liberties lawyer Bruce Rogow, was sitting in his sauna when it hit him what to do:

Ask the Florida Supreme Court.

■

More lawyers!

They came first for a recount—scores of lawyers rousted from bed and diverted from business trips and dispatched to any Florida county where machines were tabulating, from the boulevards to the backwaters. They came expecting short duty. The lucky ones went to places with nice hotels and good restaurants, but others were sent to places where Hardee's was haute cuisine.

In less than a week, though, everything had changed. Now, it was clear, there could be no recounts without lawsuits. Litigation was king. Before this was over, one firm—Steel Hector, representing Katherine Harris—would handle 40 lawsuits over 36 days, plus appeals before the Florida Supreme Court, two cases before the 11th U.S. Circuit Court of Appeals, a couple of federal district court cases and two appeals to the U.S. Supreme Court.

One firm. There would be dozens of firms involved before it was over.

When this tidal wave appeared, Ron Klain pondered the calendar and perceived a problem. He had asked his Harvard mentor, the legendary constitutional scholar Laurence Tribe, to handle Gore's case in federal court. This decision came almost immediately, when Klain still imagined that one man could do all the appellate work. But as he contemplated the likely next step, and the next, and the next, Klain now realized that it was entirely likely Gore would be fighting in federal and state appellate courts at the same time.

He consulted with Duke University law professor Walter Dellinger, a close adviser to Gore, former solicitor general, another of the leading liberal constitutional theorists in America. "Who's the best appellate lawyer we don't already have?" Klain asked. The answer, they both knew, was arguably Dellinger. But with a pair of Supreme Court cases looming, and a keen realization that this dispute was not a way to win friends, Dellinger had taken himself out of consideration. So they thought a while.

"Joel Klein," one of them said—referring to the recently departed head of the Department of Justice's antitrust division, the slayer of Microsoft. Klein's name reminded them of the private attorney Klein had hired to press the Microsoft case, David Boies.

They decided to call both men in hopes of finding one who was available. Klain discovered that Klein was on an airplane, unreachable, while Dellinger got through to Boies.

With the arrival of David Boies, Gore had the rough framework of an instant superfirm, despite the successful efforts of the Bush camp to lock up the big Florida law firms. The vice president liked to call it his "virtual law firm"—a description that appealed to his technoid side. But it was also a fitting description of a very deep talent pool separated by distance and affiliations and even interests. There was the core group with Klain in the frat-house quarters in Tallahassee. Just down the street was their Tallahassee insider, Dexter Douglass. (Eventually, Klain's group would move into the empty space at the back of Douglass's office.) Gore had Tribe and his nationwide network of brilliant liberal former students—all the Supreme Court clerks and law review editors he had managed to inspire and cultivate over the years. Gore had Boies, the Clarence Darrow of modern commerce, a quicksilver and endlessly quotable advocate for himself and all his wealthy clients, the sort of man who could eat dinner with reporters and settle a multimillion-dollar lawsuit by cell phone at the same time. ("It wasn't a very complicated negotiation," he said suavely when he clicked off and returned to his companions.) Gore had the recount guys, and he had the wise old counselor Warren Christopher (who faded from the dispute when his wife suffered the death of her best friend). He had his brother-in-law and pal, the wealthy class-action lawyer Frank Hunger, and his sage from Duke, Dellinger. And Gore had a faithful fundraiser and key Florida supporter, attorney Mitchell Berger, who offered his firm as a home base for Gore's efforts.

Klain and company moved into the cramped quarters of Berger's Tallahassee branch—so many lawyers in so little space that people were working in the hallways. It was a hodgepodge, but a stunning hodge-podge, and if the only thing really binding them all together was Gore, well, he was fine with that. Gore liked running things.

■

The teams clashed first in Miami on Monday, November 13, before U.S. District Judge Donald Middlebrooks, a distinguished Democrat. The Republicans were not optimistic, and their instincts were correct. In a fairly extensive opinion, Middlebrooks rejected their request for an order blocking all hand counts. One of the virtues of the American political system, Middlebrooks wrote, is its "decentralization." It was a good thing, he felt, to have 50 states, and 67 counties in this particular state, and each county exercising some real discretion over the presidential process.

The ruling left James Baker and team with a dilemma—the Republicans could appeal the loss and run the very real risk of another loss, with attendant public relations damage. Or they could shelve their federal claim. He put the options in a memo addressed to Bush and running mate Richard B. Cheney.

They "had no hesitation," Baker recalled. "They said keep the case going."

Meanwhile, in Tallahassee, the parties clashed in the Leon County courtroom of Judge Terry Lewis. A young-looking, athletic 47, rarely seen without a smile beneath his jet-black moustache, Lewis was a Democratic appointee who had recently angered conservatives by ruling that a law requiring minor girls to notify their parents before having an abortion violated the Florida constitution. But he also was generally regarded as a fair judge—the word in Jeb Bush's office was that Lewis could be expected to stick to the law.

The suit at hand asked him to prevent Harris from certifying the election results the following day. At issue was the Florida election law that said counties "must" certify results to the state within seven days after the voting. The law also said the secretary of state "shall" reject late-filed returns—then in another place said more flexibly that she "may" ignore late filings.

To Bush lawyer Mike Carvin, the law was "as clear as a goat's ass"—a deadline is a deadline and confusion in South Florida was no excuse. As Harris herself had argued, Hurricane Andrew—the mammoth storm that devastated South Florida in 1992—was an excuse for late filing. Confusion over ballots or whether to conduct a hand count was not.

The issue seemed just as clear to the Democrats—the law was inconsistent, allowing for candidates to request hand counts, but setting a deadline that did not allow enough time for a populous county to examine every ballot. That was the reason for saying that the secretary "may" accept late filings—because some counties could not possibly get a protested election resolved in just seven days.

For a hard-charging Washington appellate lawyer such as Carvin, the hearing was a lesson in North Florida courtroom style. While Carvin arrived with a detailed brief and supporting documents, the old Tallahassee hand Dexter Douglass came in with a thin pleading that he off-handedly offered to the judge. Douglass preferred colorful aphorisms to case citations; he dealt with the Hurricane Andrew precedent thusly: "Let me tell you, this is not only a hurricane, this is a bark-splitting, North Florida cyclone with a hurricane tacked onto the end of it."

Then, midway through the hearing, Lewis took a break to hear another case, proving that a mere presidential election would not interfere with the smooth running of Leon County justice.

The judge ruled promptly the next day. It was a mixed bag for both sides. Harris did have the authority to certify the results, he found, but she could not rule out late returns without good reason. Steel Hector lawyer Jonathan Sjostrom read and reread the opinion, and it gradually dawned on him that Harris had won the key fight. The counties would have to submit some hard numbers. But there was a problem for Mac Stipanovich, whose goal was to keep "narrowing the funnel": What would prevent the county boards, controlled by Democrats, from taking their sweet time thinking up reasons for being late, and all the while continuing to count?

Harris often consulted with her husband, Anders Ebbeson, a millionaire in the yacht business, when plotting strategy. "He's so strong," she said. "He's just so calm." She found it hard to sit still during meetings, leaping up from the table to throw away empty pizza boxes and soda cans. But now she had an idea of her own: She could send a letter to the county elections supervisors demanding that they spell out their reasons for wanting to file amended returns after the deadline.

Harris had made clear earlier that only a broken machine or "an act of God" would be acceptable reasons. The Steel Hector lawyers got busy searching Florida case law for others. They found precedents in which courts and other agencies justified late filings due to vote fraud, machine malfunction, substantial negligence on the part of election officials and natural disasters. Never voter error. This became Harris's list.

She sent letters to Palm Beach, Broward and Miami-Dade counties, where the canvassing boards were all in various stages of deciding whether, and how, to hand count. In their responses, no county cited machine malfunctions or natural disasters. Two and a half weeks later, the Gore campaign would present evidence in court that aging Votomatic machines are plagued by problems—the rubber strips can harden, the punched chads can pile up, all sorts of things can happen to make it more difficult to vote properly. But at this point, no one thought to allege in court that there had been a mechanical problem. The secretary of state was relieved. Had they done so, in the words of a key lawyer for Harris, Donna Blanton: "It would have been a different story."

As it was, Harris felt free to reject late filings. On Wednesday, November 15, she announced that the election results would become official that coming Saturday, when the overseas absentee ballots would be counted. Some of her advisers would worry in retrospect that Harris appeared too eager. She should have taken longer in answering the county letters. There were Bush lawyers who hoped she would simply say nothing—just come out at the deadline and certify the election, leaving Gore to try to undo it after the fact. By acting early, Harris hurt herself and, in a narrow sense, helped Gore, because his supporters now had time to sue Harris before the deadline. On the other hand, the strong stand made her a hero in her own party. Bouquets filled Harris's office, more than 60 of them, including one from a church in Sarasota. The card said, "You are our Queen Esther to America. God bless."

At this point, George W. Bush led Al Gore by just 300 votes—one-half of one-hundredth of 1 percent of the Florida total.

■

That night, Al Gore went before the television cameras in a speech timed to interrupt the evening newscasts. "We should complete hand counts already begun in Palm Beach County, Dade County and Broward County," he said—slightly exaggerating the state of affairs in those highly conflicted counties. Only Broward was entirely committed to counting at that point. "If this happens, I will abide by the results," Gore said.

Then he dropped his bomb: "I am also prepared, if Governor Bush prefers, to include in this recount all the counties in the entire state of Florida."

With the deadline approaching, Gore and his advisers concluded that he had to shake up the equation. Early in the dispute, Gore and his advisers had established the phrase "count every vote" as a central part of their message. Later research confirmed the power of that phrase. Gore's consultants had studied focus groups to test possible messages for the American people. The only one that worked was: In America, we count every vote. Attacking the Republicans, by contrast, turned people off. So Gore's speech included a pointed scolding of his press secretary, Chris Lehane, for his harsh anti-Harris rhetoric. From that day forth, Gore became an unrelenting, but always upbeat, advocate of vote-counting.

The proposal for a statewide recount was Gore's idea. For days the Bush team had hammered Gore for attempting to prolong the re-count. "The Bush people were saying these guys are trying to destroy America, they don't care about anything," a senior Gore adviser said. "The statewide recount sounded like a reasonable thing. We would have been shocked if he had accepted. But turning it down showed he was less reasonable."

Gore also proposed a meeting with Bush as a way to reassure the country that the Florida battle would not be too disruptive to the political system. He was surprised that Bush rejected that idea as well— and amazed when no one criticized Bush for doing so.

The speech caught Bush unprepared. The Texas governor was at his ranch, a quiet spread outside Waco, where the modest house has no cable television, where Bush was free to relax. Now Bush's aides bundled him into a motorcade for the two-hour ride southward along the prow of the Texas Hill Country. As he drove, he and his staff tried to figure out what he should say when he reached Austin.

First they sized up the offer. It wasn't much, really. Just basic recount theory—the candidate who is behind pushes for the broadest counts and the most favorable possible standards. The one in front has everything to lose and nothing to gain by going along.

The motorcade arrived in Austin about 9 p.m., and Bush quickly went before the cameras. "Everyone in Florida has had his or her vote counted," he said. "Those votes were recounted. In some counties they have been counted a third and even a fourth time." Hand counts, he maintained, could only introduce human error.

In short: No deal.

"So long as the Florida Supreme Court was rewriting the law and people were divining intent, we had a battle on our hands," Bush said later. "And if he [Gore] wasn't willing to address that, then all the rest of it was PR. That's why I rushed back: PR."

■

On Friday, November 17, a day before Harris was set to certify the results—with Bush's lead growing again as the overseas absentee votes were counted—Judge Lewis ruled again for Harris. Her decision not to accept late returns was a reasonable exercise of her discretion, he determined.

For Warren Christopher, who had seen many ups and downs in a life of law and politics, it was a memorably low moment. "The worst result imaginable," he later said. The afternoon was fading in Tallahassee, and the mood in the overpopulated offices of Mitchell Berger was extremely glum.

Then, out of nowhere, a whoop and a cheer went up. The Florida

Supreme Court was taking the case—and, without anyone asking, the seven justices ordered Harris not to certify the election and, even more unnerving to the Bush team, the justices let the recount go forward. They scheduled a hearing on the case for Monday.

■

Now it was the Republicans' turn to sweat. They simply did not trust the Florida court—that was part of the reason they had filed in federal court. When the justices blessed the hand counts without anyone asking them to, the Bush team felt its suspicions had been confirmed. Some even envisioned the hand of Dexter Douglass behind the whole thing—after all, as chief legal adviser to the late Democratic Gov. Lawton Chiles, Douglass had blessed the appointment of most of the court's justices. James Baker, who had hunted turkeys with Chiles and Douglass, was keenly aware of the man's influence. (Douglass scoffed at the notion that he engineered anything.)

In any event, conservative lawyers around the country had a sense, regardless of whether they had ever set foot in Florida, that the Florida Supreme Court was liberal and activist. In recent years, the justices had bedeviled the Republican-dominated legislature in its efforts to speed up the death penalty and limit abortion. It was, James Baker later said, simply a given that the court would be against them.

Mike Carvin had the lead for Bush in this case. After a week in Florida, the attorney believed he had figured out the Gore strategy: They had to get the count going in South Florida, their strongest area, and keep it going until Gore was ahead. Every Republican lawyer believed that, given a chance, the Democratic authorities in South Florida would devise a ballot-reading standard that would lift Gore into the lead. Then, he figured, Gore would switch gears, press for certification, and force Bush to contest the election. The public relations battle would shift in Gore's favor, and time would start working powerfully on his side. "All their eggs were in that basket," Carvin thought.

On the other hand . . .

If the Bush team could stretch things out a little longer, and keep Bush ahead, Gore would begin to face an impossible calendar. The trailing candidate could not file suit officially contesting the entire election result until that result was certified. By delaying the certification, the Democrats were taking a calculated risk that they could gain a lead—otherwise, they were chewing up precious time they would need to win the battle in a later phase.

Bush Inc. drafted briefs for the Florida high court, but in many ways they were speaking directly to the U.S. Supreme Court. Yes, they addressed Florida law and defended the deadlines. But they salted their argument with references to federal law. They cited Article II of the Constitution, giving the power to choose presidential electors to the state legislatures. They brought in Title 3 of the U.S. Code, Section 5—a remnant from the disputed presidential election of 1876—which gave preference to states that got their electors chosen by December 12, using rules set forth before the voting. What Gore wanted to do, the Bush lawyers argued, amounted to a change in the rules.

Boies, meanwhile, thought he might be coming to the end of his task. The Florida justices obviously were not opposed to hand counts. If Boies could persuade them to extend the deadline for hand counts in South Florida, he could pack up and go home.

As preparations for the hearing went on, some Bush advisers worried that the Florida court would hear only from a tough, abrasive Washington lawyer—Carvin. The Tallahassee hands knew how reluctant Southerners can be to taking instruction from visiting Yankees. So—while many in the Republican camp were leery of Barry Richard because he was a Democrat—Jeb Bush personally went to bat to assure that Richard would get time to address the justices.

■

On Saturday evening, November 18, Anne Johnson got a surprise call in Austin from Laura Bush. Anne's husband, Clay, was an old school chum of George W.'s who had agreed to manage his prospective transition team. At the end of a tough week, the Bushes were eager to get out of the house. There were moments when, for the candidates and their wives, the deadlock period felt like a prison sentence. A lot of time feeling trapped—and waiting.

Anne invited the Bushes to join them for dinner at the home of Mary and Tim Herman. Herman was an Austin attorney freshly home from volunteer duty for the Bush team in Florida. The candidate seemed intrigued, but hardly consumed, by the furor in Florida. He quizzed Herman lightly about election law and the separation of powers, but "it was not a detailed or prolonged conversation," Herman recalled. "We spent more time on the new Joe DiMaggio biography." Bush was unaware that *Newsweek* had splashed on its cover an unusual illustration blending his face with Gore's. He knew only vaguely that *Saturday Night Live* was causing a sensation with its withering satires of the two men and the crisis.

Dinner was Chinese carry-out. At the end of the evening, Bush refused to open his fortune cookie. His friends prodded. No chance. Finally, Anne Johnson tore it open and read it aloud: "You are entering a time of great promise and overdue rewards."

"You made that up!" Laura Bush cried.

But that's what it said.

■

On Saturday night, Tallahassee got down to business it really cared about—the annual Florida–Florida State football game. Hundreds of lawyers and reporters were booted from their hotel rooms to make way for fans with year-old reservations. For a few hours, a pause was called in the war for the White House. Katherine Harris emerged from near-seclusion to sip red wine with Democrats in the private box of FSU President Talbot D'Alemberte. And Harris's chief advocate, Joe Klock, finagled a ticket for his courtroom adversary David Boies.

■

You could put the most expensive tailored shirt in London on Mike Carvin's back, and within about three minutes, the front would be rumpled and the tail would be flapping. So his final preparations for oral argument were purely mental. He was reviewing cases on Monday morning, November 20, when he received a note.

A knowledgeable source close to the Florida high court had alerted the Bush team that the case was already decided. A draft opinion was circulating among the justices, and they had at least six of the seven in favor. They intended to rule in Gore's favor and extend the deadline five days.

Bush lawyers learned about it in a note passed to them shortly before the arguments were to begin. The news spread all over Republican Tallahassee. Joe Klock at Steel Hector heard it—though he wanted not to believe it. There was nothing illegal or even unethical about the justices making their decision based on written briefs, but if they were about to go on the nation's television screens and act as if their minds were still open . . .

"Just stand up there and answer their questions," James Baker counseled Carvin.

If someone had suggested, a generation ago, that the Florida Supreme Court might decide the biggest case in the world, the reaction would have been horror. The court, in those days, was a dismal and humiliating laughingstock. One justice, a bright and promising young man, had been forced from the court in a scandal and was a federal fugitive on drug smuggling charges. Another ex-justice was exiled to ignominy for having allowed an electric company lawyer to write his opinion—in an electric company case. A third justice had clung to his seat on the court by agreeing to a psychiatric evaluation. This was the man who liked to say that his preparation for his job was judging a local beauty contest.

The disasters of the 1970s persuaded Florida to stop electing Supreme Court justices, and gradually a more distinguished court accumulated, comprised of men and women nominated by a committee of lawyers and private citizens and appointed by governors. Over time, the end of directly electing justices greatly enhanced the court's reputation—and diminished its accountability. Of course, no state Supreme Court, anywhere, ever, had come under the scrutiny the Florida Supremes were about to endure.

Promptly at 2 p.m., the seven justices filed onto the bench for the most-watched appellate hearing thus far in history. Network television cancelled the soaps to broadcast oral arguments in *Palm Beach County Canvassing Board v. Katherine Harris*.

Wielding the gavel was Charles T. Wells, a lifelong trial attorney and occasional politician from Orlando. A lot of folks had thought Charlie Wells would end up being governor, but his electoral career never took off. He rose, instead, in the law. Wells was, perhaps, the perfect image of the Florida courts: He had the drawl of a Central Florida native, evoking the days when cows outnumbered tourists. But like a lot of homegrown Floridians, Wells was hard to sandbag.

He started with a warning to the hotshot lawyers: "The court, of course, has considered the papers carefully which each of you have filed." Translation: Let's cut to the chase.

And the chase, as quickly became clear, was this: How long could the South Florida counties keep counting before Florida's votes in the electoral college might be in danger of being ignored by Congress? Quizzing the first attorney up, Paul Hancock of the attorney general's office, Wells asked bluntly: "What's the date that—the outside date that we're looking at which puts Florida's votes in jeopardy?"

This move—sprinting right past the dispute to discuss the remedy—confirmed for Carvin and other Republicans that the case was indeed already decided. For David Boies, the tone of the questions was pure music. Gore's lanky lawyer realized immediately that things were going his way; he struck an answering note of cooperation. When Wells put the question of timing to him, Boies answered that "as long as the manual recounts will not impair the final certification in time to permit the selection of electors by December 12—those manual recounts must be included."

Indeed, most of Boies's time was spent discussing schedules. For political reasons, he later said, it was critical that he appear reasonable and accommodating. He referred directly five times, and indirectly several more, to the December 12 deadline. Underlying all his answers—and many of the questions from the bench—was an unspoken assumption that the count was sure to give the lead to Gore. Then the ticking clock would be Bush's problem.

At least Boies embraced some deadline, Carvin thought. December 12 sounded a long way off, but in the ongoing Republican quest to tighten the vise and narrow Gore's options, it was good to have Gore's own lawyer draw some limits.

Though Carvin tried to do as Baker advised, he was in a sour mood when his turn came to answer questions. Perhaps through exhaustion, or a sense of futility, Carvin was unfocused; repeatedly, he began his answers by saying no, then yes—or yes, then no. Justice Barbara Pariente, a transplanted New Yorker, a recent appointee and a liberal vote, demanded to know what the standard was in Bush's Texas for counting chads.

What does Texas have to do with Florida? Carvin seethed to himself. To the court he answered briskly, "I don't really know what the Texas law is." Later, Carvin insisted he was "the only person in America, I guess, who hadn't read that statute," but it was cited in the briefs and the justices now sensed that Carvin was lying to them. They came crashing down like panthers. It was left to Barry Richard, in his few minutes, to issue a ringing defense of Bush's position.

Boies, by contrast, was smooth and calm and avuncular. He had the voice of Bob Newhart and the manner of every freshman's favorite professor—as relaxed and helpful as a fellow giving directions to a lost motorist. The next day, the unanimous court ruled for Gore. "The will of the people, not a hyper-technical reliance upon statutory provisions, should be our guiding principle in election cases," the jus-

tices wrote, citing a 25-year-old precedent. The hand counts were free
to continue until Sunday, November 26, at 5 p.m. It was a five-day
extension, just as the secret source had predicted.

Gore praised the decision, calling democracy the winner that night,
and renewed his appeal for a meeting with Bush. And, in what he saw
as a significant concession, the vice president said he would disavow
any efforts by Democratic allies to persuade electors pledged to Bush
to switch their votes. That concession, he believed, would prevent
chaos when the electors met on December 18.

Boies made plans to head home for Thanksgiving—he thought he
might not even have to come back. They were going to examine the
ballots. He had won the case.

Bush was at the governor's mansion in Austin finishing a dinner of
fried chicken and mashed potatoes with the golfer Ben Crenshaw and
his wife, Julie, when the Florida Supreme Court decision came down.
They walked into the library and watched it on television. Bush immediately called Baker for clarification and to talk about next steps.
"While he was disappointed, he was very pragmatic, very collected,"
Crenshaw recalled. "He was very assertive under pressure." They all
knew that this was not the end.

James Baker was furious. The patina of diplomacy he wore was already well-chipped by the dispute. Now it collapsed. Baker went before the cameras in Tallahassee to accuse the court of lawlessness, and
to threaten escalation of the fight. "Two weeks after the election, [the]
court has changed the rules, and has invented a new system for counting the election results. So one should not now be surprised if the
Florida legislature seeks to affirm the original rules."

Baker was effectively calling Florida lawmakers to take over the
process. The legislature was controlled by Republicans. If necessary,
Baker seemed to be saying, they would elect George W. Bush themselves.

CHAPTER FOUR

■

Counting in Casablanca

America's closest election hinged, during the crucial Thanksgiving week, on the indescribably complex political machinations of three South Florida counties. The presidential race became as local as local could be. Famous lawyers, senators and governors descended on the state, but they lacked the power to make anything happen. Power was now vested in local officials on county canvassing boards, people who normally would handle zoning variances, custody disputes or fire department pension plans. By national, or even state standards, these people were unknown—yet suddenly their every utterance was on national television, bounced off satellites and relayed around the planet.

The battle between Bush and Gore would be fought precinct by precinct and ballot by ballot. In one county, things went very well for Al Gore. In one, they went fitfully. In another, they went very badly, so badly that Gore concluded he'd been knifed in the back.

Miami-Dade, Broward and Palm Beach counties make up the dominant metropolis of Florida. It's a teeming, sweaty, sunbaked and rather bizarre conglomeration of communities, a mess of humanity crammed onto a strip of land between the Atlantic Ocean and what's left of the Everglades. For years it was called the Gold Coast. That name evoked the glitzy side of South Florida: the swank hotels, the swimming pools with waterfalls, the yachtsmen tooling into harbor, the women in diamonds lounging in cabanas. In recent decades a new set of images took hold: Cuban exiles smoking cigars on Calle Ocho,

Judge Charles Burton oversaw the recount in Palm Beach County, where he and his fellow canvassing board members were charged with determining "the intent of the voter." Sometimes this process involved holding a ballot up to the light, to determine whether a hole was sufficiently punched through. (AP / Wide World Photos)

drug dealers racing around in Lamborghinis, drowned Haitian refugees washing up on the beach—a sort of exurban Casablanca. It is an area without a common language, or cultural center, or singular downtown.

But the election dispute finally gave it an identity—an incredibly simple, absurdly reductionist label: "Democratic stronghold." Miami-Dade, Broward and Palm Beach were cast together in one strategic throw by Gore's lawyers. The number of "undervotes"—ballots that registered no vote for president when fed through the counting machines—was in the tens of thousands. Some of those ballots bore discernible markings. Gore strategists believed that if the ballots were recounted by hand, the vice president would gain 1,000 votes, maybe more. That was the theory.

The issue that became the crux of the War for Florida was: What marks would qualify as a vote? This was a question that had never been raised in a presidential election. Until now, few people had ever paused to consider the actual mechanics of voting. Only a few experts understood just how many things can happen when a pointed instrument strikes a perforated card. The tab can fall cleanly away—a vote in anybody's book. Or the tiny paper, the "chad," can become partially detached. It can dangle. It can swing. It might be slightly pierced. It might be merely dimpled. It might be barely scratched.

Somewhere along that sliding scale lay the presidency.

■

The tale of the counting begins in Palm Beach County. In the first hours of the deadlock, when information was scarce and rumors were legion, the Democrats hoped this one county might yield thousands of additional Gore votes all by itself. Gradually the Gore lawyers lowered their sights. They figured they could get about 500 votes in a hand count.

In Palm Beach, Gore believed, he would be among friends. Take the lawyer for the county canvassing board: Bruce Rogow was a well-known law school professor who'd won an acquittal of the rap group 2 Live Crew in a nationally publicized obscenity trial. He was a rather dashing Democrat—thin, balding, bearded, at ease in flashy linens. And he was indeed helpful to Gore's team in the early hours of the dispute. The courts were already filling with lawsuits. There was no organization behind them, just a great deal of rage. Rogow rolled up his sleeves and tried to clear away the underbrush. Racing to the Palm Beach courthouse, he tracked down two lawyers who'd handled a couple of the suits. You need to talk to the Gore team, Rogow told them. Do it now. You can use the phone in that little room over there off the hallway.

The local lawyers disappeared into the room. Three minutes passed. They came out, looking a bit awed.

"Professor Rogow, as an officer of the court," he recalled one of them saying, "were those the real people we were talking to?"

Yes, Rogow answered.

They dropped their lawsuits.

"It was kind of like a scene out of *The Godfather*," Rogow said later.

But as the days went by, Rogow came to feel that the interests of the canvassing board were not identical to Al Gore's interests. Rogow wanted to proceed in an orderly fashion. The Gore hawks wanted to find votes fast.

The public face of the Gore effort in those early days was calm, colorless Warren Christopher. But the ground troops in Palm Beach were a different, more ferocious breed. Jack Corrigan, Dennis Newman and David Sullivan were members of Michael Whouley's crew from his Boston stomping grounds. They hit town and immediately began training volunteers who had poured in from across the country to help with the recount. There was a state senator from Massachusetts, an assemblyman from New York. Most were young, launched on the heady cause of a lifetime.

They discovered that nothing in Palm Beach would happen simply or on schedule. They were up against Republicans like Reeve Bright, a local lawyer who pursued a strategy he liked to call "mudballing."

"You draw it out. You keep it from happening. You throw up every roadblock. You get the flu, whatever you have to do," Bright said later. He found the tactic amusing.

■

Activity in Palm Beach County was split into two sites. Legal matters were handled at the courthouse in downtown West Palm Beach—a massive structure with a dramatic, arched breezeway, the kind of place that seemed architecturally suited to weighty decisions of national import. The courthouse sat amidst trendy downtown restaurants selling $20 slabs of fish, $10 glasses of merlot and $3 scoops of gourmet ice cream. But though the key players arrived regularly for this court hearing or that one, the courthouse was not where the serious action transpired. The lawsuits were merely tools to influence the counting, which took place miles away, out past the airport, among the strip malls and strip clubs.

There, the Palm Beach canvassing board had commandeered the county's Emergency Operations Center, built to withstand a hurricane. Which, in a sense, was exactly what hit it. Palm Beach became a bona fide 24-hour-a-day, round-the-globe Big Story. The roads around the EOC were always choked with traffic, lined with protesters and busy with vendors hawking T-shirts. For scenery there were incoming planes, power lines and a microwave tower. Across the street one could find a hubcap emporium, and next to that a pet shop selling a wide variety of reptiles, including a couple of fairly monstrous albino pythons. Barely 100 yards from the EOC, the Mermaid Lounge offered nude dancers all day long. You could argue that this was a crazy, chaotic, undignified setting for decisions of enormous importance for the future of American democracy. But maybe it was just right—Americana at its least pretentious.

The foreign media showed up in force. Also on hand were packs of political operatives, the spinners, waiting for a chance to denounce or applaud the latest incremental development. The recount kept getting delayed, first by hours and then by days, everything frozen by legal uncertainty. The press grew impatient and befuddled. An entrepreneur set up a massage chair in the parking lot, cashing in on the accumulating tensions.

Because there wasn't room inside the operations center for all the news crews, the canvassing board held its meetings on a flatbed trailer in the parking lot, under baking sun or twinkling stars. A week after the election, the board held a globally televised meeting in the parking lot, trying to figure out how to proceed. A knot of protesters gathered behind the flatbed and began chanting. "Let us be heard—thank you," Judge Charles Burton said sternly.

Burton explained the board's dilemma. It had two conflicting legal opinions, one from Secretary of State Katherine Harris saying don't count, and one from Attorney General Bob Butterworth saying count. All three board members wanted to do a full recount, but Burton and Theresa LePore were cautious. Only Carol Roberts wanted to plunge ahead. Roberts, 64, was a brash, relentless county commissioner. With her pink lipstick and voice made throaty by a quarter-century of politics and cigarettes, she bordered on caricature. She was the most partisan Democrat at the table—it did not go unnoticed by critics that she had a "Gore/Lieberman" bumper sticker on her car. Suppose the Harris opinion was legally binding—so what? she said.

"Do we go to jail?" she asked. "Because I'm willing to go to jail!" The Gore partisans erupted in cheers.

"This is not a political rally!" exploded Burton.

Roberts, warming to the occasion, made a formal motion to start the recount. But no one seconded her motion. It was hard to know exactly what LePore was thinking—she wore dark sunglasses and a blank expression. She said almost nothing during the meeting. "Depressed," is how a local Gore attorney, Lance Block, described her. He said LePore had told him, "This is as low as I've ever been in my life." She had tried to design a ballot that old folks could easily read, and instead she was a national laughingstock. A petition began circulating, demanding her resignation. The Florida recount was not a time of forgiveness and generosity. One day LePore had the experience of seeing a friend, Rep. Robert Wexler, a local Democrat, attack her on television. He was "slicing and dicing" her, LePore complained to a friend. LePore couldn't sleep. She barely ate. "The local Democrats were patting her on the back one minute, telling her it would be okay—the next minute, talking about the ballot, shoving it up her ass," board chairman Burton said later. "It was an outrage."

The meeting broke up with the recount still delayed. In the hours and days that followed the Democrats would become delirious with impatience. That Thursday morning, Bruce Rogow got a call from Alan Dershowitz, who'd been his ally in federal court just a few days earlier. Dershowitz told Rogow he was blowing the election. Bush would win and it would be Rogow's fault!

In the midst of this spat, Rogow's secretary informed him that Warren Christopher was calling on another line. Christopher was going to lobby Rogow as well, though in a completely different style.

"Bruce, this is Warren Christopher," the gentle voice said.

"Bruce?" thought Rogow.

"How do you do, Mr. Christopher," Rogow answered.

"I want to thank you for all you are doing for us," Christopher said.

Up to this point, the conversation would have confirmed everything the Bush team feared about South Florida—that the officials in charge of the hand counts were in league with the Gore campaign and, given a chance, would conspire to lift the vice president into the lead. But Rogow said: "You've got it wrong, Mr. Christopher. I'm not doing anything for you; I'm just trying to do right by my client."

Christopher later insisted that he was only asking that the canvassing board move expeditiously, one way or the other. But Rogow did not take it that way. "This was putting pressure on me," Rogow said. "I guess the assumption was that I would just bend."

What was possible for Al Gore in Palm Beach? Very little, ultimately, until the Florida Supreme Court gave the green light.

■

Things moved more quickly in Broward County. The canvassing board began by hand-counting a few Democratic-leaning precincts. Gore netted four votes. That didn't seem like much, and so, on Monday, November 13, the board voted against recounting the entire county. Then—in keeping with the apparent rule that everything in South Florida must change every day or so—Butterworth issued his advisory opinion in favor of counting. Butterworth had Broward roots. The county listened to him, and decided to bull ahead.

Lawsuit gridlock nearly paralyzed the process. Just finding a judge willing to hear some of the cases proved problematic. Seven judges in a row recused themselves from hearing Palm Beach County lawsuits. Democratic lawyer Leonard Samuels spent much of his time talking on two cell phones at once. "It's like playing in the Super Bowl," he said. "Only it's not just one day. It never ends."

Broward was Florida's most Democratic county. Gore had carried it roughly 2 to 1, and that was the margin on the canvassing board, too. The two Democrats got things rolling—Judge Robert Lee, a dark-haired, mustachioed Hispanic with a quick laugh; and Suzanne Gunzburger, a curly-haired county commissioner. Objecting to the recount was the board's lone Republican, Jane Carroll, the supervisor of elections. Carroll was a no-nonsense veteran. She wore pastel suits and jumbo clip-on earrings. Carroll had seen every sort of election squabble imaginable over the course of three decades on the job—or so she had assumed. She'd even gone through a manual recount, in a tiny municipality called Lauderdale-by-the-Sea. In a mayor's race involving barely a thousand votes, they recounted, recounted, and recounted again—ultimately confirming the original result. Like most elections supervisors, Carroll didn't approve of that kind of process. Too arbitrary. Too chaotic. It also taught her that human beings can make mistakes, even in counting a relatively small number of ballots. "I think machine counts are more objective," she told a reporter one day as she sat at her station, ready to examine another pile of punch cards. Carroll was preparing to retire when the cyclone struck. It was Monday afternoon—almost a week after the voting—before she managed to make her way back to Fort Lauderdale from her vacation home in North Carolina.

She gave a crash course on vote-counting to some 200 county employees and observers crowded into the Emergency Operations Center in the suburb of Plantation. She didn't recognize most of the people. Everything was being done on the fly, and it made her nervous and sapped her spirit. "In 32 years, I certainly never ran anything like this. I love organization," she lamented. One day she confided over the phone: "It's Jane. I'm dying. It's miserable. What's the earliest you can cut my hair in the morning?"

The counting in Broward County took place in an open room with a pair of counters at each table, plus an observer from each party to monitor the tally. Supervisors patrolled the tables like pit bosses at a casino. The press watched the action through plate-glass windows. The press room nearby had no television during the early days, making it just about the only news-free zone in Florida. The counters, by contrast, could watch four national networks simultaneously on enormous wall screens.

In a third room, the canvassing board did its monotonous work at one intensely scrutinized table. Judge Lee sat in the middle, with Carroll on his left and Gunzburger on his right. Partisan observers sat across the table. They could look at each ballot as Lee held it up, but they couldn't touch. The partisans would lean so far forward they could almost sniff the ballot; they were as purposeful as hunting dogs.

"Four-J-one, a clear overvote," Lee would say. "Four-J-two is a clear overvote."

"Wait, where's the overvote? Oh."

"Four-J-four is a dimple for Gore, nothing detached, that's an undervote."

And so on, and on. The board's decision to count votes was a form of self-imprisonment. They worked morning, noon and night, for days on end. "I had a field trip today—I got to see fresh air," Gunzburger said one evening. Dinner meant a pizza delivery.

"Forty-two-R-four is Gore."

As the vice president's recount team watched the progress, they began to fret. By the evening of Sunday, November 19, with more than 40 percent of the precincts counted, Gore had picked up only 79 net votes. At this rate, they would never get the 500 or more they were depending on from Broward County.

■

In the beginning, Miami-Dade was supposed to be a sort of insurance policy for Gore. But relying on metropolitan Miami for insurance is a bit like buying an annuity from a man who sleeps in the back seat of his car. "Insurance" suggests something dependable, a piece of the rock. The only sure thing about this particular county is that there are no sure things.

Gore's recount guys believed that if everything went right in Broward and Palm Beach they ought to get enough votes to pull ahead. Those were, no doubt, legitimate Democratic strongholds. But no one could be sure what Miami-Dade was, exactly. The Cuban community leaned heavily to Bush. The election had been close, with Gore on top by only 6 percentage points. Maybe there were a couple hundred votes hiding there—if only Gore could get the ballots counted by a favorable standard.

Equally uncertain was the sentiment of the Miami-Dade canvassing board. It didn't seem in much of a rush to do anything on Gore's behalf. On November 9, the Thursday after the election, Gore asked for a recount. The canvassing board dawdled, declining to consider the matter until the following Tuesday.

Membership on the canvassing board was famously undesirable. This was scut work for local officials. Every election night, instead of cruising around to parties and rubbing shoulders with the people who matter, board members had to hang out at election headquarters with the people who count—votes. The judge who leads the board is generally among the newest on the bench. It's a bit of hazing. That was certainly true of Judge Lawrence D. King, the Miami canvassing board chairman.

King had been appointed to the Dade County court in 1997 to handle misdemeanors, domestic squabbles and traffic offenses. The 44-year-old Democrat's primary fame was that he was the son of U.S. District Court Judge James Lawrence King, who for many years was chief judge of the Southern District in Miami. He had overseen the construction of a palatial federal courthouse that, in turn, was named in his honor—even though he was very much alive. Lawrence King was constantly shadowed by the big block letters on the federal courthouse, and salted his conversations with mentions of his illustrious dad.

The county elections supervisor, David Leahy, was the board's second member. Like his colleagues in Broward and Palm Beach, Leahy was an experienced bureaucrat who opposed hand counts almost on principle. Hand counting implied something was wrong with the system, which, in turn, implied something was wrong with the system supervisor.

Another county judge, Myriam Lehr, completed the roster. She was the most mysterious of the three: Born in Belgium to an Orthodox Jewish family, Lehr was a registered independent, married to a prominent Republican, with many close friends among Miami's Democratic elite. Her election to the county court in 1996 was generally chalked up to the fact that she appeared to be whatever the observer wanted her to be: Her name, for example, sounded half-Jewish, half-Cuban. She had hired a brace of political consultants, liberal and conservative, to help her reach out in all directions. One of her consultants was Armando Gutierrez, an anti-Castro conservative best known as a spokesman for the Miami relatives of Elian Gonzalez. The Gore team couldn't be sure that Lehr would be a friend.

The board convened on Tuesday, November 14, on the 18th floor of the county office building in downtown Miami. Leahy, the elections supervisor, complained that the state law was screwy. If the goal of the sample was to determine the need for a recount, test precincts should reflect the whole county. Instead, the complaining candidate—Gore—got to hand-pick the sample precincts. Still, even if it was a bad law, it was the law. Leahy joined the other two in approving the test.

The counting began. Unlike Broward and Palm Beach, Miami-Dade didn't even provide chairs for the partisan observers. Lawyers for Gore and Bush were forced to stand for hours, peering over the shoulders of the board members as they, in turn, examined the ballots. Bush attorney Miguel De Grandy found the whole process bizarre: "How do you evaluate a ballot that had a clear punch for Bush, a clear punch for Gore and then, in pen, a check mark next to one, and an X next to another? How do you argue that? Is it that the check mark is their selection, or X marks the spot?"

At least 16 times, the board members could not agree. At day's end, the sample produced a net gain of six Gore votes. The Democrats immediately argued that six votes in 1 percent of the ballots could mean 600 votes in the total sample. De Grandy countered that these were Gore's best precincts—they had gone 10 to 1 in his favor. A full recount, he predicted, would yield only 36 votes for Gore, not nearly enough to be worth the trouble.

The board had to vote. Leahy voted no. King voted yes.

Everyone turned to the inscrutable Myriam Lehr.

No, she said quietly.

■

At 11:30 in the morning on Friday, November 17, Jason Unger, the lawyer in charge of monitoring absentee votes for the Bush forces in Florida, was in his Tallahassee office when he received a fax from one of his team in Pensacola. It was a memo, drafted by a member of the Gore team. Somehow, the GOP had gotten hold of it.

According to an agreement reached many years ago between the state and the federal government, overseas ballots cast by Election Day—postmarked by November 7—could be received up to 10 days later. Bush's election night lead of 1,784 votes had shrunk to just 300 votes a week later. How much of a cushion could Bush regain from the absentees?

Unger knew there were rumors that Gore's camp planned to aggressively challenge them. When the fax arrived, he was able to prove it. Mark Herron, a Democrat in Tallahassee, had outlined the strategy in the memo that Unger was now holding. The memo laid out in detail the best way to disqualify overseas ballots. No postmark, the memo said, no vote.

Unger took Herron's memo to David Aufhauser, a Washington lawyer who was monitoring the overseas ballots, and it was quickly passed up the Bush chain of command—to lawyers Benjamin Ginsberg and George J. Terwilliger III, campaign manager Joseph Allbaugh, James A. Baker III, Austin and then to the press. By Friday afternoon, it was moving on the wires.

This Democratic effort to deep-six absentee ballots outraged the Republicans. But then it dawned on the Bush team that it had been handed a big stick. Bill Kristol, editor of the conservative *Weekly Standard* magazine, got on the phone with Dorrance Smith, a former ABC News executive working with the Bush forces in Florida. "Have you seen this military ballot story?" Kristol asked. "You ought to have someone look into it." Smith got on the phone to Austin. Then he went over to the bar at the Doubletree Hotel, a media watering hole, to tell any reporters he could find about the story.

"Count every vote" was the Gore mantra, and it was a powerful weapon in the war for public opinion. But it wasn't entirely sincere. In the midst of the South Florida struggle to gain votes, Gore needed to minimize the erosion caused by votes from predominantly Republican servicemen serving overseas. What's more, both sides suspected the other was scheming to slip illegal votes in through the absentee process. Republicans passed whispers that Gore votes were being

manufactured and postdated in Israel. Democrats retailed similar stories about Bush votes being ginned up on aircraft carriers. At one
point, Gore strategist Michael Whouley got a call from a friend who
warned that 1,000 absentee votes were about to appear miraculously
in Escambia County, home of Eglin Air Force Base. "Oh, my God,"
Whouley said. "We're about to get screwed." Unproven fears were
the currency of the Florida recount.

After the midnight deadline for receiving overseas ballots passed,
officials in all 67 Florida counties began opening the envelopes and
counting the votes. Very soon, Unger's phone began ringing. You
won't believe what's going on, his network of local lawyers reported.
Gore's representatives were executing the plan in the memo. They
eventually protested 41 percent of the military ballots.

Across Florida, the count of the absentees was high drama and
great theater. In Fort Lauderdale, the canvassing board members fired
up battery-powered letter openers; one of them pulled out a huge
magnifying glass. As Judge Robert Lee pored over signatures and
postmarks, there was a whiff in the room of Sherlock Holmes, or
maybe Inspector Clouseau. Ballots had come from Guyana, Costa
Rica, Indonesia, Israel, Lebanon, the Philippines, Denmark, Trinidad
and Colombia. One, from Canada, carried a cry on the envelope:
"Please help make my vote count. Get it to South Florida by Nov. 6."
At one point, a lawyer for Broward County dashed to the press room
for help. "Does anybody here read Arabic?" he shouted. No one did.

For the Bush team, though, it was time to start wielding the stick.
The idea that Gore was targeting military ballots compounded a
week of pictures from South Florida, images of ballot counters holding punch cards up to the light, turning them this way and that,
squinting, frowning, debating unseen nicks. The Bush team had gotten a slow start in the PR war, but here was a powerful new arsenal
to fire off at Gore.

That night at the Texas governor's mansion, Montana Gov. Marc
Racicot dined with George W. and Laura Bush, Richard B. and Lynne

Cheney, and Bush campaign chairman Don Evans. The youthful, little-known Racicot had become a pal and staunch supporter of Bush
during the campaign. During the meal, he pressed Bush to turn up the
volume in Florida. "He was appalled and amazed," Bush recalled.
Bush told his communications director, Karen Hughes, to "put him
out there."

The rollout began with a news conference on Saturday, November
18, featuring Hughes at Racicot's side. The Montana governor
poured on the gasoline: "Last night, we learned how far the vice president's campaign will go to win this election. And I am very sorry to
say but the vice president's lawyers have gone to war, in my judgment,
against the men and women who serve in our armed forces." And he
condemned the entire recount process, offering up a laundry list of
facts, stories and tall tales from South Florida—everything from Bush
ballots with the chads taped back in place to elderly counters with
flashlights reading punch cards in poorly lit rooms.

"There was a resonant chord struck on Saturday," Racicot said
later. "The media started to understand it, we started to understand it
and the American people started to understand it." The Bush message: Gore's supposed devotion to accuracy is a smoke screen for
power politics. Racicot suddenly was everywhere, arguing against the
unfair and arbitrary standards of the hand counts and blasting away
on the military ballot issue. Within a few days, by his own count, he
did 16 interviews on national television.

He wasn't the only one pressed into service. New York Gov.
George Pataki, Indiana congressman Steve Buyer and retired Gen. H.
Norman Schwarzkopf all weighed in. The party's 1996 nominee, Bob
Dole, didn't even need to be asked; he simply called Bush headquar-
ters and said: I'm on my way.

Log after log went on the bonfire. In North Florida, Bush lawyers
compiled a list of names of sailors and airmen whose ballot envelopes
had never been opened. They began e-mailing the list, looking for servicemen or spouses willing to go on camera to discuss their plight.

"We found the wife of one guy and said, 'Did you know that your husband's ballot is being protested?'" Marty Fiorentino, a Bush lawyer, recalled. "Then we put her on *Good Morning America*."

■

The Gore forces watched in horror. They decided their best chance to tamp down the story was on the Sunday morning public affairs shows. Joe Lieberman was chosen to carry the message. He was a smooth, calm, persuasive spokesman. On the other hand, no one ever knew exactly what he would say.

His devout religious practice meant that he was unavailable for prep work until sundown on Saturday, the end of the Jewish Sabbath. After that, he was happy to listen to the talking points prepared by campaign staffers, but once the cameras started rolling, he tended to speak his mind. Saturday evening, the Gore team in Florida faxed documents to Washington to help with the coaching. Then Ron Klain, Michael Whouley and Mark Herron joined in a telephone call to brief the would-be vice president. Context was everything, they counseled. A flood of absentee ballots had arrived in the last days before the deadline—a flood that made them suspicious that people were voting even after Election Day had passed. That's why they became so interested in postmarks.

Beyond that, there was no way to tell, by looking at the outer envelope, whether a vote had come from a member of the military. Overseas ballots came from employees of the State Department, from foreign correspondents, from oil company workers.

But most of all—this was war. And yes, they had taken a hard line to try to win it. Every vote mattered. "If we had not done this, Bush would have had 700 to 2,000 more votes," one key Gore operative later explained. Senior staff had been kept apprised every step of the way. Herron's memo circulated at "the highest levels" of the Gore operation, one senior Gore aide said. This was not the time to get cold feet. Gore could not win if Bush was allowed to pile up votes. The ground troops, fighting every Bush ballot, needed Lieberman to defend them, to take a hard line.

Late that night, the far-flung Gore lawyers gathered by conference call. Already, there was rising pressure to cave on the absentee ballots. Someone asked: "What happens if we let all these ballots in?"

The response from the ground troops was wary: "What do you mean by all of them? The ones who are registered? The ones who already voted once? What's the definition of all of them?"

"All."

"We would lose."

On the other hand, there were voices in Washington asking why Gore could not give in magnanimously. "Don't we have a margin of a gazillion in Palm Beach County?" the theory went. Even at this relatively late date, some people close to Gore apparently didn't understand that hand counts in South Florida would, at best, yield votes in the hundreds, not thousands. And it wasn't a sure thing that the hand counts would even be completed. "There was a huge disconnect" between Gore's team in Florida and the Washington crowd, one Gore adviser recalled.

What would Lieberman do? Sunday morning, November 19, everyone tuned in to see. On *Meet the Press*, host Tim Russert served up the expected question.

"If I was there," Lieberman began, "I would give the benefit of the doubt to ballots coming in from military personnel generally." Lieberman commiserated with Florida's beleaguered elections officials, and urged them, "Go back and take another look. Because, again, Al Gore and I don't want to ever be part of anything that would put an extra burden on the military personnel abroad who want to vote."

In Florida, the Gore operatives were in shock.

"What the fuck is going on?" exploded one senior staffer.

Mark Herron saw what was happening: He was being hung out to dry. Lieberman was asked: Did he know anything about the person who wrote the controversial memo? No, he said.

"This is not what we briefed him on," one staffer said. Lieberman's appearance had momentarily knocked the stuffing out of the Florida operation.

But the senator's stance was shared by others. Florida Sen. Bob Graham, the state's senior Democrat, and Attorney General Butterworth both repudiated all or part of the absentee ballot strategy. The tide was all in Bush's direction until retiring Nebraska Sen. Bob Kerrey—who had a Medal of Honor and an artificial leg to vouch for his military service—took to the airwaves to say that the rules should apply to people in uniform just as they do to civilians.

The absentee ballot issue, one senior Gore strategist said later, was "where the warriors and the non-warriors separated." Some people on the team seemed to care more about reputation than about victory. And now there was reason to suspect that the non-warriors— not just Lieberman, but also the cautious Christopher and the skeptical Daley—were closer to Gore than the warriors.

■

The late Republican master strategist Lee Atwater used to say, "Never kick a man when he's up." Seeing Gore reeling on the overseas ballot issue, the Bush team kept kicking and kicking. At a news conference on Wednesday, November 22, Bush himself took up the cry. "Our men and women in uniform overseas should not lose their right to vote," the candidate said. "I hope the vice president will personally support me in this call."

The Gore team was so ground down that it did little to resist the next Bush move, which became known as the "Thanksgiving stuffing" operation. Bush lawyer Jason Unger's legal team pushed the canvassing boards in strongly military counties to get the count reopened. Eventually, he succeeded in 12 counties—most of them heavily Republican, and half of them home to huge military bases. Bush picked up 176 net votes in the stuffing, mainly when boards agreed to ignore missing postmarks or missing absentee applications, which are required by Florida law.

The all-Republican canvassing board in Duval County, home to several large naval bases, initially threw out absentee ballots that were not dated or postmarked. This decision pained Rick Mullaney, a member of the board and son of a Navy man. And he didn't care much for the Gore lawyers' ferocious tactics, which he likened to "watching a criminal defense lawyer try to toss out the confession of a guilty man." But Florida law was the law, and the law said no postmark or date, no vote.

Then came the call from Lieberman and Butterworth to reconsider military ballots. And then the Florida Supreme Court's November 21 decision—the one that said that "hypertechnicalities" should not disqualify a ballot.

On Friday, November 24, the board reconvened. Mullaney quoted Lieberman and asked Gore's lawyers exactly what their position was. "They were in a box," Mullaney said. "Those lawyers were in a difficult position, and their attitude had completely changed." Duval County counted the vast majority of ballots that had been excluded because of postmark issues, and almost all went for Bush. So after weeks of complaining about the unfairness of recounts, the Bush campaign had succeeded in obtaining one simply by convincing the canvassing boards that Florida law should be ignored because military personnel had rights protected by the federal government.

The time would come when the margin between Bush and Gore dipped briefly to just 154 votes. Without his Thanksgiving stuffing, Bush would have fallen behind. Gore would have had a lead of 22 votes—a lead that could have changed the entire public relations dynamic.

Furthermore, GOP lawyers feared that if Bush ever trailed, the courts would be reluctant to intervene in his favor. "If we were behind, Gore would declare it over," explained Frank Donatelli, an old chum of James Baker who flew from Washington to help out in Florida. "It didn't matter whether the margin was 500, 900, 1,000 or some other number.

"It was just critical to stay ahead."

■

Palm Beach wasn't delivering for Gore. Soon after the county began examining ballots on Thursday, November 16, Gore's Boston pols saw that they weren't getting the bonanza of votes they'd expected. They had developed a precinct-by-precinct estimate—the necessary "yield rate," as they called it—and they compared their estimates to the actual counts as the ballots were judged. At a point where they expected to be up 400 net votes, there had been almost no change at all. Gore lawyers decided to take the canvassing board back to court—one of a seemingly endless number of hearings before Judge Jose LaBarga over the proper standard for judging Palm Beach ballots.

LaBarga already had urged the board to consider all sorts of marks on ballots as possible indications of the "intent of the voter." But the Democrats felt Burton and LePore were ignoring him. Because there was no specific standard expressed in Florida law—only the vague "intent" guideline—LaBarga was unable to command that, say, dimpled chads be counted. He could only nudge and coax.

Now he nudged them again. But for all the time spent in LaBarga's courtroom, discretion remained with the canvassing board. And its standard loosened only slightly. In Tallahassee, Ron Klain fumed as he watched LePore vote time after time with Judge Burton to deny Gore votes. Little by little, the board worked its way through Palm Beach County's half-million ballots, until there was no way to hit Gore's goal without going back and redoing ballots that already had been counted.

The Bush lawyers felt confident the board would never do that. It had been too hard to do all the ballots even once. Here, in enemy territory, Democrat territory, they were holding the line.

■

As the deadlock wore on, Gore's team grew more and more frustrated. Twelve days after the election, nothing was going the way

Gore thought it should. He and his friends worked the phones constantly, soliciting information, decoding motives, seeking the pressure points that might influence the South Florida boards. They finally made a breakthrough in Broward County.

For many years, the Broward elections office got its legal advice from assistant county attorney Norman Ostrau. He was a particular authority on voting law, having served as a legislator on the Florida House elections committee. Assistant county attorney Andrew Meyers, on the other hand, had never advised the canvassing board. He was an appellate lawyer for the county. When Gore requested a recount, Meyers was out of town working on a case concerning citrus canker, a disease menacing Florida's orange groves. Meyers did have access to a lot of information about the election dispute, though. His wife was a lawyer with Mitchell Berger's firm, which had become a key part of the Gore effort in Florida. She was a strong Gore supporter even before the deadlock.

Ostrau had advised the canvassing board to follow a narrow standard for counting ballots. "Hanging chads"—that is, partly perforated rectangles hanging by no more than two corners—should be counted as votes, but nothing else. Ostrau said this standard was based on the law in Texas. Meyers felt his colleague had it wrong, that the Texas statute was much broader, allowing for pierced chads, even dimpled chads, to be counted—if the board felt that was the voter's intention. So, without consulting Ostrau, Meyers drafted a brief for the Florida Supreme Court urging the justices to order the South Florida counties to adopt that more liberal approach.

Then, on Sunday, November 19, Meyers showed up at the counting session and told the board what it ought to do. The two-corner rule, he said, "is impermissibly narrow." He also met privately with each board member. Meyers recalled Judge Lee complaining that perfectly clear votes were being cast aside because of the hanging-chad rule. Meyers had the answer: "Why don't you change the standard?"

They did.

The Broward canvassers went back through the ballots they al-

ready had counted, and suddenly the votes poured in for Gore. Six
days later, when the Broward effort finally wheezed to a stop, the canvassing board and its deputized counters had examined more than
500,000 ballots. Result: a net gain of 567 votes for Gore. Broward
was the only county that delivered on Gore's expectations. Indeed,
Broward exceeded Gore's hopes.

The abrupt change in the counting standard convinced Republicans that the fix was in. They came to view the Broward recount
room as nothing less than a crime scene. The GOP even got permis-
sion to supply fresh tapes for the surveillance cameras so that the existing tapes could be extracted and used, potentially, as inculpatory
evidence. Ed McNally, a local lawyer and Bush volunteer, carried
with him snapshots of a Broward sheriff's deputy counting chads, in
clusters of five, on a tabletop. They'd become detached during the
handling of the ballots—a sign, McNally insisted, of "extraordinary
irregularities."

Nothing was more irregular than the Case of the Immaculate
Chad. A punch card turned up with a chad lodged snugly in the hole
for Gore—but it was backward. The rectangle was plainly on the
wrong side of the card. This chad wasn't dangling, or hanging, was-
n't one-corner or two-corner—it simply appeared to have left one
card and found its way back into a hole on another card. When it
went through the machine, the card had registered as a Gore vote, so
the board gave it to the vice president once again. The board members figured the speck of paper must have migrated.

Meanwhile, Jane Carroll, the elections supervisor, never did quite
figure out where Andrew Meyers had come from, "but I know he
didn't fall out of heaven," she said later. "Someone sent him."

As for Meyers, he agreed that perhaps he should have alerted the
board that he had family ties to the Gore campaign. "In a legal sense,
there was no conflict," he said afterward. "But in hindsight, I probably should have mentioned it earlier."

■

Miami had a lot of ballots to recount, roughly 650,000. They were locked in blue metal file boxes along one wall of the spacious, soulless, climate-controlled Tabulation Room on the 19th floor of the county building. They started on Monday, November 20. Elections supervisor David Leahy brought in a fairly small corps of counters, just 25 teams, but there was little need for more, he felt. There always would be a bottleneck in the process. Florida law required all disputed ballots to be judged by the three-member canvassing board. It was impossible to move faster than those three people could go. In Miami, the canvassing board members started with a mountain of undervotes, more than 10,000 of them, examining each card, one by one by one.

Leahy would look at each ballot and announce his verdict. The other board members would examine it, as would the partisan observers. Objections would be made. Some ballots were clear, some were hard to decipher. A number would be scrawled on the back of each challenged ballot, and a court reporter had to record the number. Using this process the board managed to count roughly one ballot per minute—60 per hour. Twelve hours a day was about the limit of their endurance: "It's just eyestrain," Leahy later explained. "You look at ballots for so long and comes a point where you just get bleary-eyed."

By the end of work on Tuesday, 139 precincts had been manually counted, resulting in a net gain of 157 votes for Gore. It was slow going, but Leahy believed they could achieve their goal of finishing by December 1.

That night, the Florida Supreme Court ordered all hand counts completed by November 26.

■

On one of the wildest, and most important, days of the deadlock— Wednesday, November 22—David Leahy rose early and began punching numbers into his calculator. Then he went to an 8 a.m.

meeting of the Miami-Dade canvassing board. The members had to examine their options in light of the new deadline.

There were, Leahy told the board, three choices. One was to keep counting as before. If they went 24 hours a day for four straight days, they might make it. But that wouldn't leave any time to resolve disputes. Plus it was a holiday weekend. Could they find the bodies to handle 650,000 ballots? The full count seemed impossible.

Alternative two was simpler: Count the undervote ballots, the ones that hadn't registered a presidential vote when passed through the machine. There were about 10,750 of them. Leahy figured that, under this scenario, he and his fellow canvassers could handle the ballots by themselves and send the counting teams home. When they found an overlooked vote, they'd prepare a duplicate, clearly punched card and put it in the precinct pile. At the end of the process they would run all the cards—the clear votes and the duplicates—through the counting machines to get a result. He did the math: If the canvassing board examined 300 ballots an hour—five every minute, or one every 12 seconds—it would take 36 hours, not counting sleep and coffee breaks, to scrutinize all of them.

Then came alternative three. It would be politically explosive. The canvassing board could simply stop the process. Give up. Go home.

Leahy didn't think that would be practical. It didn't jibe with what the board had decided: "We have already determined there are some votes in the undercounted ballots."

So they'd take the middle course, just counting the undervotes.

To save time, Leahy proposed changing the venue of the counting. The county had already started separating the undervotes from the other ballots, but had never finished the job. Why not move to the Tabulation Room, one floor higher, and count ballots while the machines separated out the rest of the undervotes? It seemed a simple, harmless decision. At 8:50 a.m., the canvassers rode the elevators to the 19th floor.

That's when things began going wrong. Following the board to the

19th floor was a crowd of Republicans, upset that the proceedings were moving from the large public space on the 18th floor into the smaller, sealed space on the 19th. There were windows in the Tabulation Room, but access beyond the doors was limited. Reporters also were angry at the sudden shift, and circulated a petition threatening to sue the board if it didn't let them in the room.

Then the elevators began disgorging angry Republican protesters, 30 to 40 altogether. They were mostly young congressional staffers and other volunteers from Washington who had served as observers in the recount. Republicans had deployed volunteers with military efficiency in Florida, flying and busing them in, paying for hotels and food. At one point more than 700 were in the state.

"We are civic-minded people and we were there to observe the process and suddenly we weren't allowed to do that," said Layna McConkey, 31, a lobbyist and former Republican congressional staffer. The protest began with people chanting that the media should be allowed in. Quickly, chants of "Let them in" became "Let us in."

The board, meanwhile, had paused in the elections office to discuss the new plan with party leaders. They began to hear muffled chants. They heard scattered thuds, the random sounds of anger.

"Stop the count! Stop the fraud!"

This was getting hot.

"Chea-ters! Chea-ters!"

With this soundtrack, the canvassers began their momentous counting of the presidential ballots in the Tabulation Room. They began with Precinct 1. "Punch number 7, number 7." That corresponded to no candidate. "This would be a no-vote . . . "

"Let us in! Let us in!"

"Hopefully," Leahy said, "the mood out front will settle down."

Outside, the local Democratic Party chairman, Joe Geller, visited the elections office looking for a sample ballot. He had a theory about the large number of punches in hole number 7 on Miami ballots. He wanted to run a little test to see if, by improperly inserting the card, he could make hole number 7 line up with Gore's line, number 6. Suddenly, a well-dressed Republican woman with a clipboard yelled: "He's stealing a ballot!"

Bedlam ensued. The crowd gathered around Geller and began jostling him. He eased his way to the elevator, and got in, but then several jumped in with him. Now he was trapped in an elevator with a bunch of screaming Republicans.

"You're not going anywhere," one man said. "Me and the colonel won't let you."

The colonel? thought Geller. He almost asked, "Which colonel?"

The elevator descended, and Geller tried to leave the building.

"You're a lawyer, you're going to get disbarred," someone shouted.

How did they even know who he was? Suddenly one of the protesters moved forward and shoved his chest against Geller's. "If you touch me again," the man said, "I'll defend myself." Touch him? thought Geller.

He made a prudent calculation that he would never make it to his car without getting into a full-fledged fistfight. Geller retreated into the building.

Inside the Tabulation Room, everything started to break down. There was the ruckus. The angry news media. And, on top of it all, they were not getting through anything close to five ballots per minute. The members decided to break and reconvene at 10:30 on the 18th floor.

The who-what-why of the Miami-Dade protest became one of the great controversies of the entire election dispute. Democrats spoke of the "riot" or the "mob" in Miami. Gore's Florida warriors seized on the protest and pressed the angle that this was a mob action orchestrated by Washington Republicans. Gore himself conferred regularly with his researchers at the Democratic National Committee who were trying to identify the rabble-rousers from news photographs. He relished the hunt for the secret agents of the opposition. After all these years, Al Gore was once again an investigative reporter.

The Miami protesters included a policy analyst in House Majority Whip Tom DeLay's office, a majority chief counsel on the House judiciary subcommittee on criminal justice, a political division staff member at the National Republican Congressional Committee, a former House Republican conference analyst, a former aide to Tennessee Sen. Fred D. Thompson, a Bush campaign staffer, an aide to Rep. Van Hilleary (R-Tenn.), an aide to Chairman Don Young (R-Alaska) of the House Resources Committee, a legislative assistant to Rep. Jim DeMint (R-S.C.), and a former aide to former Rep. Jim Ross Lightfoot (R-Iowa). These weren't ordinary Miamians taking their case to their elected officials.

But Republicans later scoffed at the idea that a group of clean-cut Hill staffers—the "Brooks Brothers" protesters, as one Republican called them—could intimidate the canvassing board. "I'm 5 foot 5, 120 pounds—I don't think I look like a big thug," said Layna Mc-Conkey, who was pictured in papers around the country next day shaking her fist with the other demonstrators.

And yet, it didn't matter. David Leahy insists he was never really worried about the protesters in the foyer. He was worried about the people who were covering the protesters in the foyer—the journalists.

"If we hadn't relented," he said, "the media would have reported that we were making decisions behind closed doors."

■

Ron Klain liked to say a good day in Florida was a day you wake up and people are counting ballots. Wednesday, November 22, was the best morning so far. For the first time, all three South Florida counties were busy examining punch cards.

If this could just keep up, he thought, they would win. Gore would be ahead by the Sunday certification deadline. Klain figured Katherine Harris would then try to avoid certifying the result, and Klain would sue to force her. Bush would have very little time to contest the result.

As he walked out of his office around lunch time, he glanced at the television screen. The Miami-Dade canvassing board was on CNN. He figured it was taped from an earlier meeting. He would have heard if the board was meeting now.

But it was live. The board was meeting, and suddenly it was not a good day anymore, not for Gore. Sometime during the lunch break, in the Miami-Dade government center, Al Gore's recount hopes were sunk. The reasons remain mysterious in a classically Miami way: There's not a shortage of theories, there's a surplus. There are simple explanations and complicated conspiracy theories. There are crosses, doublecrosses and triplecrosses.

First, what happened:

The three board members split up so no one could accuse them of violating Florida's open meeting law. Leahy went to his office, King went to the copier room and Lehr went to the storage room. Murray Greenberg and his boss, county attorney Robert Ginsburg, came downstairs to consult with the members one by one. Leahy wanted to know whether there was any hope of a deadline extension from the state Supreme Court. "I was told . . . that was not going to happen," he said. Greenberg then went upstairs and fell asleep in his chair.

During these consultations, the members seemed frustrated, but not defeated. When they reconvened at 1:30 p.m., however, they seemed to have lost hope. Circumstances had "somewhat changed," King said, and Leahy expanded on that. There was simply too much work for the available time, he said. The idea of counting on the 19th floor was not practical—people didn't trust the process. "As we just began to begin the process, we had objections from a number of the members of the news media, some members of at least one political party and citizens who felt that they needed to be present as we were undergoing this historic venture," he said. The Tabulation Room just wasn't large enough for all those people.

The goal of 300 ballots per hour was impossible, Leahy said. One per minute was more realistic. Based on this, King voted to stop counting. "We cannot meet the deadline of the Supreme Court of the state of Florida, and I feel it incumbent upon this canvassing board to count each and every ballot." Leahy also voted no—he had never been entirely persuaded that a hand count was warranted.

Lehr made it unanimous: "I would have loved to provide the people of Dade County with a vote, but that's the best I can do this morning."

■

Looking back, after the war was over, both Republicans and Democrats point to the decision of the Miami canvassing board to stop counting—a severe blow to Gore's hopes of gaining the lead—as one of the critical moments. And because it happened in Miami, the City of Mystery, the Mecca of Conspiracy, everyone has wondered why it happened. The idea that there were too many ballots and too few hours is not quite juicy enough to satisfy every partisan.

The answer may never be entirely clear, but many believe it starts with that cute little boy in the inner tube, Elian Gonzalez. Of all the members of the Clinton administration, Gore had been among the most sympathetic to the idea that Elian should remain in America. He had a long record of fierce opposition to Fidel Castro, rooted in his horror at the 1980 Mariel boatlift, when Castro emptied his prisons and asylums of Cuba's most violent criminals, mixing them into the much larger numbers of law-abiding citizens that he allowed to leave the country. Gore had never lost the feeling that only a monster could do such a thing.

So he wasn't fooled when Castro appeared on television expressing grandfatherly concern for little Elian. The case, Gore argued—in opposition to the administration's position—should be handled in American family courts, not as an immigration matter. Despite flak from the liberal wing of his own party, Gore stuck to that view. Indeed, his feelings deepened during a car ride in early 2000 with Bob Butterworth and his wife, Marta Prado Butterworth. As they drove, Marta told Gore her own story of fleeing Castro as a small child. "I felt such a sense of pain for this little boy should he have to return,"

Marta Butterworth later recalled of the conversation. She recalled that Gore shared her pain. "I remember him saying, 'What an incredible show of love—this woman so loved her son that she went to the straits of the ocean to bring her child to freedom.'"

Gore had hoped that he would do well with Miami Cubans on Election Day. True, they had been angry at the Democratic Party for almost 40 years, ever since the Kennedy administration went soft, they felt, at the Bay of Pigs. But in 1996, Bill Clinton had scored an impressive 40 percent of the Cuban American vote, and Gore thought he could build on that.

Then came the predawn raid to seize Elian, and all the fine points of Gore's anti-Castroism were washed away on a tide of rage. It made no difference when he later chose a running mate with a history of good relations in the anti-Castro community. Miami firebrands such as the political consultant Armando Gutierrez made it their cause to defeat Gore out of spite for Clinton. Gutierrez whipped up anti-Democratic sentiment at street rallies and on the all-powerful Spanish-language radio shows. Ultimately, Gore's share of the Cuban vote was little more than half what Clinton had managed four years earlier.

Elian fury burned so hot that few Cuban American leaders felt they could stand by Gore. For years, Alex Penelas—the ambitious young mayor of Miami-Dade County—had done everything possible to be seen with Gore. But after Elian, he vanished. Some people figured Penelas would come back after securing his own reelection in the September primaries. Instead, the mayor skipped off for a 12-day junket in Spain.

What if Penelas had stuck by Gore? What if Penelas had vouched for Gore on Miami radio? In a deadlocked race, a last-minute endorsement by Penelas might have given Gore the votes he needed to reach the White House. Instead, Gore's year-long dance with Miami's Cuban leadership—through Elian, through the long campaign—had carried over into the recount, an endless samba.

When the Miami-Dade canvassing board voted to stop the count, Gore almost immediately called Chris Korge, a Democratic fundraiser.

"Chris," said Gore, "did Alex kill the recount?"

Gore smelled a conspiracy. He was convinced that Penelas—his former friend—had leaned on Leahy, either directly or indirectly, to end the recount. That would be a direct, final, devastating betrayal— a powerful vice president sunk by the machinations of some hot-shot mayor.

Some of the signs pointed to betrayal: Penelas, a Democrat, hadn't faced any significant Republican opposition in his own September re-election campaign. Was that in exchange for shafting Gore? In the midst of the recount, while his city was seething, Penelas had hot-footed it up to Tallahassee to meet with Carlos Lacasa, a powerful Republican legislator, to talk about the creation of a strong-mayor position in Miami—a change in the county charter that could allow Penelas to escape the term limits bearing down on him. Leading up to the fateful day, Leahy said, Penelas repeatedly telephoned him.

The vice president was so obsessed with the local rumors and the minutiae of Miami's Byzantine politics that when the county manager resigned about a week after the count was aborted, Gore began dig-ging into whether that was somehow tied to the board's decision.

But Korge refused to feed the vice president's paranoia. He be-lieved, he said later, that behind the scenes Penelas was a strong sup-porter of the recount. Trust me on this, he told Gore. Penelas is trying to help you.

"Well, I'm hearing otherwise," Gore said.

"I think you ought to call Alex Penelas," Korge said.

Gore did just that. The conversation would prove unfruitful—and, like so much else in this strange drama, prone to dispute, with the parties describing the call differently.

"Hey, what happened?" Gore asked Penelas.

The mayor explained that the elections supervisor just didn't have enough time to complete the recount before the Sunday deadline. Penelas assured Gore that he'd offered the canvassing board sufficient resources. He'd already issued one statement to that effect, and would be willing to issue another.

Gore got the impression that Penelas had promised to help him get that troublesome board counting again. It was an impression that would later prove false, but for the moment, Gore seemed placated.

"Thanks for doing that," Gore said, "because this is going to kill me if it doesn't get recounted."

■

That left Palm Beach.

The canvassing board members took Thanksgiving off, and when they returned to work on Friday, they quickly realized they were falling farther and farther behind. In Palm Beach, the pile of protested ballots grew like a skyscraper, up, up, up, because both sides saw virtues in complaining.

Gore's team complained because they felt the board was not counting enough ballots as votes. They believed Judge LaBarga favored a much more liberal standard. So they objected to every ballot that the board "missed," thus creating a record for a possible future lawsuit. This, in turn, inspired the Republicans to object, as a defensive measure, to every uncounted dimple for Bush. If dimples and piercings ever became votes for Gore, then Bush wanted his share, too. The Republican lawyers began referring to this as the "Democratic Dimple Principle." Then it was shortened to just the initials: "Objection," they would say. "DDP."

"They were begrudging objections," Bush attorney Mark Wallace said, "because we didn't think they were right." But all these objections added up to an inexorable force: The pile of disputed ballots became crushingly large. As Burton put it: "I have never seen so many nicks, dings and indentations—sometimes we are dealing with marks that are barely discernible to the human eye."

Images from the Palm Beach recount were beamed to mystified millions of Americans, who saw the board members holding ballots up to the light, peering at them, turning them this way and that. And many viewers agreed with Bush spokesman Tucker Eskew, who said:

"You have dozens of cameras peering through the window, like parents of newborns. It is one ugly baby in that room."

■

The November 26 deadline set by the Florida Supreme Court was fast approaching. Only Palm Beach was still counting. The Gore team had pretty much given up on the recounts. It carefully tracked the "yield rate" in each county—namely, the percentage of unread ballots that the canvassing boards converted into votes. The enthusiastic re-counters of Broward managed a yield rate of 20 to 25 percent. In Palm Beach, it was a modest 5 percent. "There are hundreds of votes that are not being counted," local Gore attorney Ben Kuehne said brusquely.

As the deadline approached, the Palm Beach board members realized they might not be able to finish at all. On the afternoon of Sunday, November 26, hours before the Florida Supreme Court's deadline, Judge Burton faxed a letter to Secretary of State Harris seeking an extension until 9 a.m. Monday. This was the backup deadline allowed by the court in case the secretary of state's office was not open on Sunday. But Harris's office most definitely was open.

At 3:15 p.m., having received no answer, Burton stood up from the counting table and walked to a back office in the Emergency Operations Center, where he made a call to Clay Roberts, the state's elections director. A short while later, the canvassing board received a letter from Harris holding firm to the deadline. Burton was miffed: "I don't know what the difference is between sending it at 5 p.m. or at 7:30 p.m."

After all they had been through, for all the board's ambivalence about the count, the Palm Beach canvassers were now deeply committed to having their work validated. They'd plowed through half a million ballots—the idea that their new tally might be ignored was hard to take.

The board picked up the pace. But at 4:25 p.m., Burton announced that the count could not possibly be completed by 5 p.m. Soon afterward, county officials began feeding a hieroglyph of partial results into a fax machine to Tallahassee. Just before 5 p.m., the machine jammed. But it was quickly fixed, and word came back that the papers had been received one minute before the deadline: 4:59 p.m.

And they kept counting, just in case—faster and faster. The party observers now seemed more cooperative. Then, at 6:05 p.m., a wave of gloom came over Burton's face. Katherine Harris, he had learned, would not even accept the partial results they had sent. (Harris's lawyers would later laugh at the idea. They couldn't even read the partial results, they insisted.)

Finally, at 7:06 p.m., almost exactly 19 days after the polls closed, the Palm Beach board finished counting its votes. Gore wound up netting 174 votes—far fewer than the Gore team believed he was entitled to. There were 5,924 ballots left in dispute, according to Gore strategist Dennis Newman. Of those, 4,987 were "dimpled" ballots, he said—2,971 for Gore and 2,016 for Bush. If these had all been counted as votes, Gore would have gained another 955—more than enough to win Florida and the election.

"I believe they did a real good job to be evenhanded and fair, to be consistent," Newman said of the Palm Beach board. "They were just consistently wrong."

Judge Burton was more philosophical:

"This has been an amazing experience," he said afterward. "This is democracy. . . . This was the best and worst of politics."

CHAPTER FIVE

■

Turning Point

Al Gore had a grim Thanksgiving. Instead of counting his blessings, he was counting his enemies.

Enemies such as Katherine Harris, the Florida secretary of state—or, as Gore liked to call her, "Cruella De Vil." But she was a Republican; he expected her to be an enemy. When Gore found himself on the phone with an old friend and the topic turned to enemies, he was more interested in the former friends who had let him down. His list was growing steadily. There was Alex Penelas, the mayor of Miami-Dade County, where the canvassing board abruptly stopped counting ballots on the eve of Thanksgiving. And Bob Butterworth, the Florida attorney general, who went wobbly in the battle over military ballots. And Sen. Robert G. Torricelli, whose public hand-wringing over the amount of time Gore was taking made him the most skittish Democrat on Capitol Hill. And former White House chief of staff Leon Panetta, who was quoted day after day, fretting that the fight was stretching out too long. In the constant struggle for public opinion, Panetta was a nagging thorn in Gore's side.

Through most of the ordeal, the vice president was a model of composure and good humor. Again and again, his aides found themselves amazed by his consistency, his decisiveness during the War for Florida. He participated in conference calls with the foot soldiers. He was more solicitous of his aides, cracking jokes and repeatedly expressing gratitude for the long hours they were putting in. He was a

N. Sanders Sauls, a judge of the Leon County Court in Tallahassee, Florida, heard the Gore campaign's challenge to Florida's election results. On December 4, he ruled in favor of letting the results stand. (John Pendygraft / St. Petersburg Times)

new man. His calm, inspiring, thoughtful leadership during the deadlock confirmed something that Gore's troops had long suspected—he was happier and more effective when he wasn't asking people for their votes. Al Gore was a professional politician with an aversion to politics. He liked running things, not running for things. His staff liked him so much better now that the voters were out of the picture.

But the pressure of this unprecedented struggle was enough to get to anyone, and this was the lowest weekend for Gore. He had banked everything on the recount, which was petering out without discovering enough votes to boost him into the lead. Gore's whole strategy— legal, political, public relations—hinged on getting the lead. Instead, come Sunday, Katherine Harris would certify that George W. Bush had won the election.

Adding insult to injury, there were dozens of Republican protesters outside his house on Massachusetts Avenue, chanting, "Get out of Cheney's house!" over and over and over. He could hear them as clear as a church bell in Hades. "Get out of Cheney's house!" Finally, on Saturday morning, Gore decided he had had enough. He wanted some counterprotesters and he wanted them fast. Some people to shout something nice, to drown out the Bush crowd—maybe even drive them away. He started placing calls to find the only person he knew who could round up a hundred chanting Democrats on short notice to chant on Thanksgiving weekend: John Sweeney, president of the AFL-CIO.

Gore started looking for Sweeney at 9 a.m. Saturday. But the diminutive, white-haired power broker does not carry a cell phone or wear a pager, and he didn't bother to tell aides that he was going to visit his son and namesake in Tennessee. This is true power in Washington—the power to vanish. By midafternoon, Gore had at least five union staff members hunting for their boss, leaving messages up and down the Eastern seaboard.

Get out of Cheney's house! Get out of Cheney's house! Gore began to worry. Perhaps he was being abandoned. Maybe labor, the core constituency of Gore's campaign, was giving up without even telling him. At 7 p.m., he asked an aide to call Sweeney's staff again. He had to know: Was Sweeney mad at him? After all, the whole day had gone by and Sweeney never called.

Yes, a grim, unhappy Thanksgiving.

■

The next day, Sunday, November 26, the election ended. For a moment, anyway. Florida's designated officials gathered at the state Capitol to certify the results. At 5 p.m., the Florida Supreme Court's deadline passed. Harris was there, and her appointed head of the elections division, Clay Roberts, and the state's agriculture commissioner, Bob Crawford. Crawford was nominally a Democrat, but he supported the Bush brothers. He took Jeb's place on the state canvassing board when the governor decided to recuse himself, and now Crawford was happy to sign his name to a George W. victory.

After the paperwork was all assembled, the board members went before the cameras at about 7:30 p.m. Crawford made a little speech: "People call me and say—particularly from out of state—and say, 'What's going on down in Florida?' And I have to keep reminding people, the only thing that's going on here is that we've got a razor-thin election for the most important job in the world, and that's all it is. After all the jokes, after all of the anguish, we've just got a close election. . . .

"But I think it's over. It should be over," Crawford rambled. "And Yogi Berra once said, 'It's not over till it's over.' Well, it's over. And we have a winner, and it's time to move on."

A huge crowd on the brick plaza outside the Capitol heard Harris announce the official margin: "The certified result in the presidential race in Florida is as follows—Governor George W. Bush, 2,912,790; Vice President Al Gore, 2,912,253." Out of 5.825 million ballots cast for the two main candidates, the gap between them was 537. It defied all probability. Imagine an electronic counter that ticks off a number every second—one, two, three and so on. In one minute, the count would reach 60. After an hour, it would reach 3,600. In a day: 86,400. If this counter began at the stroke of midnight New Year's Eve and ran nonstop through all of January, and all of February, through the first week of March, the count would, finally, on March 9, reach 5.825 million. The decisive margin between Bush and Gore would go by in just nine minutes.

When Harris declared the results, the Republicans on the plaza erupted in such a cheer that even the television microphones inside the building caught it clearly. That was about all they heard. After Crawford's speech, the official ceremony was painfully, awkwardly quiet, just the scritch-scritch of pens on official documents as the board members signed one set of results after another. "There was all this dead time when all you could hear was the pens scratching on and on," recalled Harris adviser Mac Stipanovich. "Someone got so nervous about all that dead airspace that they decided it had gone on too long. So Clay didn't even sign the last set until afterward."

Then it was over.

But it was never over.

The Bush team feared that this was a moment of extreme danger. Election law required that the governor sign a "Certificate of Ascertainment," naming the state's presidential electors. This was to be sent by registered mail to the National Archives. But if Gore subpoenaed the ascertainment before it could leave Florida, George W. Bush's electors would not become official in the eyes of the federal government.

Looking down the road, Bush's lawyers could imagine a time when Congress might be forced to choose between dueling sets of electors. Which slate bore the governor's signature could be significant. It was crucial that they get a Bush slate signed, sealed and safely off to Washington. The Bush team did not believe for a second that Gore was about to quit. No, the next step was for Gore to file a lawsuit contesting the certified results. And if he won that, he would get his own document certifying his own set of electors.

Reporters had the statehouse surrounded. Three aides to Jeb Bush sneaked from the building into a car that took them quickly from downtown to the Governor's Mansion. Jeb Bush signed the documents at his dining room table as soon as he got them, at 8:41 p.m., before Gore's team could seek an injunction.

Now what? Bush's lawyers had scoured Florida for a post office open on Sunday night of a holiday weekend. No luck. Someone suggested having a young lawyer drive with the certificate a half-hour north from Tallahassee into Georgia to spend the night. A Florida subpoena would have no force in Georgia. Someone else suggested chartering a plane to fly the document to Washington, where it could be registered at a post office near the Archives building. That might get it there faster. Finally, Frank Jimenez decided to give the certificate to a staff member entirely unrelated to the election dispute—someone the Gore team would never think of serving with a subpoena. This staff member took the document home and slept with it. Then, the next morning, she took it straight to the post office and mailed it.

When she arrived at the office that morning, Jimenez and deputy counsel Reg Brown asked how it had gone. Fine, she said. In fact, the nice clerk at the post office had offered her an option that was better than registered mail—Express Mail.

The people on the Florida governor's legal team rushed out the door to the post office. They flashed all sorts of identification, begged and pleaded and cajoled, until finally the clerk let them retrieve the package. They tore off the Express Mail packaging and relabeled it as registered mail. At last, George W. Bush's deciding votes were on their way to Washington.

■

On Sunday night, the Texas governor made his strongest statement so far on the election results. There was a lot of hand-wringing in the Bush camp over just what to say after the results were certified. This was a big moment: the official apparatus of the state of Florida certifying that Bush had won the 25 electors that he needed to be president. Even though Gore was not going to fold his tent, Bush felt he should seize the moment to appear presidential, and to make the case that the dispute was entering an important new phase.

But what should Bush say about Gore himself? It didn't seem right to call on the vice president to concede. That would risk making Bush look pushy or grabby. He needed to fly above that. At the same time, the Bush team did want to portray Gore as stubborn, recalcitrant, a man whose insistence on challenging the results was endangering the country. It settled on language warning Gore not to heed the advice of his lawyers to fight on. When in doubt, attack the lawyers.

"The last 19 days have been extraordinary ones," Bush began. "The election was close, but tonight, after a count, a recount and yet another manual recount, Secretary Cheney and I are honored and humbled to have won the state of Florida, which gives us the needed electoral votes to win the election."

Bush laid out a set of agenda items that he said could be a basis for bipartisan governing: improved schools, prescription drug coverage for senior citizens, a stronger military and a tax cut. It wasn't a policy speech, though. The point was to get Americans used to the experience of hearing an executive agenda coming from Bush's mouth. He talked about his White House staff, and called on the Clinton administration to start working with Cheney on transitional matters.

But he deliberately stopped short of mentioning names of Cabinet members, and he never specifically claimed victory. Some of his advisers thought the format was all wrong—Bush in a formal setting, staring straight into the camera. He was better if they could find an excuse to shoot him from an angle. From straight-on, his eyes looked too close together.

As for the fancy footwork: "The vice president's lawyers have indicated he will challenge the certified election results. I respectfully ask him to reconsider. Until Florida's votes were certified, the vice president was working to represent the interests of those who supported him. I did not agree with his call for additional recounts, but I respected his decision to fight until the votes were finally certified. Now that they are certified, we enter a different phase."

■

This all came as a surprise to David Boies, Gore's superlawyer. Five days earlier, Boies had figured his work was done. Election law is generally a matter for the states to worry about, and Boies had won his team's case in the state Supreme Court. He expected that the counties would get busy, examine their ballots, find the winning votes for Gore—and that would be that. He was so confident he packed his bags and flew home to Armonk, N.Y., for Thanksgiving. But by the time he landed, the wheels were off Gore's wagon. Boies turned around and headed back to Florida.

The Gore team's calculated risk had backfired. Boies—along with Ron Klain and the rest of Gore's senior legal advisers—had gambled by asking the Florida court to extend the deadline for counting votes. It was a complicated risk.

Under Florida statutes, the postelection period was divided into two phases. The "protest" period came first. The trailing candidate had certain narrow opportunities to challenge the results to the county canvassing boards—mainly by requesting recounts. This period ended when the results were certified. Then the "contest" phase began. During this process, the losing candidate could file suit in Leon County Circuit Court, alleging problems with the election. The judge had wide leeway to examine the complaint and to "fashion any remedy" that might be necessary to set things right.

Because this was a presidential election, federal law also came into play. A specific date was set for presidential electors to cast their votes—December 18. (Another federal law gave preference to electors chosen by December 12.) When the state laws were combined with the federal calendar, the presidential candidates were left with a total of about five weeks to complete both phases of the election challenge.

Five weeks. Gore's gamble was to stretch the first, "protest," phase by seeking a later deadline for counting, thus shortening the time available for phase two, which was a lawsuit contesting the results. Some lawyers for Gore thought this strategy was a mistake. Dexter Douglass, Gore's old Tallahassee hand, believed that they should let Katherine Harris certify the results and go straight to the lawsuit. In the protest phase, all the power rested with the county canvassing boards. As Gore had learned, they had wide discretion. They could count or not count. They could drag their feet. They could set hard standards for counting or set easy ones. Better, Douglass felt, to get the whole election in front of one judge with the power to order a recount and set the standard. And if the judge wouldn't deliver results, they could appeal to the Florida Supreme Court—Gore's favorite court in the land.

But Douglass didn't have to factor Washington into his equation. At the time when this decision had to be made, a scant seven days into the deadlocked election, Gore was under intense pressure to get the whole thing over with. The Bush machine was relentlessly on message: We've counted and recounted, and it's time to close the book. Many leading news outlets were wringing their hands over the risks of a long dispute. Gore's support on Capitol Hill was shaky. Official certification of a win by Bush could sink him. He needed a win to keep going, so he chose to appeal to the Florida Supreme Court sooner rather than later, on the issue of extending the deadline.

One more thing: Gore thought he had an advantage in South Florida. If the predominantly Democratic canvassing boards delivered quick counts using the standards Gore preferred, he would move into the lead, and the shortened contest phase would be Bush's problem. So Gore challenged the deadline. And won. His public support held steady.

But while Gore gained ground thanks to the extended deadline, he didn't get enough votes to take over the lead. Now Boies, Klain and company had to live with the consequences of their gamble: They had little more than two weeks to get the results thrown out.

■

So Al Gore had to make some tough decisions. Of all the strange elements of the Florida election, which ones should he include in his contest lawsuit? He had a range of choices on the table:

- *The on-again, off-again South Florida recounts.* In the official certified results, Katherine Harris and the state canvassing board included the Broward County hand recount, but not the Palm Beach County survey—Palm Beach had missed the deadline. As many as 215 net votes for Gore were found there: Shouldn't those votes count? In Miami-Dade, more than 150 net Gore votes were discovered before the board quit counting. Surely Gore should sue to have those votes tallied, and the remaining 9,000 or so undervotes examined.

- *The strange results from Nassau County.* When officials conducted a mandatory recount in this little county in Florida's far northeast corner, they came up short several hundred votes. Instead of accepting the smaller number, they simply reverted to the first count, which gave Bush an additional margin of 51 votes. Gore could challenge the inclusion of those votes.

- *Continuing reports of racial intimidation.* Although Gore had done little to promote these complaints, African American activists struggled to focus media attention on the charge that blacks were given a hard time at the polls. Tens of thousands of ballots in predominantly black precincts registered either too many votes for president or no vote at all. Hundreds of names, many of them black voters, had been purged from the rolls in a campaign to strike felons from the registry. There were allegations that voting equipment was inferior in poor neighborhoods, that poll workers were inadequately trained to assist inexperienced voters, that ballot designs and instructions were confusing. Gore could include some or all of these complaints in his challenge.

- *Shenanigans involving absentee ballot requests in Seminole and Martin counties.* This one gave Gore and his people their hardest decision.

In the weeks before the election, the Florida Republican Party sent out absentee ballot application forms to hundreds of thousands of voters statewide. The GOP prided itself on its absentee efforts. As far back as 1988, in an extremely close Senate race, the party elected Connie Mack on the strength of a huge absentee advantage. The GOP's grassroots people loved absentee voters. They are the easiest voters to track from first contact to cast ballot. The party apparatus can determine which citizens have mailed in their ballot applications, and which ones have yet to return their ballots. Then it's a simple matter to telephone the laggards, pester them with postcards, even go and ring their doorbells. Pushing the absentee vote is the most efficient element of a modern political campaign.

But in two counties—Seminole in Central Florida and Martin on the Atlantic coast—the printing company that prepared the GOP applications failed to include voter identification numbers on the application forms. In Seminole, one of Florida's most Republican counties, elections supervisor Sandra Goard permitted a party employee to take the forms and add the missing information. Martin County officials also allowed a local Republican operative to add information to the ballot application forms. Democrats in the two counties yelled foul. They said the law invalidates forms that lack proper information. Republican elections officials, they contended, gave an unfair advantage to their own party by allowing the applications to be fixed.

They sued.

For the Gore team, these cases now posed a tricky problem. If these lawsuits worked, Gore would hit pay dirt. George W. Bush's lead in the absentee voting was 4,700 in Seminole County and 2,815 in Martin County. But the only plausible remedy was to throw out all the absentee ballots. If a judge decided to do so, it would hit the election like a neutron bomb—only Al Gore would be left standing. But the lawsuits cut against everything Gore was espousing in his public statements. As they passionately pursued their South Florida recount strategy, Gore and his spokesmen repeated ad nauseam that their only concern was to count every vote. Their spin condemned "hypertechnical" reliance on rules, as the Florida Supreme Court had put it. And in neither Seminole County nor Martin County was there any suggestion that the voters themselves had done anything wrong. It was a question of accurate information added to otherwise legal ballot request forms.

Boies looked over the smorgasbord of lawsuit options and argued for a streamlined case. The goal, he said, remained the same: to get the South Florida undervotes counted. Gore's recount experts still believed that, given a favorable standard for counting ballots, the vice president could win on the basis of hand counts alone. If Gore got a judge to give him the Palm Beach ballots, and the partial Miami-Dade results, and the results of the Nassau recount, all told, Bush's 537-vote winning margin would dwindle to little more than 100 votes. That could be erased by counting the rest of the undervotes. Counting ballots had always been Gore's strategy. This was no time to change course. "We focused on the absolute easiest, cleanest contest points," Boies explained afterward. "Until we really were able to be sure we could get those issues done, there was a reluctance to try to take on Seminole County, or Martin County or any of the other places."

The political lawyers basically agreed. William Daley and Warren Christopher felt that Gore's argument had been consistent for weeks. To the extent that he had public support for contesting the results, that support rested on the foundation of count every vote. Ron Klain took a more nuanced tactical view. He believed that by adding the Seminole and Martin cases, Gore's team might force Bush's lawyers to talk out of just one side of their mouths. As it was, the Republicans were free to argue in the recount cases that every little mistake by a voter is fatal to the ballot, then shift to the absentee cases and argue that mistakes should not matter. If Gore put the cases together in front of a single judge, the Bush team would have to choose one argument or the other, Klain believed.

Gore was tempted. In his inimitable way, Gore had immersed himself in the details of every option. He knew the minutiae of the misbegotten effort to purge felons from the rolls. He knew the contours of the absentee cases. He saw that the racial issue was a polarizing morass with no clear end to it. But he was intrigued by all the pundits who thought that Seminole and Martin could be the "sleeper" cases that would decide the election. He was torn.

Ultimately, Gore chose an uneasy middle ground. Officially, the vice president and his people would not participate in the absentee cases. But they offered encouraging words. In fact, their stalwart supporters in the labor movement took over the absentee cases. They hired the lawyers and handled the PR as Gore looked on approvingly.

So it was settled: Gore's lawsuit would demand that every recounted vote be included, and that all the remaining South Florida undervotes be looked at. There were enough ballots outstanding, Boies would argue, to call the result into question, and that was what the law required. The absentee cases, meanwhile, would get no official sanction but a lot of backdoor support, while the racial complaints were on their own.

On Monday, November 27, Gore went on television to answer Bush's muted victory speech of the night before, and to justify his continued fight. "Ignoring votes means ignoring democracy itself," he said. "If we ignore the votes of thousands in Florida in this election, how can you or any American have confidence that your vote will not be ignored in a future election?

"That is all we have asked since Election Day, a complete count of all the votes cast in Florida—not recount after recount, as some have charged, but a single full and accurate count. We haven't had that yet."

■

George W. Bush had his own hard decisions to make: first whether to appeal his case to the U.S. Supreme Court, and then whether to withdraw the appeal.

The first choice came after the Florida Supreme Court's 7–0 decision to extend the deadline for certification. The Bush team crafted a highly theoretical criticism of the Florida court aimed directly at the slim conservative majority in Washington: that the Florida justices had usurped the power of the state Legislature by fashioning new rules for counting and certifying the votes.

A second argument was that "the use of arbitrary, standardless, and selective manual recounts" violated the equal protection and due process clauses of the U.S. Constitution, though some lawyers for Bush worried this argument might strike a bad note with those same Supreme Court conservatives.

Outside the Bush team hardly anyone, least of all Gore's lawyers, expected the U.S. Supreme Court to take the case—precisely because the political stakes were so high. Gore's team of law professors noted the general reluctance of this court to involve itself in matters that did not require immediate attention. No matter who was ahead on November 26, there was sure to be a contest challenging the vote, and that challenge was sure to be appealed, and that appeal could very well reach the Supreme Court. In other words, the justices could count on another chance to intervene.

Bush turned for advice to his appellate lawyers. The team was led by Theodore Olson, who had argued 13 cases before the court. More than that, he was a Supreme Court scholar who also happened to know some of the justices socially.

As a senior partner at the huge firm of Gibson, Dunn & Crutcher, Olson could marshal help from his partners and an army of younger lawyers. Many of them were former Supreme Court clerks—Helgi Walker, who had clerked for Justice Clarence Thomas; Columbia law professor John Manning, who had clerked for Justice Antonin Scalia;

R. Ted Cruz, a Cuban American from Texas who worked in the Bush campaign and had clerked for Chief Justice William H. Rehnquist. After a year or two spent discussing cases and drafting opinions with a justice, a clerk learns to see the world through the justice's eyes.

Olson had gone to Tallahassee at the beginning of the recount, but after two weeks found it impossible to concentrate on drafting Supreme Court arguments amid the chaos of the Republican Party headquarters. Now he was doing his thinking in a windowless hide-away within Gibson, Dunn's Washington office. Handicapping the case, Olson recalls, "I felt that we had a very respectable argument for the court, and I believed that we had a decent chance."

But the risks were inescapable. If the court refused to take the case, Bush's only real backstop was the Florida Legislature, and its intervention would inflame the opposition and escalate the conflict immeasurably.

As members of the Bush team surveyed the high court, it was the conservatives who worried them most. "There were a number of people who had a concern about . . . Justice Scalia," recalled George Terwilliger. Scalia was known to take a very hard line on technical questions about who has the legal standing to bring an appeal before the court, "who the parties were and the standing of these claims."

James Baker laid out the issues for Bush during a November 21 conference call, with other lawyers chiming in. "There was some concern raised about [Justice Sandra Day] O'Connor, as a former state legislator, that she might believe that the Supreme Court should not intervene," recalled Benjamin Ginsberg. Also, people talked about Rehnquist's writings on the 10th Amendment, which reserves for the states authority not granted to the federal government.

On balance, however, Bush's lawyers were relatively optimistic. The many former Supreme Court clerks were more confident than outside legal experts that the high court would take the case, and at that point it wasn't clear whether Bush or Gore would be ahead in the count come November 26. Bush listened to the discussion and decided to go forward.

Three days later, the Supreme Court announced that it would take the case, though only on the issue of whether the Florida court had changed the law after the election, not on equal protection or due process grounds. The high court set oral arguments for Friday, December 1.

Now with Harris having certified the election results, Bush was faced with an even more difficult choice: Should he continue the appeal to the Supreme Court, or drop it and hope the certification would push the whole dispute to closure? Bush later called the decision the most significant he was asked to make during the 36-day struggle.

"That was the gamble," he said later. "If we lose, we're in trouble."

Hours before Harris's certification ceremony, Bush and his legal and political advisers discussed their options in a lengthy conference call. Many of Bush's lawyers remained bullish about their chances of winning the case, and some worried about offending the justices by withdrawing the case after the court had accepted it. But to others on the call, winning the presidency outweighed the question of ruffling the feathers of a few justices.

By dropping the case, Bush could claim the high ground politically and put more pressure on Gore. Staying in the Supreme Court, Bush was told, would freeze public opinion and give the Democrats more time to get the counting resumed. And if he were to lose in the Supreme Court, Bush was told, he then would be far more vulnerable to the decisions of the Florida courts. Beyond that, an adverse ruling in the U.S. Supreme Court could undermine any pending action by the Florida legislature.

Bush listened for about 20 minutes as his team presented the options, and then, with very little hesitation, told the lawyers to keep going. Josh Bolten, who was part of Baker's team in Florida, recalled Bush's response. "He said, 'Here's what we're going to do. We're going to stick with the appeal because it's the right thing to do,'" Bolten said. "He said our arguments are correct, and he wanted that ratified by the Supreme Court so that people will believe this is legitimate."

Bush worried aloud that intervention by the Florida legislature could undermine the legitimacy of the presidency.

That night, after Harris certified the election, Baker appeared before reporters. "What will this do to the Supreme Court hearing this Friday? Are you going to press on with it?" he was asked. "Absolutely," Baker replied.

Bush's lawyers had one more idea. As an insurance policy, Tim Flanigan and Ted Cruz came up with a way out for the court if it didn't buy their argument. They cited case law that suggested the court could vacate the Florida court's decision and remand the case for further instructions. They called Olson and his team at Gibson, Dunn with the language. Olson's lawyers wrote it into the brief. "It was a back door for the court," Flanigan said later.

■

Gore filed his contest. Then, more bad news. Case No. CA–2808 was assigned by the courthouse computer to the only eligible member of the Leon County bench appointed by a Republican: Judge N. Sanders Sauls. He was a lifelong Democrat, the well-connected son of Democratic activists, but native North Florida Democrats are not always of the liberal variety. There in Dixie, the lineage of a lot of Democrats runs straight back to the anti-Lincoln days of the vanquished Confederacy. Sauls was a conservative soul with a linear mind; he was unlikely to warm to legalistic leaps of faith in the cause of Al Gore. "From the time we knew he was the judge, from that very moment, we knew we had a serious problem," Gore attorney Mark Steinberg said later.

Sauls almost didn't get the case. Shortly after 8 a.m. on Monday, November 27, as the Gore team was preparing to file its papers, George S. Reynolds III, chief judge of the Leon County circuit, called together several judges eligible to preside over the landmark case. Reynolds had become chief two years earlier, after the Florida

Supreme Court forced Sauls to resign in a messy squabble. The
episode had embarrassed and infuriated Sauls. Nominally, at least, the
issue that got Sauls in trouble was his decision to fire a court administrator. But Cindy Sauls, the judge's wife, had another view of the
high court's motivations. "It has nothing to do with whether you're
correct on the rule of law," the judge's wife said. "It has to do with
them doing whatever they feel is in the interest of their own political
agenda and promoting their own pet projects. They're over there leg-
islating from the bench."

Cases in the circuit were ordinarily assigned by computer program
to the next available judge. But Reynolds now proposed to his colleagues that they abandon the computer and allow him to assign the
case to a judge of his choosing, the better to consolidate knowledge of
the high-profile presidential case in one jurist. The idea did not get far.
The judges balked; the computer ticked through the dockets, and the
contest went to the only judge on the court who didn't already have a
piece of the election litigation: Sandy Sauls.

"He was probably the worst of the judges we could draw," Boies
said later. The selection of Judge Sauls gave a new shape to the Gore
lawyers' strategy. Instead of trying to win at trial, Boies decided he
must push the case past Sauls as quickly as possible. The appeal was
everything: "We thought we could win the issue in the Florida
Supreme Court," Boies explained. The worst thing that could happen
was not to lose in Sauls's courtroom—the worst thing would be to
lose slowly.

■

David Boies was born to be a trial lawyer. He was blessed with the
twin gifts of tactical cunning and prodigious gab. He could hatch a
case and spring it like a bear trap in court, and he could sell his theories fluently in relaxed but relentless streams of press-friendly con-
sciousness. Boies was a movable feast for reporters working the
twinkly lighted pre-Christmas streets of downtown Tallahassee, but

he also had time for paying customers. In fact, so many wealthy clients clamored for his time that he set up a luxury ferry service to bring them all to Tallahassee. Choosing a president was just one of the myriad tasks competing for his time, but it was the one he couldn't massage or delay. The great David Boies was very busy trying to get one very important lawsuit past one very unfriendly small-town judge.

To expedite the case before Judge N. Sanders Sauls, Boies and the rest of Gore's legal team distilled their claims into a few arguments they considered simple and winnable. They argued that Sauls had the power to consider the election afresh—it didn't matter how local canvassing boards applied their discretion, whether they had done well or done poorly. What mattered, Boies said, was that Florida law provided for a remedy in any case in which enough "legal votes" were "rejected" to "place in doubt the result of the election." Gore's team maintained that the very narrowness of Bush's lead itself created sufficient doubt, and the only way to resolve the question was to examine the ballots.

Bush, on the other hand, dug in deeper. Baker introduced a tough-minded new litigation team in Tallahassee with a speech lamenting Gore's decision to challenge the election "after 19 or 20 days of counts and recounts and more recounts." The stakes were painfully clear to the former secretary of state. Bush's election-night margin had dwindled to a relative handful; Baker was determined to make sure that no more votes would be found and the best way to do that was not to look for any more. To reporters, Baker offered the polish and experience of Houston colleagues B. Daryl Bristow and G. Irvin Terrell, and Chicago law partners Philip S. Beck and Fred H. Bartlit, Jr. as proof that Bush would fight to protect his lead.

The opposing approaches were obvious on Tuesday, November 28, when the teams for Bush and Gore met in Sauls's third-floor courtroom in the Leon County Courthouse near the state Capitol. The judge wore half-moon reading glasses perched way down his nose, and liked to peer over them when he was delivering the ruralisms he was so fond of. "They drugged me out of Wakulla County," Sauls said at the beginning of the proceeding—a reference to the more mundane duty he had been pulling in the piney country outside the capital. Sauls addressed Gore's local attorney, Dexter Douglass, as "Squire Douglass," and philosophized, with a sigh, that "trial lawyers live a dreadful existence. You're always in some crisis."

The first issue was the trial schedule. Hurry up, said the Democrats. Slowly, slowly, replied the Republicans—they offered a timetable that would have run the trial through December 11, the very last minute. When Boies spoke, there was a brittle edge to his usually genial voice. He all but begged Sauls to order Palm Beach and Miami-Dade to renew immediately their counts of roughly 14,000 ballots. He wanted the counting to proceed even as the trial was underway. In Washington, Gore underlined the request, going before the cameras to say: "I believe this is a time to count every vote and not to run out the clock."

Barry Richard, the local Tallahassee Democrat in the Republican camp, answered for Bush. Boies's request was absurd, he said. It would give the Democrats everything they wanted even before the judge considered the disputed facts. What was the point of a trial if Gore was going to get his entire wish list right away? Sauls agreed—but he was not as hard on Gore as some people expected. He set the trial for the coming Saturday, December 2—a fairly swift timetable, though Boies vowed to appeal the matter immediately to the Florida Supreme Court. On Friday, on the eve of the trial, the Florida justices refused to intervene.

But the Gore team managed a second small, but significant, victory ahead of the trial: It persuaded Sauls to order the disputed ballots moved from South Florida to Tallahassee. "Pack 'em up and ship 'em up," ordered the judge. In the long empty hours on cable TV, cameras tracked the all-day progress of a Ryder rental truck bearing the punch cards. It was the longest, slowest, most famous truck ride since O. J. Simpson in the white Bronco.

The courtroom was packed at 9:20 Saturday morning when Sauls took the bench. Lawyers were double-parked in the well of the court, and the jury box overflowed with broadcast crews. In a futile show of independence, Joe Klock—lead attorney for Katherine Harris—planted himself in a chair some distance from Bush's legal team. But he encroached on the Gore team's space, and ultimately Sauls ordered him to the Republican table.

Gore had hired Deeno Kitchen, a former law partner of Judge Sauls, to make a crucial pitch. Kitchen asked his friend to admit the Palm Beach ballots into evidence. Even if things went badly with Sauls, the existence of the dimpled ballots in the court record might be enough to persuade appellate judges to examine the ballots, Gore's lawyers figured.

Sauls accepted the cards as evidence, but still refused to have them counted.

After that, Boies moved swiftly. Keeping one eye on the clock, he ran a hurry-up offense, summoning only two witnesses—a voting machine specialist and a statistician. He considered calling no witnesses at all. "The issue was whether we put anyone on at all," Boies explained afterward. "Our point of view was—look at the ballots and count them." Simple. But there was a purpose in calling the two witnesses. Two purposes, actually: to build a record for the appeal, and to entice Bush into summoning his own witnesses, who were then available for cross-examination. And yet Barry Richard, representing Bush in court, was "pleasantly surprised at the weakness of their case," he said.

The first Gore witness was Kimball Brace, a loquacious elections expert from Fairfax Station, Va. Brace was hardly getting warmed up when Gore's team began to feel the trial slipping away. The clock ticked. Brace volunteered long answers about "chad buildup" and the deterioration of rubber on voting machines. "This is like watching an antitrust trial," Klock said during one recess, "except it's not as interesting."

The next witness, Yale statistician Nicolas Hengartner, did better.

He offered a concise explanation of the fact that far more punch-card ballots than other types went uncounted when run through a machine. Still, Hengartner consumed a lot of time. It was 4 p.m. when the Democrats rested their case. The trial was clearly going to spill into a second day.

The people on Bush's team had originally threatened to call 95 witnesses. But when it came time to present their case, they kept things streamlined. Richard called Judge Burton, chairman of the Palm Beach canvassing board, who testified that local officials had been diligent in following the law. Sauls seemed to agree—he hailed the witness as "a great American." But the Republicans did not run a perfect case. Their botched witness was John Ahmann, a California rancher and former IBM engineer, who designed and sold thousands of punch-card machines to Miami-Dade County in the 1970s. Ahmann started well for Bush, scoffing at Brace's notion that tiny paper scraps from punched ballots could accumulate in the machines and make it difficult for a voter to punch a proper hole. He also dismissed the idea that machine deterioration could impede the punch mechanism.

Then came the cross-examination. And just moments before he rose to question Ahmann, Gore attorney Stephen Zack was handed a folder. A note on the outside shouted: "Urgent! Read this immediately!" Inside was a 1981 patent application from Ahmann. It was so dense that Zack almost quit reading—but buried in the document was Ahmann's explanation that problems with old voting machines could lead to "potentially unreadable votes." Bingo. Even if Sauls didn't find that meaningful, it would be added to the record for the friendlier Florida justices.

When it was over, Sauls ruled quickly. He worked through the night on Sunday and into Monday, then ruled from the bench on Monday afternoon, December 4. The timetable was so tight that there had been no time to type his opinion.

Sauls gave Gore nothing. Gore lawyer Dexter Douglass called the ruling a "slam dunk" for Bush. Sauls refused to order an examination of the undervotes. He felt Gore had failed to show a "reasonable probability" that more counting would change the outcome. If any ballots were to be examined by hand, Sauls ruled, then all the ballots should be looked at. In all, it was a memorably bad day for the Democrats. The only consolation for the gloomy Gore lawyers was the hope that perhaps Sauls had gone too far, and a higher court would rein him in.

■

While Sauls was handling the Tallahassee trial, the two teams clashed in the U.S. Supreme Court. People waited all night on a Capitol Hill sidewalk to get one of a handful of tickets for the general public. The lucky few sat on hard-backed chairs among the marble pillars of the court's surprisingly small courtroom. Theodore Olson, the reigning champion of conservative constitutional lawyers, faced Laurence Tribe, his liberal counterpart. For the first time in its staid history, the high court made a tape immediately available after oral arguments ended, and for the first time the American people heard on network television the rapid-fire give-and-take of a Supreme Court presentation.

Olson was deep-voiced and deferential, and scarcely got a sentence out before he was interrupted for the first time. Tribe tried to open with a reference to popular culture and was instantly cut off by Justice Anthony M. Kennedy. In the end, both men were put through their paces in an oral argument marked by obvious and fundamental differences of opinion between liberal and conservative justices.

Justice Ruth Bader Ginsburg, a Clinton appointee, was the most vigorous of the liberals. She seemed shocked that the case was even being considered by the high court. "I do not know of any case where we have impugned a state supreme court the way you are doing in this case," Ginsburg scolded Olson. Florida's seven justices "may have been wrong; we might have interpreted it differently, but we are not the arbiters—they are." She seemed to have an ally in Justice

David H. Souter, who was appointed by George W. Bush's father—to Bush Senior's lasting regret.

When Olson's time was up, and Tribe reached the lectern, it was time for Chief Justice William H. Rehnquist and Justice Antonin Scalia, two rock-ribbed conservatives, to turn up the heat. They latched onto a case that had appeared in passing in the Bush brief: *McPherson v. Blacker*, an 1892 dispute over presidential electors. They read that century-old precedent to say that there is no basic constitutional right of citizens to vote for president. The Constitution instead gives the choice of president to the electoral college, and the power to set rules for choosing electors to state legislatures. In its opinion, the Florida Supreme Court referred to the rights of Florida voters—but unless those rights were given by the legislature, they weren't relevant to the presidential election. It was a fresh interpretation of the issues at hand, and Tribe had trouble finding a satisfactory answer.

In all, the liberals seemed most uncomfortable—and though the court generally does not tell which justices voted to accept each case, it was clear that this had been a choice by the conservatives. As the oral arguments progressed, Ginsburg and another Clinton appointee, Justice Stephen G. Breyer, mulled over actions the justices might take short of deciding the case for Bush. "I suppose there would be a possibility for this court to remand for clarification," Ginsburg mused to Tribe—meaning, we could send it back to Tallahassee with some questions.

And that is ultimately what happened. On Monday, December 4, the Supreme Court issued an unsigned "per curiam" opinion that vacated the Florida court's deadline-changing decision and asked the Florida justices to explain their thinking better. To a number of former clerks, the opinion bore the unmistakable stylistic hallmarks of Rehnquist's writing. "There is considerable uncertainty as to the precise grounds for the [Florida Supreme Court] decision," the opinion said. "This is sufficient reason for us to decline at this time to review the federal questions asserted to be present." The justices had taken the back door marked out by Bush lawyer Tim Flanigan.

Both sides claimed victory. The Bush team pointed to the fact that the Florida court's decision was vacated. The decision was a clear rebuke, the Republicans maintained. The Democrats pointed out that the high court had not ordered anything different to happen in Florida. That, they said, was a boost for Gore.

But they agreed on one thing: The decision had taken the Supreme Court off the hook. The justices had found a way to appear harmonious while avoiding divisive action. They were flying above the fray—at least for now.

■

George W. Bush's ranch is a quiet, modest spread by the standards of millionaire Texans. There is a low-slung house built around a central room, a few head of cattle. The main luxury is a manmade pond not far from the front door, stocked with bass, so the governor could just grab a pole and his tackle box and have a lure in the water in a minute or two. The place is a couple of hours north of Austin near the big road to Dallas, just outside Waco. The closest town is Crawford, which—like a lot of places out West, like a lot of rural towns everywhere—prides itself on not bothering neighbors. As Bush realized that the election deadlock was not going to be over any time soon, he began to spend more and more time at the ranch. He had more privacy there. It was easy to get out of the house. In Austin, there were reporters ready to track any move he made—to the office, to the gym—but at the ranch he could climb into his truck and drive off to work up a good sweat hacking away the cedar saplings that sprang up all over the place, gulping precious water. In Austin, it was hard not to get bogged down in the constant stream of information, most of it useless. This judge ruled this; that board overruled that— all of it likely to change with the next hour. There were days in Florida when a half-dozen lawsuits were born or died. Bush liked to think of himself as a big-picture guy.

The world could just come to him. And it did—potential Cabinet members, including retired Gen. Colin L. Powell; possible White House staffers, led by Bush's designated chief of staff, Andrew H. Card Jr.; governors and legislators and family and friends. On Saturday, December 2, the Republican congressional leaders, House Speaker J. Dennis Hastert and Senate Majority Leader Trent Lott, made the trip to the ranch. It was a cold prairie morning. The announced purpose of the visit was to plan business under the future president, but the real value was just the photograph.

Truth be told, this had been a harrowing and dismal election for the Republican Party. Hastert's majority had gone from small to infinitesimal—five seats out of 435. Lott was in even more parlous shape—he remained majority leader only if Bush held on to Florida, and then only in the most theoretical sense. The Senate was going to be split 50–50 for the first time in history, and the Republican edge would rest entirely in the tie-breaking vote of the vice president. Meanwhile Bush, if he won, would become the first president in 112 years who failed to win the popular vote, and his victory margin in the electoral college hinged on about 500 ballots out of more than 100 million cast nationwide. Pretty thin soup. Perhaps there would be some small public relations value in a photo op showing the three leaders hatching strategy together in a cloud of relaxed confidence. Bush, Hastert and would-be Vice President Cheney gathered around the ranch fireplace wearing comfortable clothes. Lott looked vaguely uncomfortable in stiff new denims and a cowboy hat sprouting an enormous eagle feather.

That night, after the big men from Washington had gone, Bush settled in with family and old friends. His house guests—Mike and Nancy Weiss, cousin Debbie Stapleton and her husband, Craig—craved the latest news from the tube. But Bush didn't even have cable television at the ranch—no 24-hour blowhard shows, just the local Waco stations, which the governor watched mainly for the weather forecast. "He could be a Texas weatherman, he knows so much about the weather down there," Craig Stapleton later said. The electoral crisis was barely mentioned.

Even with a house full of guests, Bush stuck to his early-to-bed schedule. "It was a late night for him—maybe 9:45 or so," recalled Mike Weiss, laughing. "He gave us an extra 30 minutes." As soon as Bush was out of sight, his guests made a move for the television. Later, they tuned the set to NBC for *Saturday Night Live*, home of the savage election parodies.

"TURN THAT THING OFF!" Bush roared from the adjacent bedroom.

They heard his feet hit the floor.

"Turn it off!" Bush bolted through his bedroom door.

His friends scattered. One of them dove under the table. Another dashed into the kitchen and pressed his back against the wall, pretending to hide. Then they all burst out laughing—though deep down they knew that Bush was not entirely joking.

■

On Sunday, December 3, the phone rang at the office of Gerald Richman, a prominent Palm Beach attorney. A Mr. Steven Kirsch was calling. Richman had never heard of Steven Kirsch.

So the billionaire introduced himself.

Two years earlier, Kirsch explained, he had sold an Internet search engine called Infoseek to the Walt Disney Co. for the equivalent of $2.5 billion in stock. He had a new business now, called Propel, which created software and services for e-commerce sites. But that was not the reason for his call. He was calling because, although he was a Republican, Steven Kirsch was a devoted believer in Al Gore. He had given $150,000 to the Gore effort during the general election, then spent $5 million on his own television ads bashing Bush's record.

And there was more. On the morning after the deadlocked election night, Kirsch had awakened in his Nashville hotel room to find a note had been slipped under his door. "It's not over yet," the note said, and it was signed by Peter Knight, a powerful Washington lobbyist and principal fundraiser for Gore. Knight invited Kirsch to join him—and a few of Gore's other deep pockets—for a meeting to discuss the recount. More specifically, the funding of the recount. Kirsch went, and pledged $500,000.

Since then, Kirsch had become obsessed with the recount. He stayed up late at night reading the Florida elections code. He worked the phones incessantly, trying to get tips and theories to Gore. He called Knight daily, sometimes two or three times a day. He called Gore lawyer Mitchell Berger several times a week. He even called Joe Lieberman. Kirsch had become extremely interested in the Seminole and Martin county absentee ballot cases. These were the killer apps, he believed. These cases would decide the election for Gore.

And that was why Kirsch was calling. Gerald Richman, he understood, was the trial muscle for the Seminole case. It so happened that, after Gore decided not to take over the absentee ballot cases, his team arranged to have them run by their friends in the labor movement. Jack Dempsey, the general counsel of the American Federation of State, County and Municipal Employees (AFSCME), took the lead. AFSCME was the largest single donor to the Democratic Party, and Dempsey had been a key figure from the start of the recount. His union helped to round up volunteers to watch the ballot counting, and his union contributed lawyers to track down voter complaints. In Dempsey's view, the labor effort was one leg of a three-legged stool supporting Gore in Florida—one was the campaign, one the Democratic party, and one was labor. They shared a single purpose: "The objective was to get Gore elected," he said.

Seminole was one way of achieving that goal, so Dempsey sought out a courtroom killer. He found Richman, of the Palm Beach firm of Richman Greer Weil Brumbaugh Mirabito & Christensen. The Democratic Party's chief lawyer, Joe Sandler, was detailed to recruit Richman. Ostensibly, the case was being filed by a flamboyant local Democrat in Seminole County, lawyer Harry Jacobs. But Sandler made it clear the party wanted someone dependable. "Gerry," Sandler told Richman, "there is a lawsuit pending in Seminole County, and they need a good trial lawyer to come in and take over that case and take it to trial." There was a catch, though. Gore was not going to offer any public support. The official team would keep the absentee cases at arm's length.

And it did—most of the time. Gore's team made a big deal of its distance from the case. In one meeting with the press, Gore made a point of explaining that his campaign had nothing to do with the Seminole lawsuit. "I'm not a party to it, but I've read about it," he said modestly.

But his team was doing a lot more than just following the case in the newspapers. There was a "clandestine meeting" at one point with Mitchell Berger and other Gore lawyers, Richman said afterward. Richman visited Berger's office and discussed the difficulties of finding an acceptable remedy to the problem of improper ballot requests. How could you punish the unsuspecting voters when the offense, if there was one, was committed by local bureaucrats? Berger gave him a pep talk, Richman recalled. "We're England and you're the United States," Berger said, evoking World War II. "We're beleaguered here, and you're the one that has the chance to come through."

Now this phone call came from out of the blue. "Do you need money?" the Silicon Valley billionaire asked Gerald Richman.

"Sure," Richman answered. He threw out some numbers: $50,000 in costs and $50,000 in fees.

"I'll wire $150,000 to your trust account tomorrow," said Steven Kirsch.

Kirsch also called the attorneys handling the Martin County case and wired $150,000 to them, too. He hired a public relations manager for $50,000 to get the word out on the absentee ballot cases. Suddenly, the press filled with stories about the "sleeper" cases. Kirsch hired someone to purchase computers and printers—which he paid for—to equip war rooms for the lawsuits. Kirsch was indefatigable in his support for the two cases. Eventually, a lawyer on the

case would need a plane ride to Tallahassee. Kirsch delivered a chartered jet. He constantly urged Gore's people to believe in the cases.
These were the ones that could turn everything around.

But even a man who put roughly a million bucks of his own money
into the War for Florida could not get the Democrats to embrace the
cases fully. When Kirsch got Lieberman on the phone and pressed his
theory, the hawkish running mate was noncommittal. "Thanks for
your efforts—I really appreciate your efforts," Kirsch remembered
Lieberman saying. "We're hoping for the best."

■

But the day after Kirsch called Gerald Richman was Monday, December 4, which was a terrible day for Al Gore and Joe Lieberman
and all Democrats interested in winning Florida and with it the White
House. It was the day that the U.S. Supreme Court flashed its "Go
Slow" sign in the path of the Florida justices.

It was also the day Judge N. Sanders Sauls took to the bench and
recited his grim litany of no's. No further examination of South Florida undervotes. No changes ordered in the certified election results.
No rebuke, even, to the election officials in Nassau County with their
botched mandatory recount and their ad hoc decision to restore the
original numbers—the numbers more favorable to Bush.

No. No. No.

Nothing.

Gore campaign chairman William Daley was in his Washington office when Sauls issued his ruling. He telephoned Gore. "Hey, Al," he
said.

"Well, I didn't think it went so bad—did you?" Gore joked dryly.

"No," Daley parried. "And I thought his taking a shot at your
clothes was a bit much, but the rest of the opinion I thought was
pretty moderate."

It was the day when the punditocracy concluded that time was
running out for Al Gore, with his losing contest case, his stalled re-

counts and his scolded, scalded friends on the Florida high court.

Joe Klock, the lead attorney for Florida Secretary of State Katherine Harris, looked across the Capitol plaza in Tallahassee and down a steep hill to the state Supreme Court building, and imagined that he saw three heavily armed destroyers pulling up outside the court. And though the ships did not open fire, they rode at anchor with guns primed and bristling: the *U.S.S. State Legislature*, the Florida House and Senate, ready, if necessary, to convene in special session to declare George W. Bush the winner; the *U.S.S. 11th Circuit*, the conservative federal court of appeals, which was quietly maintaining a very watchful eye over the Florida proceedings; and the *U.S.S. Supreme Court*, with its obvious skepticism concerning actions on Gore's behalf. Klock beheld this vision and concluded that the vice president's hopes were completely blockaded.

This was the day when the absentee ballot cases suddenly began to look a whole lot better, because they were very nearly Al Gore's last hope.

The seven justices of the Florida Supreme Court, all of whom had been appointed by Democratic governors, assembled on December 7 to hear oral arguments in the Florida ballot recount case. The following day, they would rule in favor of a statewide hand recount. (Scott Wiseman / The Palm Beach Post)

■

CHAPTER SIX

Hail Mary

There is a play in football called the Hail Mary, attempted only at the very end of a close game—the last, desperate play, when the trailing team sends its receivers racing to the end zone and the quarterback heaves the ball as far as he can. The odds are that the pass will fall incomplete or be intercepted, but there's nothing to lose. The pass just might connect for a touchdown, an event almost as amazing as an intervention by the Virgin Mary herself.

By the first Monday in December, Al Gore had won much, but not the victories that mattered. He had a small but indisputable lead in the popular vote. More American voters wanted him to be president than wanted George W. Bush. Take Florida out of the equation, and Gore had won more electoral votes. But not enough to be president, not without Florida. Gore also had won many court cases during the month of deadlock, and he had carried certain arguments in the court of public opinion. But he was not converting his victories into enough votes.

And so he remained behind in the decisive state by—how many votes? The answer wasn't even clear anymore. The certified results said 537 votes. But that certification was tied to a deadline created by a judicial opinion that was now vacated. What did that mean for the vote count? Perhaps the Bush lead was 930. But there were disputed vote counts and partial vote counts and repudiated vote counts to reckon with. In the last stages of America's closest election, no one

could say with certainty exactly how large or small the gap was between the would-be presidents.

Gore's lawsuit challenging the results was emphatically rejected by
Judge N. Sanders Sauls. So he lofted the Hail Mary pass. With a wink
and a nod, he approved as a team of labor lawyers and hired guns
went into the local courts of Tallahassee to try to have thousands of
absentee ballots thrown out. At the same time, Gore filed an appeal
to the Florida Supreme Court, which had helped him once and might
help him again—although there were powerful forces stacked against
another intervention.

■

Gerald Richman had filed suit challenging the actions of the Seminole County elections supervisor on Monday, November 27, the day
after George W. Bush was certified the winner of the Florida vote. By
mutual consent, the parties to a similar suit already filed agreed to
have the case moved to a Tallahassee court, where all election contests were to be heard. Richman's case charged that special favors had
been granted to the Republican Party in Seminole. Namely, the GOP
was allowed to add voter identification numbers to incomplete applications for absentee ballots. This same opportunity was denied to
Democrats, he maintained—although the Democratic forms had not
lacked any information.

Attorneys for both parties waited eagerly to learn which judge
would get the case from the computer that made the judicial assign-
ments. Judge Nikki Ann Clark's name came up, to the great satisfac-
tion of the Democrats and to the Republicans' dismay. Clark, a native
of Detroit, was a Democrat, and she was the only black woman on
the circuit court. Her resume included service to the late Democratic
Gov. Lawton Chiles, the vanquisher of Jeb Bush in his initial bid for
the Florida governor's mansion. Only a few weeks earlier, Jeb Bush,
now governor, had passed Clark over for a promotion to the local appeals court. Tallahassee buzzed with speculation that Clark might

have her revenge. If any judge might use the bench to elect Gore, Clark seemed like a good possibility.

Certainly the Bush camp believed that she might. In fact, they were so worried that over the next week attorneys for Bush and the state Republican Party worked desperately to get Clark off the case. They asked the judge to recuse herself. When she refused, they asked an appeals court panel to order her to step aside, and when that didn't work they took their case to the full court of appeals. They just wouldn't give up. When the appeals court backed Clark, the Bush team tried to have the case consolidated with Gore's lawsuit before Judge Sauls—and when that failed, they persuaded the Seminole County attorney to file a motion requesting a jury trial, which Clark rejected.

"It is my firm belief that Judge Clark will not provide a fair trial to the Republican Party and its nominees for president and vice president because Governor Jeb Bush did not appoint her to the First District judgeship," Florida GOP chairman Al Cardenas argued.

The Bush camp ignored the attorneys on its team who knew Clark best. The local Florida lawyers—Tallahassee litigator Barry Richard and Orlando trial lawyer Terry Young—refused to join the assault on Clark. "I think she was erroneously stereotyped by both sides," Richard said later. "She was a black woman, so she was presumed to be liberal and pro-Gore, plus she had been turned down by Jeb Bush. These are people from outside of Florida," he said of his Bush teammates, "and they don't know her from Adam."

Judge Clark was annoyed by all this, understandably—but not, she said later, for political reasons. She felt she had earned a good reputation as a judge, which was not—whatever the political lawyers might think—a partisan role. "I was surprised that someone in such a major case would think I'd be so childish and upset that I would not be able to do my job," Clark said later. "Either they had a very unfortunate misperception of what a judge's job is or they had a very unfortunate perception that I wasn't able to do my job for some reason—even though I had done my job for seven years."

Terry Young had heard a story about Judge Clark that deeply impressed him. The judge's sister, Kristin Clark Taylor, had been director of White House media relations under George W. Bush's father. And yet, Young had learned, the judge had never mentioned the connection during her interview with Jeb Bush for the appeals court job. "The interview was about me, not my sister," Judge Clark said afterward. This was a complex and dignified woman of integrity, Young concluded. But the tide of anti-Clark passion was running strong among his colleagues, who basically believed the entire Florida court system was stacked against Republicans. From James A. Baker III on down, the Bush team feared Florida judges, with few exceptions. Young wasn't willing to ride that wave of suspicion, but neither would he pretend that he could stop it.

Once Clark was finally running the trial, she made it clear from the start that she would cut no favors for the Democrats. In a pretrial hearing, the judge revealed her skepticism about finding a remedy for the absentee ballots scandal. Even if the Democrats proved that laws were broken so that GOP applications could be completed, there was no suggestion that any actual voters were involved in a fraud—or even knew that anything was wrong. The voter identification numbers that had been added to the applications were all accurate numbers identifying real voters. The ballots that were requested using these applications were then legally cast by eligible citizens. Clark was uneasy about tossing out legal ballots to correct a screw-up, or even a scandal, in the elections office.

That doesn't mean Clark wasn't troubled that the Seminole County Republicans got special treatment. In lengthy sworn testimony, taken by deposition, elections supervisor Sandra Goard acknowledged that she allowed a party operative, Michael Leach, to come to her office for long stretches of loosely supervised time. He brought his laptop, loaded with voter ID numbers, and transferred the numbers onto the incomplete applications. This had never happened before, Goard testified.

Her staff culled out the incomplete GOP forms as they arrived, storing them in a separate box for Leach. Goard ordered this done, she said, because the Republicans asked her to. There was nothing in her office's written manuals or policies to justify her actions. Indeed, she testified, her office did not have much in the way of written procedures.

The process for dealing with incomplete applications that were not from the GOP was different, she said. There, her staff tried to call the voter to get the information, but if that didn't work, the request was discarded.

With the clock ticking toward the final date for choosing electors, Judge Clark was determined to move the trial along quickly. She pushed the parties to agree to many of the key facts even before the trial began. What remained for Richman to prove was that the Democrats received disparate treatment. And if he proved that, then he had to propose a remedy. To that end, once the trial was underway, Richman called to the stand a statistician from the University of California at Berkeley who had tried to calculate the effect of the altered applications. Of the 15,000 absentee ballots cast in Seminole County, he testified, as many as 1,932 were the fruit of the altered applications. It might be possible, he said, to guess statistically how many of them were votes for Bush—and throw that many out.

This complicated theory didn't move the judge. As Barry Richard noted on cross-examination, when votes are assigned according to statistical models, real voters risk having their actual ballots counted for the wrong candidate. Voters are people, not factors in an equation, and their votes are, in the end, secret by law. "There is a distinct possibility," Richard argued, "that the voters will end up supporting a candidate they did not wish to vote for."

"Wouldn't it be easier if we just adopted your formula and skipped all of this voting business?" Richard sarcastically demanded of the expert. And though the Democratic attorneys objected, the point had been made.

Despite Clark's skepticism, there were signs throughout the trial that the Democrats had misjudged her just as the Republicans had. They evidently thought she might join them in putting on an anti-Bush show. Richman asked to have long stretches of prior testimony read into the record—all for the benefit of people watching the trial on television. Clark hauled him into her chambers for a dressing down. "Mr. Richman," she began, according to lawyers who were present, "this case is not being tried to the media. This is not the court of public opinion. This is my court." But the Democrats failed to get the picture. In closing arguments, Richman asked the judge to "send a message" with her verdict.

Again, Clark let him have it. "My job is not to send a message," the judge scolded. "My job is to rule on the case that is before me."

Her ruling was expected on Friday, December 8.

■

The members of the Bush legal team operated under a carefully enforced "no gloat" rule, so after Judge Sauls's ruling on December 4, they had to wait until they got to a conference room down the hall to express the elation they felt. There were handshakes and hugs and a sense from Barry Richard and the other Florida lawyers that the Leon Circuit Court judge had left very little room for Gore to appeal. Even though they soon would be returning to the hostile environs of the Florida Supreme Court, they were optimistic.

Bush's inner circle in Austin approached the appeal with more reservations. Campaign manager Joe Allbaugh was the most optimistic, believing Bush had a better than even chance of prevailing. Communications director Karen Hughes, remembering what the state Supreme Court had done two weeks earlier, was more nervous.

For the Gore team, the Sauls decision was most worrisome because of its potential impact on Democrats in Congress, particularly Sen. Robert C. Byrd of West Virginia and Sen. Max Baucus of Montana, who seemed the most likely to break with Gore and call for him to concede. "I'm surprised there are no defections," a senior Gore adviser said the morning afterward. But if there were no defections, there was a chorus of doubters within the party who were making their views known in the newspapers.

Micheal Whouley was disgusted at the lack of loyalty. He thought Sauls had done Gore a favor. An across-the-board rejection would require an across-the-board remedy. "The [Florida] Supreme Court is going to rule, they'll count the ballots this weekend, we'll be up" when the counting ends, he said. "And then the ball will be in the other guy's court. The Supreme Court is going to be hard-pressed not to decide that we should actually count the ballots."

Ron Klain often felt that the election dispute was like a tough primary campaign. Every few days there was a new life-or-death battle. Gore's team would score a victory, lurch forward, bog down and then the papers would be full of a new round of stories: Is it time for Gore to get out? And then they'd need another win. "Legal victories were to this process what primary victories are in the winter of a presidential campaign," Klain said later.

The extension of the deadlines was a huge public relations victory. Now Gore desperately required another win. The press was measuring Gore's life in mere hours. Klain thought their chances were good. The case before the Florida court, he believed, was "as close to bulletproof, legally and politically" as anything they'd done. While Gore was asking for a hand count of the Miami-Dade undervotes only, there was time enough, he believed, to count all the undervotes—and the overvotes—in two or three days.

The Florida Supreme Court set oral argument for Thursday, December 7, three days after the Tallahassee judge had slam-dunked the vice president.

For Al Gore, this was a period fraught with political danger. With Bush the official winner in Florida, the public opinion polls had begun to turn, if only slightly, toward the idea that Gore should concede. Gore stepped up his media campaign, enduring—among other appearances—a rather unfriendly interview with Lesley Stahl of *60 Minutes*.

"You're not really reaching the public with this argument," Stahl asserted during America's Sunday news institution. "You've been making it over and over—every vote has to be counted. There's more of a sense that you are asking to change the rules of the game. Can you go on if you lose the public?"

Gore: "The public I think has shown a remarkable amount of patience, and a determination to see that all the votes are counted. Of course it is split . . . "

Stahl: "But it's flipping. It's flipping."

Gore: "Well, you know, this isn't easy for any of us in this country, and I know that the Bush family, same as my family, is wanting this to be over. I know the American family wants it to be over. But as strongly as people feel about that, they feel even more strongly that every legally cast vote should be counted."

Stahl seemed mainly interested in getting Gore to promise a graceful concession, if and when his options ran out—which, she seemed to expect, might happen with a loss in the Florida high court later that week. But Gore set himself a much longer deadline, not days away, but weeks and weeks: "Whoever is sworn in as president on January 20 should have the support of all the people," he said. "And if that's not me, I will not question the fairness or legitimacy of the final outcome."

Two days later, still worried about rallying support, the Gore campaign sent Joe Lieberman to the Senate to buck up his colleagues. There, again, the questions focused on whether support was slipping away from the Gore effort, and whether a loss in the Florida Supreme Court would bring down the curtain.

"There is no erosion of that support," declared Thomas A. Daschle, the Democratic leader in the Senate. "There is extraordinary belief that the vice president and Senator Lieberman have conducted themselves in a way that makes us very proud." But Lieberman, more than Gore, seemed to buy the idea that the critical moment was fast approaching. "I think that we're going to put our faith in the Florida Supreme Court," he told reporters.

■

Republicans, meanwhile, played their own brand of public relations. Their strategy was to add, day by day and brick by brick, to an eventual fortress of Bush inevitability. The state legislature's GOP leaders announced on Wednesday, December 6, that they were calling the House and Senate into special session to consider the need to pick electors.

The idea to involve the legislature came from Don Rubottom, the lawyer for the Florida House and a former legislator from Oklahoma. On the morning after the election, he got to thinking about the constitutional power the state House and Senate would have in deciding how presidential electors were chosen.

That afternoon, House Speaker Tom Feeney authorized Rubottom to "sell the idea to the Governor's people," according to an e-mail Rubottom sent at 2:07 p.m. on November 8. He presented the idea to Rep. Charles Canady, who had been named legal counsel to Jeb Bush but who had not yet assumed that post. "He was appreciative and will consider it as a possible route later," Rubottom reported in his e-mail. "While there, the Governor came in, I said nothing but listened. He expressed his trust in the processes at work. I have done all I can or should and will desist from any more advocacy at this time."

Nevertheless, Rubottom continued to press his case, sending e-mails outlining the legislature's argument to Jeb Bush's acting general counsel, Frank Jimenez, and Deborah Kearney, a lawyer for Secretary of State Katherine Harris. He faxed the argument to Bush lawyer Ben Ginsberg.

Rubottom also began gathering up constitutional scholars from around the country to help the legislature, at one point inquiring whether Robert Bork, whose nomination to the U.S. Supreme Court in 1987 failed after a bitterly partisan fight, would be available. When Bork's son told Rubottom that his father was unavailable, Rubottom e-mailed back: "We would be interested to know who he might recommend as a substitute hero of the republic in this critical matter."

And soon, the Bush campaign began to warm to the idea as a counterweight to the Florida Supreme Court. After the court's first, unanimous ruling, Bush field marshal James A. Baker III had practically invited the legislature to step in, saying that the court "rewrote the legislature's statutory [election] system." He added: "So one should not now be surprised if the Florida legislature seeks to affirm the original rules."

From that point onward, the Bush campaign kept in close contact with legislative leaders. Bush lawyer George Terwilliger would offer advice. Florida GOP chairman Al Cardenas would later admit that he spoke with both Feeney and Senate President John McKay to advise them on the timing of their intervention. And Jeb Bush also would weigh in to offer cautious encouragement.

Now, on the eve of the second oral arguments before the Florida Supreme Court, the stakes were ratcheted up. Baker believed that the legislature was Bush's ace in the hole. The time had come, apparently, to play that card.

Feeney appeared braced for action, but McKay seemed less certain. "The action taken today is done so with considerable reluctance on my part, due to the potential far-reaching effects," he told reporters. But McKay said he would vote for the Bush electors if that's what it took to ensure that Florida wasn't left out of the election.

The leader of the House Democrats, Lois Frankel, was appalled. "This is a very sad day for the state of Florida and the Florida state legislature," she said. The Republican action was "unnecessary, unfair and unjust." The entire strategy, Frankel asserted, was orchestrated by Bush headquarters: "The only thing missing from the proclamation today was the postmark from Austin, Texas."

■

Barry Richard felt confident going into the second Florida Supreme Court argument. Just as a surgeon doesn't get jittery before an operation, Richard said, a lawyer who is doing what he is meant to do doesn't panic before standing up to make an argument.

He reviewed the issues and the case law. Then, as is his habit, he put together a very brief, unstructured outline of the points he needed to make so that he could "roll with the punches" coming in the form of questions from the justices. His outline was no more than two pages.

Some members of the Bush legal team thought Richard was a little too confident. They worried that he hadn't practiced his argument in a moot court setting. And they thought he was overextended—staying in court in the Seminole County case until 7 p.m. the night before the Florida Supreme Court argument.

That night David Boies ate dinner with Steve Zack, another Gore lawyer, at the Silver Slipper, a Tallahassee steak-and-potatoes restaurant popular among the legislative and lobbying crowd. The next morning he was up early in his hotel room, eating a breakfast of pretzels and Diet Pepsi and reading case law as a camera crew from *Nightline* started the day with him.

In Boies's view, the key to victory in the Florida Supreme Court was one small part of Sauls's opinion. It wasn't an entire sentence. It was one phrase of one sentence: "although the record shows voter error and/or less than total accuracy in regard to the punch-card voting devices utilized in Dade and Palm Beach counties, which these counties have been aware of for many years . . . "

That clause proved, Boies would argue, that people had cast ballots and they might not have been registered as votes, and that a manual recount could ascertain what that voter intent was. And for more than a century the case law in Florida, which he now pored over and memorized, says that the intent of the voter is paramount.

■

"Good morning, and welcome once again to the Florida Supreme Court," Chief Justice Charles T. Wells offered jauntily at the opening

of the December 7 oral argument. The election dispute had entered its
second month, and the chief's cheery greeting belied his unhappiness.
The chief was a practical man. Wells had deep roots in Central Florida. He was a Blue Key man from the University of Florida—that's
the honor society that grooms and launches Florida political careers.
After his elective ambitions went nowhere, he had made his name as
a commercial lawyer in the family firm. Wells had the drawl and good
manners and common sense of a successful Florida politician, and
when his turn came as chief justice he set out to heal some of the rifts
dividing the liberal court and the conservative legislature. This presidential election dispute was not going to help that project one bit.

Wells also had been the first person in a number of years to go
straight from practicing law to the high court without a stint as a
lower-court judge in between. He thought like a lawyer, and was
proud of it. In this case, thinking like a lawyer meant that when the
U.S. Supreme Court vacated his own court's opinion, he figured he'd
better pay attention. Lawyers learn to listen to judges. Judges, by contrast, quickly grow accustomed to having everyone listening to them.

"Mr. Boies, let me start right off," Wells said as soon as Vice President Gore's lawyer had introduced himself. "You know," the justice
said, "when the case was here previously . . . no counsel for any party,
in briefs or in argument, raised with this court [the case] of *McPherson v. Blacker*. . . .

"However, that case was forcefully argued to the U.S. Supreme
Court and the U.S. Supreme Court has now called that case to this
court's attention in the opinion that came out this Monday." Wells
began to seethe. "And now, once again," he said, "no counsel has argued that case to this court."

The 108-year-old *McPherson* case had indeed played a starring
role in the U.S. Supreme Court's opinion, latched onto by the court's
conservatives to prove that state legislatures—not state judges nor
even state constitutions—have complete power to decide how presidential electors are chosen. Wells clearly felt spanked by the high
court. And he seemed to suspect a bit of sandbagging was going on

among the lawyers. So right off the bat, in this second go-round, he voiced strong doubts that the Florida Supreme Court had much power to do anything about the election.

Of course, Boies tried to put his mind at ease. "What you're doing is you're reviewing, and reviewing in an ordinary judicial interpretation way," Boies said soothingly. "The legislature has provided this court with the authority to interpret these laws."

Wells was not placated, however, and he forcefully put the same question to every lawyer who spoke that morning, including Barry Richard on behalf of Bush and Joseph Klock on behalf of Katherine Harris. It seemed clear—to the chief justice, anyway—that the U.S. Supreme Court's decision had dramatically shifted the field of operations in Florida.

But not every justice was as struck by the high court's intervention. The next person to question Boies was Peggy A. Quince, the newest member of the Florida court, and its first black female justice. She seemed less interested in the "if" than in the "how." Gore's lawyers had come to the court asking for some 14,000 ballots to be examined. Quince wanted to know: Why stop there? Five days before the supposed deadline for choosing electors—the deadline endorsed repeatedly by Boies in his first oral argument to the Florida justices— Quince wanted to know: Why not scrutinize every undervote in the state?

As the oral argument raced by, this division in the court became more and more apparent. The newer members spent their questions on logistics: How many ballots should be examined? Why weren't they tallied earlier? Why would Judge Sauls admit the ballots into evidence and then refuse to examine them? How long would a recount take?

Justice Barbara Pariente was, in many ways, the antithesis to Wells on the court. She was from New York. She didn't drawl. She wasn't in the business of making peace with anyone. But she was like Wells that day in one key respect: Her view of the dispute was very easy to read. Pariente referred to the disputed ballots as "votes . . . that have

never been counted," an idea that was, in itself, a key bone of contention. The vast majority of the undervote ballots examined thus far
were not votes at all. Using the most liberal standard for counting,
perhaps one in four revealed a vote. Pariente's questions bristled with
indictment of Judge Sauls. "The circuit court is to do whatever is necessary to ensure . . . to ensure that each allegation in the complaint is
investigated, examined or checked," she recited from the Florida election statute. If that doesn't mean "look at the . . . . ballots," she demanded, "what does that section mean?"

Justice Harry Lee Anstead, a former trial judge with a professorial
air, took the same tack from a loftier altitude, while Justice Fred
Lewis, with the stolid air of an aging athlete, hammered on the vague
underpinnings of Sauls's ruling.

Two justices remained fairly quiet throughout: the senior member
of the court, Leander Shaw, and the second-longest serving, Major
Harding. Shaw was an imposing figure, a large man with a deep voice.
He was a veteran of the Florida civil rights movement, a former law
professor and lower court judge. Harding was a former domestic
court judge from Jacksonville. Both men had served as chief justice—
and there was something about having the top job that made a person
wary. The chief of the Florida Supreme Court has no particular power
inside the building. It's not like the U.S. Supreme Court, where the
chief largely controls who writes the opinions. The key job of the Florida chief justice is to manage the court's business, which means money,
which means lobbying the governor and legislature. The chief under-
stands not just the law, but also the consequences. Like Wells, Shaw
and Harding could see just how large a step Gore was asking them to
take. The trial court, the U.S. Supreme Court, the legislature, the executive branch—everyone was lining up against Gore at this point.

■

Ron Klain liked to think of himself as "the most optimistic man in
Goreworld." By the time the cases in Seminole and Martin counties

were being decided, he already had developed a plan to wipe out the Florida legislature's efforts to lock up a Bush victory. It was a canny strategy: In a number of Florida counties, the U.S. Department of Justice still supervised election rules because of past violations of the Voting Rights Act. Any changes in election laws in those counties had to have approval from Washington. If the legislature acted, Klain intended to challenge the move in federal court as an unapproved change in the law. (The Bush lawyers had investigated a similar tactic at an earlier stage in the dispute.)

In fact, Klain was so upbeat that, on Thursday, December 7, after the Florida Supreme Court oral argument, he called Monica Dixon at Gore's Washington headquarters and urged her to start mobilizing the troops for a new recount. We'll need planeloads of people, he told her, because we'll be counting by Saturday.

So he was shocked the next morning, when Dixon called to say she had been assigned to begin developing a concession plan. Klain was horrified. Dixon was probably Klain's best friend in the Gore circle, but now he unloaded on her viciously. Didn't she realize how demoralizing it was, how disloyal, to the people in Florida working themselves sick on this? How could she do such a thing? They should be getting ready for a fight, not for a surrender.

But in Washington, the smell of death hovered over Gore. For most of the week, interviewers had been pressing the vice president, demanding to know whether he would quit if the Florida Supreme Court went against him. That Friday morning, December 8, reporters asked George W. Bush the same question. He expressed his faith in "Jimmy" Baker and added: "The folks in Florida anticipate a decision, and they feel like our lawyers made a good, strong case. . . . It's time to get on with America's business. But we'll see what the courts decide today. . . . We're prepared to, if need be, take our case back to the [U.S.] Supreme Court."

In fact, Bush had good reason to protect his options. No matter how reluctant Chief Justice Wells appeared, he was just one vote. Don Evans, Bush's campaign chairman, had a bad feeling about the

Florida court. He was no lawyer—he had made his fortune in oil—but as he listened to the oral argument Evans noted on a legal pad which way each justice appeared to be leaning. He figured they had Wells. Leander Shaw also seemed to be with Bush, Evans jotted. But his gut told him they might have problems with the others.

The attorneys felt the same way. Thursday night, hours after the oral argument, a bipartisan bunch of big men sat down to dinner at Andrew's Capital Bar & Grill in Tallahassee, a hangout for lawyers and journalists. Irv Terrell and Phil Beck from Bush's team joined Miami Democrat Steve Zack and Boies from the Gore operation. It was just a friendly dinner among business rivals. As they ate, the lawyers handicapped the Florida court.

Boies believed that political pressure would keep his margin of victory small. But he did feel he was going to win. He put his money on a 4 to 3 margin.

And one by one, the other attorneys agreed. Beck said he had been trying all day to get the Bush people to start preparing for the resumption of hand counts. "Plan for the worst, not just the best," he counseled. But Beck could tell that many Bush volunteers considered such talk almost treasonous. The official loyalist position was simple: "There shouldn't be any counting," Beck remembered later, nor any talk about counting. So Beck assigned the planning job to himself. He worked on which standards to use for judging ballots. He calculated how many observers would be needed, and where. All because he felt certain that if Bush wasn't ready for a hand count, Boies and Gore certainly would be. "We would forfeit the field to Boies and [the counters] would do whatever Boies said to do," Beck theorized.

■

On Friday, everyone gathered around television sets shortly after noon, expecting an announcement of the verdicts in the Seminole and Martin county cases. A court spokesman stepped before the microphones and said the judges needed more time. At about 2:20 p.m., the spokesman stepped to the microphones once more.

"Good afternoon, ladies and gentlemen," said Terre Cass, the Leon County court administrator. "We have a ruling in both the Seminole County case and the Martin County case."

All week long, Judge Nikki Ann Clark had been conferring with her colleague in charge of the Martin County case, Judge Terry Lewis—the novel-writing, basketball-playing, boyish judge who'd handled the deadline lawsuit. The facts and allegations in their two cases were virtually identical. As the trials opened, they realized that the lawyers in the two cases would be the same, too. So they decided to use one courtroom to try both cases—rather than shuffling the lawyers and reporters from room to room, the two judges agreed to take turns in the same chair.

"When I got Martin, I wanted to compare notes," Lewis said later. "We had two cases with the same issues and, according to the pleadings, very similar facts. If she came to the same conclusion and interpretation of the law, that would be good. If she came to a different one, then so be it."

When the cases ended, Clark and Lewis realized they had reached the same conclusions: that something bad had happened, that "irregularities" had infected the elections offices in both counties, but that the ballots cast were accurate reflections of the intentions of legal voters. Therefore, they issued their opinions simultaneously, along with a rare joint statement, read by Terre Cass:

"Despite irregularities in the requests for absentee ballots, neither the sanctity of the ballots nor the integrity of the election has been compromised, and . . . the election results reflect a full and fair expression of the will of the voters. Accordingly, all relief requested by the plaintiffs has been denied."

Now Gore was down to his last hope.

■

On television it seemed as if the battle was over. The pundits weren't with the lawyers the night before, hadn't heard them tote up their Florida Supreme Court score cards and predict a 4 to 3 win for Gore. And so for a very long hour and a half, a widespread assumption settled in that the Florida high court would rule against Al Gore.

In Austin, one of Bush's closest aides, Karen Hughes, sat down at her computer. Hughes was a fine example of Fact Number One about Bush: Once he found someone he could trust, he stuck by that person through thick and thin. His inner circle was almost the complete opposite of Gore's, in the sense that friends of Bush remained forever, while serving Gore usually involved occasional banishment and exile. Hughes, a former television news reporter, had joined the first Bush campaign for Texas governor in 1994. She wrote his speeches and handled his press and traveled with him from one end of the state to the other. When he won, Hughes became press secretary to the governor of Texas.

Five years later, when Bush decided to run for president, it was simply a given that Hughes would handle communications. Bush didn't care that she had not played the game at the national level before. Hughes grew famous as one corner of Austin's Iron Triangle, with political strategist Karl Rove and campaign stationmaster Joe Allbaugh completing the team. And of all those closest to Bush, Hughes was the one who traveled with him every day. (Hughes even took her teenage son, Robert, out of school for the fall campaign so he could travel with his mom and learn a lifetime's worth of stuff.) She saw Bush up and down. She heard every campaign speech, and every candidate complaint. She knew when to leave the candidate alone— which, the gregarious Bush gradually learned, is one of the best traits a friend can have after a year and a half on the trail. Being a major candidate for president means somebody always wants a piece of you. "There's always somebody there," Bush reflected after the campaign. "There's always some elected official that just wants, you know—just in case things go well—just wants to be there."

She was rare among presidential press handlers—she never pretended, even for a moment, to be on the side of the press. Karen Hughes always, always was with Bush. And she did whatever needed to be done. When Bush and a ghostwriter failed to gel on a campaign memoir, Hughes pulled herself off the trail and pounded out the book. The candidate repaid her loyalty by sticking with her when it counted. In the aftermath of his disastrous New Hampshire primary, Bush heard a rising shriek from Washington for someone's head on a platter. Hughes's name was frequently mentioned. No chance. They weathered the storm together.

Now, at the computer, Hughes called up the draft of a victory speech. It was time, she figured, to get the words ready. The draft had been written by the campaign's wordsmith, Mike Gerson. But Hughes had some thoughts of her own to add—or rather, thoughts of the governor's; they'd been together long enough she had learned to think like him. She began revising heavily. Surely the end of the ordeal was near, Hughes thought. She wanted to be ready.

In Tallahassee, Frank Donatelli, an old friend of James Baker's, also waited hopefully for the release of the Florida Supreme Court decision. "We had won the Sauls decision," he recalled later. "We had won the contest case in Martin and Seminole that day." The Bush lawyers started to believe they were going to win a tripleheader. Ben Ginsberg always had believed the Florida Supreme Court was the right body to resolve the election battle, and now it looked like it might happen that way.

Then, just before 4 p.m., Richard got a call from the clerk's office: The court was reversing Sauls, 4 to 3. "Everybody was just shocked," Ginsberg said later. The legal team, about 20 people in all, jammed around the television in Ginsberg's office to watch Florida Supreme Court spokesman Craig Waters deliver the news. Still boyish at 44, Waters radiated a gee-whiz charm in the middle of the maelstrom. But as he got ready to step through the court's big metal doors, a deputy stopped him to ask: Did Waters want a bulletproof vest?

Waters shook his head no, then walked outside into the glare of television lights and the noise of chanting protesters. "That unnerved me," he said later.

As soon as Waters began reading, Boies knew he and the others had pegged it just right: The court had split 4 votes to 3, in Gore's favor. It was the young ideologues versus the older pragmatists; the new justices versus the current and former chiefs. Justices Harry Lee Anstead, Barbara Pariente, Fred Lewis and Patricia Quince had taken the court's earlier, vacated opinion and renewed it. Florida law, they asserted, preferred examining ballots over ignoring them; the law favored the will of voters over the convenience of efficiency. "The Legislature has expressly recognized the will of the people of Florida as the guiding principle for the selection of all elected officials—whether they be county commissioners or presidential electors," the four defiantly declared.

They utterly repudiated Judge Sauls's ruling, and replaced it with a sweeping order to scrutinize ballots—not just the ones in Miami-Dade County that Gore's team had asked for, but all the undervotes in Florida. The four justices took note of the fact that time was short—so short, according to the dissenting justices, that a hand count could not possibly be done with enough time left to challenge the results. However, the majority wrote:

"While we agree that practical difficulties may well end up controlling the outcome of the elections, we vigorously disagree that we should therefore abandon our responsibility to resolve this election dispute under the rule of law. We can only do the best we can. . . . We are confident that with the cooperation of the officials in all the counties, the remaining undervotes in these counties can be accomplished within the required time frame."

The justices did not offer much guidance on the standard to be used to decide what marks constituted a vote. A ballot "shall be counted as a 'legal' vote if there is 'clear indication of the intent of the voter,'" they offered. And with that, the case returned to the trial court for a massive, statewide, instant count. Stung by the reversal,

Judge Sauls quickly removed himself from the case, and the job of administering the order fell to Judge Terry Lewis.

This decision ended days of grueling debate on the Florida court, and nights of furious writing. (The justices were so worried about computer hackers that they drafted their opinions on laptops.) But it was only the beginning of the ocean of mail—paper mail and electronic mail—that buried the court. Some of it was approving, but some of it was cold with menace. "Run while you still can," one e-mail said threateningly.

In the rabbit warren of desks where the Gore team was headquartered, the ruling was greeted with cheers, hugs and highfives.

Barry Richard was shocked. The court's decision, he thought, was based on the majority's "liberal, populist" ideology and a desire to have votes counted. He was in such low spirits that he couldn't face appearing before Judge Lewis to work out the details of the recount. Instead, he asked another Bush lawyer to go in his place.

"Everybody was expecting to win in the second Florida Supreme Court hearing because I thought the law was clear and that they had put on no case," Richard recalled. "We all thought we were getting to the end at that point, and the decision was very disheartening."

At Bush headquarters, Frank Donatelli recalled, "All the air went out of the balloon." In Austin, Bush and his wife Laura were in the living room of the governor's mansion. Two photographers were there to "record the great moment," as Bush later put it. "And I'll be damned that they ruled . . . 4–3 against me in a ruling that just astounded the legal minds." Karen Hughes stopped work on the victory speech. "I just couldn't even look at it again," she later recalled.

So was Charlie Wells. Even the lawyers who, over dinner, envisioned a 4 to 3 decision did not foresee the passion with which the chief justice dissented. He launched a cry from the heart and bellowed it straight at the U.S. Supreme Court. "I want to make it clear at the outset of my separate opinion that I do not question the good faith or honorable intentions of my colleagues," Wells wrote—and then he let them have it. "My succinct conclusion is that the majority's decision

. . . has no foundation in the law of Florida as it existed on November 7, 2000, or at any time until the issuance of this opinion," Wells wrote. The court's action "propels this country and this state into an unprecedented and unnecessary constitutional crisis" that would do "substantial damage to our country, our state, and to this Court as an institution. . . . We must have the self-discipline not to become embroiled in political contests whenever a judicial majority subjectively concludes . . . it is 'the right thing to do.'"

At the core of this bitter disagreement was a question: How much evidence should Gore be required to show to win relief? To the majority, the dispute boiled down to a simple matter of doubt. Namely, were there enough unexamined ballots to shift, potentially, the result? If a hand count went in Gore's favor, could he win the election? A "yes" to these questions automatically justified a hurry-up effort to look at the ballots, the majority believed.

Wells, by contrast, thought that Florida law applied a tougher standard: Was some striking irregularity shown in the conduct of the election? "The trial judge found no dishonesty, gross negligence, improper influence, coercion, or fraud in the balloting and counting processes," he noted. The state doesn't have to count ballots simply because Gore asked them to.

But hovering over Wells's agitated opinion was the specter of the U.S. Supreme Court, whose footsteps he heard far more loudly than the other justices. "Clearly," wrote the chief, "in a presidential election, the Legislature has not authorized the courts of Florida to order partial recounts, either in a limited number of counties or statewide. This Court's order to do so appears to me to be in conflict with the United States Supreme Court decision."

The rift between the majority justices and the chief justice could not have been deeper; it burrowed past differences of interpretation to differences in core philosophy. Early in the election dispute, Bush lawyer Mike Carvin, a true-blue conservative, sized up the battlefield and concluded that the deadlock was a classic example of the gap between legal liberals and conservatives. "We talk about the law,"

Carvin said of conservatives, "and the liberals talk about doing justice." In this dramatic confrontation, the Florida court's liberals focused on the very real possibility that the elections system was veering toward an unjust result. Al Gore had carried the popular vote nationwide, and there was ample reason to believe he was the intended choice of more Floridians, too.

But, obviously, a last-minute hand count of many thousands of ballots across the state was a remedy that stretched Florida law—if it didn't, as Wells believed, remake the law completely. In the role of court conservative, Wells argued for a more cautious, constrained approach. The strict letter of Florida law, he noted, made no provision for the sort of far-reaching remedy whipped up by the majority.

The graybeards, Leander Shaw and Major Harding, were the last ones heard from. They took a third tack, the practical argument. Time, they sensed, had flat run out. To add a frantic flurry of ballot scrutiny during the long hours of a slapdash weekend was far more likely to produce confusion rather than clarity. "Speed would come at the expense of accuracy," wrote Harding with Shaw's concurrence, "and it would be difficult to put any faith or credibility in a vote total achieved under such chaotic conditions.

"The law," they noted, "does not require futile acts."

Actually, the law required whatever the majority decreed—at least until a higher court overruled them. That's the power of judges. And so no matter how electrifying the court's opinion was, the surprise gave way quickly to a fast and furious effort to get ready. In barely more than 12 hours, officials were supposed to start looking at ballots in every corner of the vast Sunshine State. The Bush lawyers rushed to get an appeal ready for the U.S. Supreme Court. At the same time, logistics experts on both sides began gathering up recount observers from every part of the country.

Gore's Hail Mary pass had been caught—but for a touchdown? It certainly looked that way that evening. Gore was not only still alive; he was closing the gap rapidly. The Florida justices had ordered that the Palm Beach hand count be certified, adding some 215 votes to

Gore's column. They ordered the inclusion of ballots already examined in Miami-Dade—roughly 20 percent of the countywide total—and decreed that ballots already counted need not be reviewed. The total impact of the orders was to cut Bush's lead to little more than 100 votes.

So it was a very jaunty Gore campaign chairman who went before the cameras at 5:30 p.m. to hail the ruling. "This decision is not just a victory for Al Gore and his millions of supporters," said the normally pessimistic William Daley. "It is a victory for fairness and accountability and our democracy itself."

Now it was time to get down to business, he continued. "We urge everyone to let the counting—supervised by the independent judiciary—proceed without interruption to a speedy conclusion," Daley said. "Let the count begin."

CHAPTER SEVEN

■

Endgame

Bright and early Saturday morning, December 9, the phone rang at Karen Hughes's house. George W. Bush was on the line. The Texas governor relied powerfully on Hughes for advice and friendship, and he often began her day with a call at dawn. "Have we won yet?" Bush asked jokingly.

If the disputed election was the first test of Bush's presidential abilities, he felt he was passing admirably. "I remained very steady," Bush said afterward, taking inventory of the things he'd done right. "I was pretty peaceful throughout. . . . I called upon the very best people I could find to solve the problem, and when called upon I was able to make decisions." Field marshal James A. Baker III, running mate Richard B. Cheney and chief of staff–designate Andrew H. Card Jr. crystallized the questions and proposed answers, and once Bush pulled the trigger, the whole team moved on.

Bush considered morale one of his most important jobs. Routinely during the War for Florida, he placed calls to people who were doing a good job pursuing his cause. After Supreme Court arguments he called his constitutional lawyer, Ted Olson, to say thanks. When a Democrat from Tallahassee, Barry Richard, did a good job for him in court, Bush called the man's house and had to convince his wife that yes, this really was George W. Bush. "Somebody had told me he had twin kids," Bush later recalled. "I said, 'It's hard to be away from your wife and the twin babies but tell your wife how much I appreciate it, tell her it's going to end. Wish her all the best. You're looking

When the election dispute moved to the Supreme Court on December 11, the fate of the candidates was left in the hands of their top litigators. For Gore, that was David Boies (top, at right), who had represented the government in the Microsoft antitrust suit. Bush's man was Theodore B. Olson (below, center), an icon of the conservative legal community who had argued 13 cases before the high court and was a friend of several of the justices.

(Bill O'Leary / The Washington Post; Stephanie Kuykendal / The Washington Post) great.'" On Thanksgiving, Bush phoned a large group of loyalists sharing a holiday dinner far from home.

So here he was, the former prep school cheerleader, trying to start a bad day on an up note for his communications director. In these waning days of the election dispute, Bush became "fully engaged," he said later. "I've got a lot of Lyndon Johnson in me, I guess. I'm on that phone: What does it mean? What are you seeing? What are you hearing?"

Bush also called Josh Bolten, his campaign policy director, who was working with Baker in Florida. Bolten gave him a pessimistic report. "I told him that counting was bad for us from a PR standpoint," Bolten remembered, "because it posed the risk that at some point Bush would fall into deficit and then we'd have serious public relations problems."

In Florida that Saturday morning, officials in nearly every county were preparing to start scrutinizing ballots, looking for uncounted votes that might just tip the election to Al Gore. When he called Hughes—"Have we won yet?"—she wondered if she had missed some big event overnight. "Not that I'm aware of yet, sir," she hedged.

Hughes wasn't in a joking mood. On Friday afternoon, Gore had been on the mat. Now, thanks to the Florida Supreme Court, he was back where he wanted to be—counting ballots.

■

Ron Klain, the hub of Al Gore's Florida wheel, had read the deeply split decision of the Florida Supreme Court with a mixture of excitement and foreboding. The excitement was simple: Just as he had expected, the Florida justices, by a 4 to 3 vote, had ordered further examination of ballots rejected as unreadable by the state's counting machines. All Gore's hopes rested on those ballots.

Klain's foreboding was more complex. Nowhere in the Florida four's opinion was there any direct mention of the fact that, just a few days earlier, the U.S. Supreme Court had vacated the lower court's previous work on the dispute. Klain wasn't sure the Florida justices intended to provoke the highest court. But as he read their opinion— and the passionate dissent of Chief Justice Wells—Klain realized that he must immediately begin preparing for a new hearing at the U.S. Supreme Court.

Meanwhile, in Washington and in Tallahassee, the Gore team began a mass mobilization, as Klain had recommended the day before. Phone calls went out to union activists and local party loyalists and Democratic attorneys around the country, pleading with them to get to Florida as quickly as possible. Observers would be needed all over the state.

Joe Allbaugh faced the same task on behalf of Bush. When the imposing Oklahoman heard the news of the Florida Supreme Court's decision, he got so angry he stalked into his cubbyhole office and fumed. Eventually, he emerged and started organizing an airlift. Allbaugh and his aides were on the phone all night rousting volunteers to come watch the counts—by Saturday morning, they had pulled in more than 450 people from across the country. "We were moving and mobilizing an army, and getting them not only there, but briefed up the next morning to go into the counties that were starting to recount," Allbaugh explained later, "and what they needed to be prepared for, and what did they need to look for, and what was the law, and what do they do in case this crops up or that crops up."

Watchers were needed in every county, and lawyers to advise the watchers, and another layer of attorneys to coordinate the lawyers, and so on. Allbaugh caught a couple of hours of sleep after 2 a.m. When he got back to the office at 6:30, he was amazed to find the first waves of recruits were already arriving. He walked into a little meeting room and there were perhaps 100 people crammed inside, sweaty and stifling, yet hanging on to each instruction.

The key, the volunteers were told, was to keep track of every interpretation by the counters, because Leon County Circuit Court Judge

Terry P. Lewis had declined the night before, when he set up the recount process, to set specific standards for counting votes. Lewis would order only that the examiners seek "the intent of the voter," whatever that might mean from ballot to ballot. For the sake of speed, though, the judge barred party observers from making objections. Instead, they were to keep a list of disputed ballots. He would let them complain later, maybe.

Bush attorney Phil Beck had protested this lack of a uniform standard—not because he thought Lewis would change his mind, but because he hoped a few U.S. Supreme Court clerks—maybe even a few justices—might be watching the proceedings on television. The seemingly hopeless issue raised by the Bush team weeks earlier in federal court—that the recounts violated equal protection standards in the U.S. Constitution—was now ripening by the minute. This hasty statewide recount would involve dozens of counties devising their own standards for discerning votes. By order of the court, roughly 20 percent of the Miami-Dade ballots would be certified according to the county canvassing board's partial count, while the rest of the Miami undervotes were to be counted in Tallahassee by an entirely different group of judges with their own set of standards. In that case, Beck believed, the standard was not even consistent in one county. "My whole point was, you must have a coherent standard that applies uniformly throughout the state of Florida," he said later.

Beck called Mike Carvin to urge that the standards issue be front and center in Bush's appeal to the U.S. Supreme Court. Carvin was already there. He had been watching the equal protection argument getting a little bit stronger—and stronger and stronger, he felt—with each step in the election dispute. Of all the lawyers in the tangled dispute, Beck mused, Carvin got the rawest treatment. Because of the battering he took in the initial oral argument before the Florida Supreme Court, Carvin had become the butt of jokes and whispers throughout the political world. Radio host Don Imus loved to dump on him. Carvin had been pulled unceremoniously from the public eye.

Yet he remained, Beck believed, one of the most creative thinkers in the crucial area of federal litigation.

Indeed, people on the Bush team began to feel that their once-doomed argument was turning into a winner. George Terwilliger and Ben Ginsberg barreled out of Lewis's courtroom so quickly that Terwilliger bumped shoulders with David Boies. Instead of apologizing, the tall, bearded Terwilliger said, "You know what, David? We just won this case."

"This is so bad it's good," Ginsberg added.

Boies looked at them as if they were crazy. "I'm sure he thought I was out of my mind," Terwilliger recalled. But as he explained to a crowd of reporters as he strode down the courthouse hallway: "It's exactly the kind of chaotic, confusing, standardless situation that we had warned the U.S. Supreme Court about."

■

Nearly five weeks after the election had ended in a virtual tie, an elections supervisor in Leon County named Ion Sancho stood up in the community room of the county public library and said simply: "The process may begin."

With scarcely a murmur, eight judges and their assistants hunkered down to tally the roughly 9,000 undervotes left unstudied when the Miami-Dade canvassing board halted its recount on Thanksgiving eve. In Duval County—greater Jacksonville—elections officials met a computer programmer from Miami bearing the software to instruct their counting machines to separate nearly 5,000 undervotes from the mountain of 292,000 ballots cast on Election Day. In Sarasota, a county judge corralled an official van and headed to a satellite office at the other end of the county to collect 65 boxes of ballots.

In Collier County, on the Gulf Coast, the canvassing board needed five hours that Saturday just to decide how to count 40 absentee ballots. "We've set up a system that has a built-in margin of error of 3 percent, one way or another," the board's chairman lamented. "To tell us on Friday to count them by Monday is ridiculous."

In Pinellas County, on Tampa Bay, Commissioner Robert Stewart pondered the recount effort and mused: "Damn, we need a better process."

And so it went all over Florida. As it was from the beginning, the reliability of hand counting was in the eye, or party affiliation, of the beholder. Democrats extolled a heroic effort moving along quickly with noble intentions. Republicans saw chaos. In Austin, Hughes felt her stomach sink as she watched on television. "Well," she thought, "once again, we're counting votes."

But no one had much chance to contemplate the matter. At 2:40 p.m., CNN reported that the U.S. Supreme Court had ordered an immediate halt to the effort. Gore was on the phone with Ron Klain when the news broke. It was the vice president's lowest moment.

In Tallahassee, the chief local judge, George S. Reynolds III, confirmed the news and issued his order 12 minutes later. At 3 p.m., court spokesman Terre Cass was once more at the microphones. "We have stayed the recount," she said.

The simmering divisions in the U.S. Supreme Court had boiled over. The stay order—and the related decision to hear oral arguments on Bush's appeal on Monday, December 11—was issued by a bare 5 to 4 majority, perfectly splitting the court's most conservative members from its most liberal ones.

The liberals reacted to the stay with a published dissent—a very rare form of writing at the Supreme Court. It read like the work of people who suspect their colleagues are not dealing with them in good faith. Citing the necessary standard for a stay order—namely, that there must be a risk of "irreparable harm" unless the action is halted—the liberals scoffed at the idea that counting ballots threatened to harm Bush. If anyone was threatened with irreparable harm it was Gore, they said, who could be deprived of his challenge if time ran out. As Justice John Paul Stevens wrote for the four: "Preventing a recount from being completed will inevitably cast a cloud on the legitimacy of the election. . . . The Florida court's ruling reflects the basic principle, inherent in our Constitution and our democracy, that every legal vote should be counted."

At that, Justice Antonin Scalia, the court's leading conservative theorist, felt he had no choice but to issue an even more unusual document—an opinion concurring with the brief, boilerplate stay order. "The counting of votes that are of questionable legality does in my view threaten irreparable harm to petitioner," he wrote, "and to the country, by casting a cloud upon what [Bush] claims to be the legitimacy of his election. Count first, and rule upon legality afterwards, is not a recipe for producing election results that have the public acceptance democratic stability requires."

In this unusually public dispute, Scalia added a so-there that his liberal colleagues could not answer. Under the court's rules, he noted, the stay grant meant that Bush had a "substantial probability" of prevailing in the case. In other words, he had five votes going into the Monday hearing. The case was Bush's to lose.

■

William Daley had just finished a joint news conference with the top House Democrat, Rep. Richard A. Gephardt of Missouri, in which they talked about Gore's solid support in Congress. Daley left the Capitol and went south a few blocks to Democratic Party headquarters, and when he arrived he got hit with news of the stay. From that upbeat note of solidarity, Daley spun right back down to his accustomed pessimism. This dispute had just about always felt like a lost cause to him.

He called Al Gore.

"He was shocked," Daley recalled. "In spite of some people saying that they thought the court would do the political thing, I think he wanted to believe they wouldn't. . . . So when they really did, he was genuinely surprised by that."

Daley was not. The son of the legendary Chicago mayor was no legal scholar—he didn't have much time for esoteric discussions of federalism or appellate jurisdiction. But he knew how to count votes. And so he told Gore: "Forget it. Five Republicans. We're going right in the tank." The decision by five Supreme Court conservatives, all appointed by Republican presidents, was enough to convince Daley that the die was cast. "They don't have to explain it to anybody, okay?" he told Gore. "They just have to write it, okay? All they have to do is find a way to say The End, and it's the end."

Gore disagreed. The issue of state sovereignty would surely peel off at least one conservative, he believed. After spending their whole careers arguing that federal courts should defer to the states, how could the rightward justices turn on a dime to overrule the Florida court?

"Forget it," Daley repeated.

In Tallahassee, Klain and Boies, the leaders of Gore's legal team, called a quick news conference. "We're obviously disappointed in the Supreme Court's decision to grant a stay against the manual recounts," Klain began. He looked tired and puffy. After being pushed out of the Gore campaign in 1999, Klain had managed to shed 30 pounds from his stocky frame, but the Florida effort had brought them all back. "Our latest information shows that 13 counties had completed or partially completed their recounts," he continued, "and in those counties, Vice President Gore and Senator Lieberman had gained a net of 58 votes. Five of those counties were heavily Republican counties, so we believe that the progress made in the count thus far indicated that we were clearly on a path for Vice President Gore and Senator Lieberman to make up the difference and to pull ahead."

Judge Lewis had ordered the night before that no partial results could be released. A Republican partisan heard Klain's statement and rushed off to file suit asking that he be held in contempt of court.

The reporters turned to Boies. What about the December 12 deadline for choosing electors—now less than 80 hours from expiring? It was a deadline Boies had vigorously espoused in his first appearance before the Florida Supreme Court nearly three weeks earlier. How

long ago that seemed now. Then, the public's tolerance for the Florida dispute seemed to be measured in hours. When the Florida justices started talking, back in mid-November, about a deadline weeks
in the future, Boies greeted it as a lifeline. Now, as one senior Gore
lawyer put it, the date loomed "like a tiger trap." It was a trap Boies
himself had helped to set.

"I think the timing issue is probably the single most disappointing
thing about what the Supreme Court has done," Boies answered. "It
has created a very serious issue as to whether that count can fully be
completed or not by December 12th."

The stay was greeted with jubilation at Bush's Tallahassee headquarters. Lawyers shouted and hugged and signed copies of the stay
order like pages from a high school yearbook. In 24 hours, they had
felt the extremes of shock, depression and desperation, of excitement
as help arrived by the planeload, of apprehension when the counting
began and now of sheer joy.

All but Bush campaign chairman Don Evans. The genial millionaire grew angry watching the Democrats' news conference. His count
didn't show Gore gaining any 58 votes. In fact, by his estimate—con-
trary to widespread assumptions—the count, if it continued, was going to ratify Bush's victory. Evans had called Bush the minute the stay
came down, and reached the governor in his car touring his Texas
ranch while chatting with Time Warner Inc.'s editorial director, Walter Isaacson, in preparation for *Time* magazine's annual "Person of
the Year" edition. Mindful that the whole scene was being watched,
Bush kept the conversation short. But later, after the journalists had
gone, Bush and Evans talked again.

"It's great news," Evans said of the Supreme Court's action. But
even if the counting resumed, he added, the standards being applied
were quite acceptable to the Bush team. Evans was an engineer, a
numbers guy, and the way the precincts were going in the Miami-
Dade hand count gave him rising confidence that Bush would not lose
votes in that county. In fact, he might even gain some. With roughly
two-thirds of the precincts counted, Evans told Bush, the Republican

had picked up 32 votes. "It was going to get close," Evans recalled, "but I was convinced that we could hold on." Others around Bush were far more dubious.

So when Evans heard Klain and Boies talking about 58 net votes for Gore—cutting the margin almost in half in just a few hours of counting—he was steamed. "We'll win the count if the count continues," he assured Bush. That, plus the show of support from Scalia made Bush feel pretty good about things. The governor decided it was time to head back to Austin. Time to get ready for the endgame.

■

One of the most substantial differences between George W. Bush and Al Gore—evident in the campaign, but now vivid in the election dispute—was the extent to which the two men tinker. Bush was reluctant to revisit decisions after he had made one he liked. He stuck by tactical decisions and, even more, he stuck by personnel decisions. Gore, on the other hand, was constantly revisiting his options. Every day, every situation, was a new set of variables requiring a new calculus. Of the two men, Gore was much more likely to shake up the organization, to juggle the lineup, to hatch a new strategy.

In the final days, this difference burst into the forefront. Although the chaos of Florida never permitted anything remotely like long-term planning, the Bush team came pretty close to that goal. There was a political operation, run in Florida by Joe Allbaugh alternating with Don Evans. The team selected a message very early, emphasizing Bush's lead and disparaging all recounts, and it stuck with that message in public.

There was a separate legal operation, divided into several divisions. One team, led by Barry Richard, handled the main cases in state court; smaller teams handled the ancillary state issues, like military ballots; and another team handled the federal case, led by Ted Olson and George Terwilliger—with help from grinds and eggheads across the country. These lawyers marched onto the field like rank upon rank of well-drilled cadets. Bush had a general counsel, Ben Ginsberg, and he had a chairman of the whole Florida effort. James Baker was a lawyer, he was a dealmaker, he was—above all else—a politician. Baker was a master manipulator of the press. He was a gambler—but poker, not roulette. He was an insider; he knew how powerful people think and act. He was experienced and cool. He had left vanquished enemies beside the road of life, and it didn't bother him. He was a partisan, a competitor, a hunter.

Once Bush had gotten his apparatus in place, the lines of command and zones of responsibility stayed fixed. Gore's organization, by contrast, devolved in certain ways over time. True, Ron Klain was always in the Tallahassee control tower, and in the early days he put together quite an efficient team of local lawyers scattered through South Florida. But as the case matured, more and more responsibility settled on one man, David Boies, who ultimately would argue Gore's cause at every level of the process, from county canvassing board to U.S. Supreme Court. Boies became the most-quoted spokesman for the campaign; he shuttled from courtroom to courtroom—and at the last possible moment, he took over the federal case, too, and had to try to master in a matter of hours territory that Bush's federal team had been marking for weeks.

This happened because Gore decided to tinker. Soon after the U.S. Supreme Court stopped the recount and scheduled oral argument, Gore gathered his key legal advisers, in person and by phone, at his residence in Northwest Washington. Warren Christopher was there, along with Daley and Duke law professor Walter Dellinger; Klain was on the line from Tallahassee. Notably absent was Harvard professor Laurence Tribe, who had been nominally in charge, with Klain, of the federal case since the first week of the dispute.

In fact, he thought he still was in charge. On Friday, December 8, Tribe had been teaching a legal seminar when news arrived of the Florida Supreme Court victory. He called Klain, one of his star students from earlier years, to ask what role he would play in the new appeal. Klain asked Tribe to get to work right away on a brief for the inevitable appeal by Bush to the U.S. justices.

Tribe started Saturday working at home, but when the stay was ordered, he hopped a plane to Washington and checked into a suite at the Watergate Hotel. There, he resumed his frantic work—usually months, and even years, go into shaping a Supreme Court case; now, one of the most important briefs of Tribe's career was being done in a matter of hours. He got help from his vast network of former students, many of whom he had shepherded into clerkships on the high court. His closest colleague on the draft, though, was probably Tom Goldstein, who did not have the Harvard imprimatur. He was, instead, a ferocious workhorse, a self-made Supreme Court authority—and, interestingly, a former associate at David Boies's firm.

On Saturday evening, Goldstein called Tribe at the Watergate. Christopher wants to come see you, he said. Figuring that he was going to receive a pep talk from the elder statesman, Tribe said, sure, have Chris come on over. Soon the phone rang again. "A Mister Christopher is here to see you," the concierge said. Moments later, the doorbell chimed.

Christopher was dressed in a two-piece suit and expensive overcoat, which he draped over a chair. Tribe wore jeans, sneakers and a purple sweat shirt. He offered to send for coffee or soda, but the older man declined.

During the conference at Gore's house, attention had quickly settled on the question of who should argue the vice president's case. Klain was loyally and emphatically for Tribe. The professor was, after all, the most experienced and among the best regarded liberal advocates on constitutional issues of his generation. While it was true that Tribe was often quoted in the press saying disparaging things about the court's conservative members, he had a well of knowledge and a degree of confidence that was unsurpassed. Among the great lawyers Tribe had beaten before the Supreme Court was one David Boies. They had clashed in the epic oil company clash, *Pennzoil v. Texaco*—Boies's only high court case—and Tribe had won a 9–0 decision.

But Gore had misgivings about the job that Tribe had done in the first Supreme Court hearing on the election dispute. Many commentators judged the lawyer to have been glib, condescending and—on the key case of *McPherson v. Blacker*—unprepared. Bush's initial appeal had been a suit that all the law school professors said the court would never take, yet when the justices decided it, the result—though mild—was more favorable to Bush than to Gore. Maybe, Gore had thought, a different lawyer would have gotten a better result. Walter Dellinger, a longtime rival of Tribe (both men, among other conflicts, harbored ambitions of becoming Supreme Court justices themselves) underscored Gore's feelings. The upcoming oral argument, he suggested, was certain to focus on the nuts and bolts of the Florida situation. Gore would be better served by a man who knew every nuance: Boies. Christopher concurred. The vice president dispatched his gray eminence to the Watergate—sometimes being the counselor and confidante of powerful men involves doing some unpleasant work.

Christopher settled lightly onto the sofa and glanced around the room at the piles of paper. Obviously, the professor had done a great deal of work already. "I have some news to deliver that is not going to be very pleasant," Christopher said, as Tribe recalled it. "I've learned that when you have a hard message, it is best to come out and say it."

Tribe began to think this was not going to be a pep talk.

"The vice president has decided that David Boies should do the argument," Christopher said. "The vice president is a very decisive man, and when he makes up his mind about something like this, he doesn't change it." Christopher expressed his admiration for Tribe's advocacy. "But this is about Florida law and not constitutional law, and it will be better to have someone who has been on the ground."

Tribe was shocked and deflated, but he tried not to show it. "I think I maintained about as poker a face as he did," Tribe said later. He was not convinced by Christopher's explanation. After all, Supreme Court justices always care about constitutional issues, he thought. Christopher seemed to be braced for an argument, but his gravity made it clear to Tribe there was nothing to be gained. "It seemed to me that a decision had been made by the client, and there was not any point in trying to shake it," Tribe explained later. The two men agreed that Tribe should finish the brief. Eager to show his humility and team spirit, Tribe also agreed to meet with Boies Sunday afternoon and coach him on the federal issues.

The former secretary of state thanked Tribe, collected his overcoat and left the room. Soon, the phone rang again. It was Gore, calling to thank Tribe for being agreeable. "You made it very easy for Chris," he said. Tribe recalled that Gore even mentioned his win over Boies in the oil company case. "But this is a Florida matter," the vice president told him.

The phone rang again. This time it was Boies. "I'm sorry that it worked out this way. You should be doing it," he said. They arranged for Boies to visit Tribe a little after noon on Sunday. But when he arrived at the suite, Boies found the professor working frantically to meet a 4 p.m. deadline for filing Gore's brief. Boies dove in and started proofreading pages. They made the deadline, barely, then spent about two hours going over questions Boies might face the next morning. They finished around 7 p.m.

■

Ted Olson was also in Washington that day. One of the best conservative Supreme Court advocates of his generation was winding up the last day of nearly five weeks of preparation for this moment.

The open antagonism among the Supreme Court justices had a crystallizing effect for the advocates. Scalia had noted that five justices were leaning toward Bush. If Olson could hold on to them, he would win. Simple.

Boies certainly perceived this. His mission boiled down to changing one vote, and to accomplish that he first had to figure out which one. "You had to work on the assumption that there was no way you were going to get Thomas, Rehnquist or Scalia," Boies said later. These three men formed the rightward end of the court's spectrum.

Antonin Scalia, appointed by Ronald Reagan, was a stocky, gregarious man, intense, a bit show-offy perhaps, but with a great deal to show off. As a law professor at the University of Chicago, Scalia had been a leading figure in the "textualist" movement, which held that everything a judge needs to know about a law can be found in the words themselves. Historical context, legislative intent, evolving mores—none of it mattered. The law meant what it said and said what it meant. Scalia had been an enormous force on the court, not by any skill for building majorities, but through force of will and intellect. Although he would be inclined to defer to a state court on matters of state law—because the text of the Constitution says so—in this case Scalia was plainly infuriated by the latitude taken by the Florida Supreme Court justices. There was nothing textualist about their approach.

Scalia had a soul mate in Clarence Thomas, a George Bush appointee, the second African American member of the Supreme Court, and a polar opposite of the first, Thurgood Marshall. Marshall had been relaxed, informal, occasionally vociferous and always liberal; Thomas was reserved, silent on the bench and strictly conservative. He voted with Scalia in virtually every case.

Then there was Rehnquist, the chief justice. A relatively obscure Justice Department lawyer when he was promoted by Richard M. Nixon, William Rehnquist had, over nearly 30 years, exercised a slow but significant influence on the court. While most of Nixon's appointees never lived up to their president's conservative hopes, Rehnquist was a steady vote on the right at a time when the right was pretty lonely turf. Little by little, the ranks on his side grew, and Reagan made him chief in 1986. Rehnquist launched a strikingly successful campaign to reduce the number of cases the court accepted. And while his sense of the chief's responsibility—and the chief's power to control majority opinions—made him more of a compromiser than he once had been, he continued to be a sure vote for the right whenever it had a winning cause.

In sum, Boies was correct: These were three of the most reliably conservative votes in modern court history, and they were unlikely to move to his side. This left two slightly squishier justices, both Reagan appointees—Sandra Day O'Connor, the first female justice on the court, and Anthony Kennedy, arguably the court's quintessential swing vote. In the battle for the court, the team with Kennedy on it was usually the winning team. One of these two would have to be Boies's quarry.

But as the parties lined up at their seats and stood for the justices filing into the courtroom, Boies felt that his case was a long shot indeed. The stay—which stopped the ballot-counting—was an extraordinary measure, Boies felt. Once O'Connor and Kennedy had signed on to that, what chance did he have of winning them over? "If they were going to take that step," Boies said afterward, "it was going to be very hard to turn them around."

The seat next to Boies did not contain Larry Tribe. When he was bumped from the oral argument, Tribe's only request was that he be allowed to skip the public appearance. He knew that questions would come up and he would want to answer them—he would know the answer and want to burst with it—and he'd be stuck there in the second chair, silenced. Instead, he boarded a plane to meet his wife in South Florida, where he kept a second home.

Olson spoke first. He began by reminding the court of the insult it had received from the Florida justices. "Just four days" after the U.S. Supreme Court vacated the previous Florida decision, "without a single reference to this court's December 4 ruling, the Florida Supreme Court issued a new, wholesale, postelection revision of Florida's election law," Olson said, in a low, deep, unhurried voice that made everything he said seem as reasonable as the time of day.

As always, the grilling began immediately. O'Connor and Kennedy pressed Olson to explain the high court's jurisdiction in the matter. Then the momentum shifted to the liberals. John Paul Stevens, appointed by Gerald Ford, demanded to know—along with Clinton appointee Ruth Bader Ginsburg—why traditional deference to a state court should not apply here. David Souter, the apostate appointee of

George Bush Senior, pointed out that the entire hearing had to do with a Florida law that, in the contest phase, was very broadly written. It seemed, he said, to give extensive leeway to the Florida courts to examine elections.

Stephen Breyer cut to the chase.

"If it were to start up again . . . what, in your opinion, would be a fair standard? . . ." Breyer asked. He was the most junior member of the court, appointed by Bill Clinton after a distinguished career as a professor and appellate judge. Breyer, with Souter's support, had taken on the job of coaxing Kennedy or O'Connor to the more liberal side. But he knew Kennedy would not permit the examination of ballots to start up again without a consistent standard to define a vote. The question of consistent standards from county to county had been a feature in the Bush complaint from the first weekend after Election Day. Boies, when he argued to the Florida Supreme Court in November, had asked the justices then to set a standard—he suggested one favorable to Gore, of course—because he knew the issue could grow in significance. Indeed, the latest actions in Florida had given question of standards a new potency.

Why did the standards issue get stronger for Bush? Because time was running out. Differing standards, applied early in the process, could always be leveled by a judge at the end of the contest, at least in theory. But here, Bush was alleging inconsistent standards in the final contest itself. With a week left before the presidential electors would cast their votes, what assurance was there that inequalities in the counting process could be weighed, argued and—if need be—fixed? The dwindling sand in the election hourglass made it increasingly likely that varying standards would not just be used in counting—they would be certified by order of the judge. In fact, some of the ballots—the hand-counted votes from Broward and Miami-Dade—had already been certified by order of the Florida Supreme Court. There was no provision for Bush to challenge those under the court's opinion.

That was very bad for Gore. If there was a silver lining, though, this was it: The equal protection claim gave Souter and Breyer a lure to go fishing for a conservative defector. Kennedy or O'Connor might find an option that would allow them to enforce order in Florida while also tabulating the votes. So the quest for an agreeable standard became the core of the oral argument.

However, neither the Bush team nor Gore's lawyer seemed eager to move away from positions staked out weeks earlier. Lawyers for the Republicans contended that nothing but a cleanly punched card should be considered a legal vote. When Breyer pressed Olson for a standard, the Bush lawyer tried to dodge, then said: "At a minimum . . . the penetration of the ballot card would be required." Attorney Joseph P. Klock, representing Florida Secretary of State Katherine Harris, put it more strongly, citing the rules posted on voting machines. "I would hold that you have to punch the chad through," he said.

For Boies, this issue posed two big problems: First, Gore needed a very open and liberal standard to feel confident of enough new votes to win. Second, the only standard expressed in Florida law was the vague "intent of the voter" admonition. Boies worried that anything more specific might expose Gore to the potentially fatal charge that he was changing the law after Election Day. Boies saw no easy way out of this box.

So he simply refused to engage the issue, no matter how hard the justices tried. Kennedy asked Boies to translate the subjective notion of "intent" into the objective, physical realities of actual ballots. "You're not just reading a person's mind," the justice said. "You're looking at a piece of paper. And yet you say it can vary" from one counting table to the next? Boies hemmed and hawed, until a seemingly exasperated Souter broke in. He seemed to be trying to alert Boies that answering the question was vital to his chance of winning.

"I think what's bothering Justice Kennedy," Souter coached, was the variation in the counting methods. If those could be fixed, in other words, the swing vote might swing Gore's direction. "Isn't it a denial of equal protection to allow . . . variation?"

Again, Boies hemmed and hawed. The standards issue, he finally said, "is a very hard question." At that, Scalia spoke up mockingly: "You'd tell them to count every vote." The courtroom laughed at this hostile twist on the constant Gore refrain. "You'd tell them to count every vote, Mr. Boies," he repeated.

Even if Boies had developed a better answer for this inevitable question, it's not clear the answer would have mattered. The targeted justices, O'Connor and Kennedy, expressed hostility toward Gore's case on other grounds. O'Connor seemed particularly bothered by the lack of any response from the Florida justices to the court's earlier opinion. It was as if the U.S. Supreme Court was a highway patrolman who had just let a speeding driver off with only a warning, and the driver climbed back in the car and burned rubber racing away. "It just seemed to bypass [the earlier opinion] and assume that all those changes in deadlines were just fine," O'Connor complained. She seemed to have no sympathy for voters who failed to mark their ballots properly. "Why isn't the standard the one that voters are instructed to follow, for goodness sakes? I mean, it couldn't be clearer."

Kennedy, meanwhile, strongly hinted that he agreed with Bush's contention that the Florida court's actions were changes in the law, and thus impermissible under the Constitution—even without the problem of standards. "Could the Legislature of the state of Florida, after this election, have enacted a statute to change the contest period by truncating it by 19 days?" he asked Boies. "I'm not sure why, if the legislature does it, it's a new law, and when the Supreme Court does it, it isn't."

After 90 minutes, Rehnquist said brusquely: "The case is submitted." The marshal rapped his gavel.

■

And then, nothing happened.

Early Monday evening, the Supreme Court spread the word that there would be no decision that day. It was perhaps the quietest night in more than a month.

Tuesday, December 12, the waiting resumed.

In Tallahassee, the Florida House of Representatives voted to confirm a slate of Bush electors, with a few Democrats breaking ranks to join the Republicans. This was, in part, a power play—a signal to the courts that no matter what happened, Bush would remain in the ballgame. "Unless and until the United States Supreme Court guarantees us that Florida's electors are protected, then it is our duty based on the best advice we could get to move forward," House Speaker Tom Feeney explained.

For weeks, strategists on both sides had been trying to figure out what would happen if the Congress received two slates of electoral votes from Florida. The Constitution provides for Congress to tally the presidential votes in early January. But which slate would the Senate prefer? When Maria Cantwell, a Washington state Democrat, won a slim, recounted victory over incumbent Sen. Slade Gorton, Florida tacticians realized that a weird event might occur. For the first time, the new Senate would be split 50–50 between the two parties. On the appointed day for counting the electors, the deadlocked Senate would still be presided over by Vice President Gore. So if the Senate had to choose one Florida slate over the other, Gore could well be in a position to select his own electors. Presumably the House, where the Republicans still held a tiny advantage, would go for the Bush slate.

And what then? The possibilities boggled the mind. Lawyers for Jeb Bush, the Florida governor, concluded that in case of a deadlocked Congress, the slate signed by the state's executive would prevail. They researched whether the governor could be compelled to sign off on a Gore slate, and discovered a 19th-century case that suggested he could not. On that slim reed, they realized, their hopes might hang. The Democrats, meanwhile, developed an argument that their own senior state official, Attorney General Bob Butterworth, could qualify legally as the "executive" signature. Tallahassee was wet with plottings and schemes.

For every move on the chessboard, a countermove, spinning out toward infinity in the canny minds of the long-range warriors. Who had the power to end it all, to prevent war with no quarter?

Everyone waited on the Supreme Court.

It was a frozen day in Washington, under a perfect blue sky, and as the sun fell behind the Capitol it threw its twilight rays on the white marble of the court facade. The orange faded to red, to purple, to gray, to black. The television spotlights came up. Everyone waited.

In Austin, George W. Bush climbed into bed. His destiny was hanging, but he was a man of routines. He snapped on the bedside television, and waited.

In Washington, Gore worked on an Op-Ed article for *The New York Times* justifying his fight, breaking for dinner with film director Rob Reiner, an ardent supporter. The house was full of family: Gore and his wife, Tipper; three of their four children—Kristin, Sarah and Albert—Gore's best friend and brother-in-law Frank Hunger; and Gayle Romansky, Tipper's cousin. Throughout dinner, Gore kept receiving messages on the tiny e-mail transmitter that was his favorite new gadget. Gore had been bracing for the end ever since the Supreme Court stopped the counting, and Daley said, "Forget it!" The long day of waiting for an opinion further drained his hopes. If the court was going to resume the count, surely the justices would move quickly. "There was a sense that waiting till 10:30 at night was not a great sign," an aide said afterward.

The heads up came about 10 p.m. A decision was imminent. A few minutes later, the television producers burst from the court's side entrance, the one nearest the clerk's office, and sprinted toward the cameras. And as all America watched, the correspondents began reading the 65-page parcel and commenting as they went. Very quickly, they bogged down.

What the court had produced was an unlovely and hastily composed pile of opinions, dissents, half-agreements and bitter recrimina-

tions. A nation accustomed to seeing the mulled, sanded and lac-
quered work of a leisurely court now caught a glimpse of the human
passions that run upstairs, behind the marble. There was a per curiam
order, an unsigned statement for the court—this was the binding order. The three conservatives had concurred, but added more fuel.
There were dissents signed by Breyer and Souter—yet they also appeared to have joined the per curiam. Ruth Bader Ginsburg and John
Paul Stevens had filed their own dissents.

What did it all mean?

Bush watched from his bed, then hauled himself out to work the
phones. The scene on his TV set reminded him of the night more than
a month before when reporters struggled to understand a jumbled
story even as the cameras rolled. "It was hectic and chaotic and it was
as much about the news broadcasters getting the story first as it was
understanding the story and reporting it," he said later.

Campaign chairman Don Evans called from Tallahassee. "Find Olson," Bush said, meaning Ted Olson, his Supreme Court advocate.
"Find out if we won."

Bush's father, the former president, called next. "What does this
mean?" he asked.

"I think we won," answered the son. "I think this is a victory."

"Call me back when you get something," his dad said. Then
everyone was phoning from everywhere at once. Karl Rove, Bush's
political guru, was in McLean, Va. He dialed in, desperate for
analysis. Bush called Bolten at the Austin headquarters. "I told him
I read this as closing the door," Bolten said later. "He was not exul-
tant. He didn't even sound happy. He was interested in the dissents.
He was plainly interested in how the American people would feel."

At Jeb Bush's office, Frank Jimenez scrambled to get a copy of the
opinions. Jeb needed to know if he should call his brother to offer
congratulations. The deadlock had been a period of excruciating pressure for Jeb Bush. Family loyalties pulled him one way—but that way
threatened severe damage to his own political future. If his brother
won, half the voters in his state would be angry. A good number of

them would suspect that Jeb personally arranged it. The story was Shakespearean, even biblical: The dutiful younger son had been passed over in favor of the prodigal brother; the feast he had expected was being laid on for the man who, whenever they were together, couldn't resist calling him "little brother."

Jimenez skimmed the printouts. We won, he said.

Jeb phoned Austin, but he didn't connect with W. through the cacophony of calls. Several days would pass before the brothers spoke.

James Baker was in Tallahassee with Allbaugh and Evans and the legal team. They got Olson on the speakerphone. A dozen people were channel-flipping and speed-reading. With each passing minute, they grew more confident. Finally, Baker took one last scan around the room, seeking nods of agreement. Then he placed the call.

"Congratulations, Mister President-elect," he said.

■

Ron Klain grabbed the pages as they spilled from the fax machine. The Supreme Court Web site was jammed and crashing. A fax from Washington was the quickest way to get the opinions. He was looking desperately for any sign of a crack in the court's conservative alliance. When he got the heads up that the decision was coming, the clerk's office indicated that there were lots of dissenting and concurring opinions, and that made him hopeful that the result would be shaky. He read the pages aloud to his weary colleagues in the back room of Dexter Douglass's one-story, peach-colored office in Tallahassee. Even as he read, the lawyers started buzzing about their next brief.

Page by page, the contours of the decision began to take shape in Klain's head. The opinion, he felt, was thin and unsound. Indeed, it seemed that the only thing David Souter and Stephen Breyer had accomplished by their attempts to set a counting standard was to create a fleeting 7–2 majority for the idea that the earlier count violated the Constitution's equal protection clause. "The only disagreement," wrote the per curiam opinion's anonymous author, "is as to the remedy." Of course, the remedy in this case—to count or not to count—was no small matter. Breyer and Souter made clear in their dissenting opinions—and they did not style them as "dissenting in part," just plain dissents—that if they agreed with the majority on anything, it was only a tiny sliver. They did not even think the court should have involved itself to begin with. "What it does today," Breyer wrote, "the Court should have left undone. I would repair the damage done as best we now can, by permitting the Florida recount to continue under uniform standards."

The conservative troika—Rehnquist, Scalia and Thomas—protested that the decision didn't go far enough. They would have preferred to decide the case on the grounds that the Florida Supreme Court changed the rules after the election was held. The most impassioned writers, though, were Ginsburg and Stevens, at the other end of the spectrum. Ginsburg argued that the court should have deferred to the authority of the state justices to decide state law. Stevens went further. "The endorsement of [Bush's] position by the majority of this Court can only lend credence to the most cynical appraisal of the work of judges throughout the land," Stevens wrote. (Two weeks later, the children of Florida Supreme Court Justice Harry Lee Anstead wrapped their father's Christmas gift in pages from Stevens's dissent.)

The targeted swing justices, Kennedy and O'Connor, did not sign any of the opinions, which apparently meant the only one they fully agreed with was the per curiam. It was the only opinion that concluded the case purely on the once scoffed-at claim of equal protection. The unsigned opinion bore the marks of hasty composition—at least one spelling error and some strange punctuation—as though the conservative bloc had fractured at the last minute. A number of former court clerks, after scrutinizing the opinions, felt certain the per curiam was the uncomfortably fast work of Kennedy, usually a slow, fitful writer.

"The recount mechanisms implemented in response to the decisions of the Florida Supreme Court do not satisfy the minimum requirement

for non-arbitrary treatment of voters necessary to secure the fundamental right" to vote, the opinion said. Furthermore, with less than
two hours left on December 12, the defects could not possibly be
remedied in time to meet the deadline for naming electors without risk
of a congressional challenge. This unsigned opinion went one step further: It asserted that the Florida courts and the Florida legislature had
expressed a desire to adhere to the December 12 deadline—although
there was no state law, and scant case law, to support this idea.

Thus, the high court majority had steered the Florida justices into
a box. On December 4, the Supreme Court had advised the state
court that postelection changes in the law were unacceptable. But
now it criticized the Florida justices for failing to set a counting standard more detailed than the vague "intent of the voter" language in
the statutes. Yet if the Florida court now tried to fix that standards, it
would be flouting the December 12 deadline.

It began to look like checkmate.

Gore joined a conference call with Daley, Christopher, Boies,
Dellinger, Klain, Tribe and other key advisers, shortly after the opinion was released. There was a mixture of panic and chaos in the air.
Things sounded worse by the minute, but still, no one had had much
time to, well, read the document. Half of what they thought they
knew, they'd heard on television. "Well, why don't we do this?" Gore
finally said. "Why don't we take a break while you guys read this
thing, and let's talk in a half-hour."

Over the next 90 minutes or so, the vice president spoke with
many lawyers, via conference calls and one to one. Their readings
were mostly bleak. Only Klain wanted to keep fighting. He was planning to put his team to work on a petition to the Florida Supreme
Court, asking it to repudiate the higher court's opinion that December 12 was final.

At about 1 a.m., after talking to Klain, Gore asked to speak to Dexter Douglass privately. If anyone knew how the Florida justices would
react to a new appeal, it was Douglass. He had been the legal adviser

to Lawton Chiles, the late governor, and he had blessed the selection of nearly every justice. Douglass took the call in his private office.

"Dexter," Gore said, "I want to talk to you about where you want to go."

"I told him I thought that the Florida court would be hard-pressed to do anything," Douglass later recounted. Even if the court defied the U.S. Supreme Court, and kept counting up to December 18 (the day the electors voted), the best Gore could hope for was a slate of disputed electors.

"It would cause one tremendous uproar," Douglass told Gore. "My own feeling is that the Florida court would not be able to go forward. I don't think they would have time to shape an opinion."

Gore was gracious. "I really appreciate your telling me exactly what you think," he said.

Very late—between 1 and 2 a.m., after his round of calls to the lawyers—Gore rang up Daley again. "Nobody's going to do anything tonight," Daley advised. If Klain wanted to keep going, let him—at least for a few more hours. "The lawyers who think we have options ought to prepare some papers," Daley said. "But let's sleep on it."

After all, a too-hasty concession had hurt Gore badly 35 days before. But the weight of the legal opinions was dire, and Daley also felt there was no point denying it. What the Supreme Court was saying, Daley felt, was simple: "You ain't going to count." Even if they managed to get the Florida justices wound up and defiant—so what? The GOP would take them straight back to Washington, where the Supreme Court would repeat: "You ain't going to count, okay? So quit bothering us."

Gore stayed up until 3 a.m., conferring, reading, analyzing. By then it was clear to him that the court had closed the door, nailed it shut and cemented the door frame. He went to bed knowing it was over, and that he would concede the election when he awoke.

■

This was a very tricky moment.

The Bush team had to figure out what to do and say. No false steps. No wrong words. It was important to get on screen hailing the opinion, to help confirm the growing sense among TV analysts that the race was over. But they could not afford to say something that might get Gore angry. The wanted him resigned, not riled.

After quickly digesting the opinions, and conducting a round of consultations, Baker decided to face the cameras with a very short statement. To have Bush himself speak before Gore could appear grasping and premature. Two sentences were drafted, one defining the decision as a 7–2 victory—certainly the most favorable possible interpretation of the angry and explosive jumble—and the other expressing hope that the election ordeal was finally near an end. Baker delivered the statement and refused to take questions. Years of sparring with reporters had taught him to think like one, and he knew the first question would inevitably be: "Is it over?" That was the one he didn't want to answer.

Some people on Bush's team suggested an expression of sympathy for Gore; that seemingly generous suggestion was shot down. It would be tantamount to claiming victory, Baker believed. Gore must be given plenty of room to make his own decision to strike the flag. It would happen, of that the Bush command was quite sure. Democratic Party Chairman Ed Rendell had already called on Gore to concede, after all. The only thing that could screw it up was if they accidentally provoked the vice president.

But the public reticence masked a private relief. Ben Ginsberg summoned the lawyers into a conference room. "You know, we've been waiting a long time to make this toast to the next president of the United States." With that, they clinked imaginary glasses and sipped imaginary champagne.

■

Ginsberg got word almost immediately that Ron Klain's team

down the street was busy working up a last-ditch appeal. That sent
Ginsberg straight to the files. He re-read the recent Florida Supreme
Court ruling, searching for footnote No. 22: "We are mindful of the
fact that due to the time constraints, the count of the undervotes
places demands on the public servants throughout the State to work
over this weekend." That seemed to say—maybe not say, but imply—
that the Florida Supreme Court thought the deadline was December
12. If the counting could continue all the way up to the 18th, why
would an opinion published on the 8th say people must work
through the weekend? It was one footnote in a dashed-off opinion,
but Ginsberg felt sure it would be enough to withstand Klain's attack—if not in Tallahassee, then in Washington. So he headed off to
Clyde's, the Florida capital's power saloon. He sympathized with the
Gore team's frame of mind, he said later: "Had the coin turned and
we were on that end, I can understand it, because you can't give up."

In Dexter Douglass's back room, Gore's legal machinery was
cranking up for one more all-nighter. About 11:30 p.m., Klain gathered the partners and associates of his "virtual law firm" and announced: "Here's what we're going to do."

There would be two lawsuits. One would address the case that the
U.S. Supreme Court had just dumped, near death, back into the Florida court's laps. Gore would argue passionately that the only issue
that mattered was the right of Florida citizens to have their ballots examined—and every legal vote counted. Neither deadlines, not convenience, nor partisan desire could overcome that priority. The second
suit would challenge the actions of the Florida legislature. Klain knew
that if Gore went back into court, the Florida Senate would immediately vote to join the state House in approving the Bush electors. That
had to be stopped.

Mark Steinberg, a partner of Klain's at O'Melveny & Myers, outlined Klain's thinking and doled out the work. Rich Cordray, an Ohio
State University professor and former Supreme Court clerk, wrote the
draft of the brief. Cordray started out hot and raised the temperature
from there.

"This Court has never . . . held that there was a hard Dec. 12 deadline," he wrote, "and Florida's elections laws cannot remotely bear such a construction." The Florida justices should make that clear. He warned that a provision designed to safeguard uncontested electors from challenges was being turned into an impediment to any challenges at all.

"A mere 'safe harbor' provision . . . cannot sensibly be transformed into a deadly vortex that sucks into its maw the rights of voters, the rights of candidates, and the legal and democratic procedures established under Florida state law."

It was a go-for-broke document. The high court wanted a ballot-counting standard? They proposed one: Count every dimple. In bold-faced, italicized type—a virtual scream by legal standards—Cordray wrote: "The Court should direct the counting of all ballots which contained a discernible indentation or mark, at or near the ballot position for the candidate." Instead of having to prove that marks on a ballot showed a voter's intention, the brief proposed turning the burden of proof on its head. Marks were assumed to be votes, unless the other side could prove that was not the voter's intention.

Shortly before dawn, Klain called David Boies, who was at home in Armonk, N.Y., outside New York City. By this time, Boies had read and reread the opinions from the night before, and "it was clear that the U.S. Supreme Court had decided that the vote counting was going to end." He was steamed. The courts in America execute people based on vague standards applied differently from case to case. That never seemed to bother the Supreme Court conservatives. It was only the counting of votes for Al Gore that disturbed them. But Boies did not see anything in the brief that would change their minds. As for the December 12 deadline—Boies still believed it had a certain validity. It might not be hard and fast in a strict legal sense, but it was a very real political deadline. By missing that, Gore had opened the battlefield for the tanks of the state legislature.

Could they fight on? Sure, Boies said. Should they? "It is not just making a decision of whether this is viable or sensible," he said later.

"It is whether the viability of it or the sensibility of it great enough to consider it. It is not just a legal question." It was a question about a divided country, and about the future of Al Gore.

All this was hashed and rehashed in early morning conference calls. At about 8:30, Daley and Gore spoke again. The spin on the morning news was "It's over," Daley noted. Even if they wanted to keep fighting, there was scant running room and vanishing support.

At 9 a.m., the senior lawyers agreed by telephone that the new lawsuits wouldn't work. For Klain, it was a crushing moment. On his wild roller coaster with Gore's campaign, he had gone from insider to exile and returned to the inside. And he came close to sinking the miracle shot at the buzzer. He arrived in Florida with Al Gore nearly 1,800 votes behind and he had helped shave that margin, at one point, to about 100. Sometimes life is not quite like a movie.

In Washington, Gore's advisers worried that the networks would push for a concession speech early in the day. Gore wanted prime time. A few feelers erased their worries. Around 9:30 a.m.—just as he had done five incredible weeks earlier—William Daley placed a call to Don Evans to arrange Gore's concession.

■

Joe Allbaugh put down the phone, walked into James Baker's office and said: "Let's go home."

Daley had told Evans, and Evans told Allbaugh that the Gore campaign was about to issue a cease-fire statement. Gore would address the nation at 9 p.m. The war was over.

At the same time, in a little room nearby, Ron Klain gathered his team and gave it the news. "I'm privileged to have worked with a group like you," Klain began. "It is time for us to stand down. This has been a difficult decision, but based on what's good for the country, and what we have before us, it's time."

Gore called the war room soon after that. Someone pressed the button on the speakerphone. Another began scribbling notes to record the moment. "Hey, Ron," Gore said in his signature deadpan, "that was some election night!" Then he turned serious. "There are no words to express my gratitude. You people are unbelievable, just unbelievable," the vice president said. "I hope and expect—in fact, I know in my heart—that you will look back on this experience as a crucible in which you were proven. Your performance was absolutely astonishing."

Dexter Douglass studied Klain's face, and he felt a wave of admiration as he saw tears well up in the eyes of the man who had held the team together.

Gore was being funny again. He said he hoped everyone would come visit him at the vice president's residence in Washington. "You'll know it," he said, "when you see a group of people shouting, 'Get out of Cheney's house!'"

When the speech ended and the phone went silent, as the lawyers shuffled from the room, one of them shouted: "Okay, let's file the brief!"

■

Austin awoke that morning to a surreal scene. An ice storm had hit overnight, and the city was glistening and silent, littered with the wreckage of snapped power lines and broken branches. Karen Hughes had been too excited the night before to go to sleep, so she sat with her husband in front of the fireplace until almost 1 a.m., talking about the wild past and a momentous future. The power failed before they went to bed, and so she couldn't set her alarm clock. It was nearly 8 a.m. when she jolted awake.

She immediately called Bush. "I've been trying" to reach you, he scolded. Gore was dropping out, and Bush needed a speech. "I showered and dressed by candlelight that morning with no heat in the house," Hughes recalled.

Throughout the campaign, Bush had presented himself as a man who knew how to bring people together. After the painfully divisive dispute, Hughes wanted to reassert that aspect of Bush's record. So she arranged for him to speak from the chamber of the Texas House of Representatives, where he had championed a good deal of bipartisan legislation. "This was not the time for celebration," she explained later. "But on the other hand, I felt that it should not be the governor alone, the lonely man." She and Bush had already arranged, more than a week earlier, for House Speaker Pete Laney—a Democrat—to introduce Bush if and when the time came.

Hughes had finished polishing the speech—the one she had abandoned in anger several days before. When the stay came and her spirits lifted, Hughes had decided that it needed a historical flourish, so she called Karl Rove, the political guru. Rove's vocation was politics, but his love was history—he had been taking classes for years at the University of Texas up the hill. "Look at the election of 1800," he told her, so she sent an aide to Rove's house to pick up a book, and she spent the day studying this bitterly contested race. Thomas Jefferson tied with Aaron Burr in the electoral college, which was, in those days, chosen mostly by state legislatures. Thrown into the House of Representatives, the dispute raged for six days through 36 ballots before Jefferson was elected the nation's third president. Hughes found the perfect sentiment in a letter Jefferson wrote soon after that: "The steady character of our countrymen is a rock to which we may safely moor. . . . Unequivocal in principle, reasonable in manner, we shall be able, I hope, to do a great deal of good to the cause of freedom and harmony." Hughes wrote the quote into Bush's speech.

In Washington, Gore worked on his own speech. When Daley arrived for lunch that day at Gore's house, he found the vice president with his familiar marking pens and easels, jotting down lines and themes and weighing them with family and friends. Other friends were faxing and e-mailing suggestions—some bitter, some grand, some designed just to help Gore laugh. The drafting went on through the afternoon and into early evening.

Loss brought out the best in Gore. His eulogy for his father was a masterpiece. The concession speech he was now completing was a concise blend of humor, grace and a touch of humility—in passing he evoked his loss in his own home state of Tennessee, a state that could have made him president regardless of Florida's votes.

His advisers were unsure, however, about his closing. Gore wanted to turn a joke on his famous campaign line from 1992: "It's time for them to go." He wanted to say: "And now, my friends, in a phrase I once addressed to others, it's time for me to go."

Daley had disappeared for most of the afternoon. Speeches weren't his thing. But now he was back, and he took in the debate. At last, he spoke up. "If you like it," Daley told Gore, "it's your goddamn speech. Give it." On that note, the vice president slipped outside to join the Christmas party in progress in a tent on his lawn.

■

Albert Arnold Gore Jr., having carried the popular vote, having come within a few hundreds ballots out of more than 100 million cast, having come within three votes of winning the electoral college, having won his case with precisely half the appellate judges he faced—eight justices out of 16 on the Florida and U.S. Supreme Courts—delivered his concession speech in an ornate office inside the Old Executive Office Building.

"Just moments ago, I spoke with George W. Bush and congratulated him on becoming the 43rd president of the United States, and I promised him that I wouldn't call him back this time," Gore began.

"Almost a century and a half ago, Senator Stephen Douglas told Abraham Lincoln, who had just defeated him for the presidency, 'Partisan feeling must yield to patriotism. I'm with you, Mr. President, and God bless you.' Well, in that same spirit, I say to President-elect Bush that what remains of partisan rancor must now be put aside."

Gore also echoed Lincoln's own words, from the grand and great Second Inaugural Address—which was also a speech of healing after a far more bitter and costly war. "Neither he nor I anticipated this long and difficult road," he said of Bush. "Certainly neither of us wanted it to happen. Yet it came . . .

"Now the U.S. Supreme Court has spoken. Let there be no doubt, while I strongly disagree with the court's decision, I accept it. I accept the finality of this outcome, which will be ratified next Monday in the electoral college. And tonight, for the sake of our unity of the people and the strength of our democracy, I offer my concession."

The word landed hard on the ears of many listeners, for much of the day had been spent by the television pundits wondering if Gore would actually concede defeat. To the last minute, theories were hatched as to how he might yet win by swaying electors to change their votes. But Gore had said it. This was a concession speech.

"This has been an extraordinary election. But in one of God's unforeseen paths, this belatedly broken impasse can point us all to a new common ground, for its very closeness can serve to remind us that we are one people with a shared history and a shared destiny. I know that many of my supporters are disappointed. I am, too. But our disappointment must be overcome by our love of country. . . .

"As for what I'll do next, I don't know the answer to that one yet. Like many of you, I'm looking forward to spending the holidays with family and old friends. I know I'll spend time in Tennessee and mend some fences, literally and figuratively."

Gore ended with the memory of the man who raised him to be president, but taught him to lose with dignity. "As for the battle that ends tonight, I do believe, as my father once said, that no matter how hard the loss, defeat might serve as well as victory to shape the soul and let the glory out. . . .

"It's time for me to go."

■

In the rush to return to Austin from Florida and Washington, some Bush soldiers found their seats in the chamber only minutes before the Texas governor began speaking.

"Our country has been through a long and trying period, with the outcome of the presidential election not finalized for longer than any of us could have ever imagined," Bush began. "Vice President Gore and I put our hearts and hopes into our campaigns; we both gave it our all. We shared similar emotions. I understand how difficult this moment must be for Vice President Gore and his family. . . . I have a lot to be thankful for tonight."

The heart of his message was a mixed promise. Bush offered himself once again—as he had in countless campaign speeches—as a man who could end the partisan rancor in the nation's capital. "The spirit of cooperation I have seen in this hall is what is needed in Washington. It is the challenge of our moment. After a difficult election, we must put politics behind us and work together to make the promise of America available for every one of our citizens. Our nation must rise above a house divided. Americans share hopes and goals and values far more important than any political disagreements. Republicans want the best for our nation. So do Democrats."

In the next breath, lest anyone forget that the GOP was back in the White House, Bush renewed his campaign agenda. For Bush, the last day of the election was the first day of a presidency—he had to begin, under inauspicious circumstances, to govern. Bush tried to begin by appealing to a national concord that time alone could validate.

"During the fall campaign, we differed about details of these proposals—but there was remarkable consensus about the important issues before us: excellent schools, retirement and health security, tax relief, a strong military and a more civil society. We have discussed our differences; now it is time to find common ground . . .

"I was not elected to serve one party, but to serve one nation," Bush continued. "The president of the United States is the president of every single American, of every race and every background. Whether you voted for me or not, I will do my best to serve your interests, and I will work to earn your respect. I will be guided by President Jefferson's sense of purpose: to stand for principle, to be reasonable in manner, and, above all, to do great good for the cause of freedom and harmony.

"I will give it my all."

■

Al Gore went home to rejoin the party on the lawn, and he laughed and danced into the night.

George Bush also went home, to a small gathering of some of the men and women who had given their all to help him across the finish line. At this gathering, there were tears. Burly, all-business Joe All-baugh was the last man you might expect to see with brimming eyes, but there he was. "Not that I walk around crying all the time," All-baugh said later. "It's just that sometimes the emotion of the moment is overwhelming."

The future president worked the room, hugging and mugging and wiping away tears with some of his most ardent supporters and ad-visers. The champagne was popped, a gift from the first President Bush to the second. The bottle from Dad had been in the house on November 7. Then it sat, unopened, for 36 of the most difficult days in American political history. Now the bubbly was poured and many took a taste.

Not George W. Bush, however. He was a teetotaler, and besides: For Bush the battle wasn't over. His work was only beginning.

A week after the Supreme Court's ruling, President-elect George W. Bush paid a visit to Vice President Al Gore at the U.S. Naval Observatory, the vice president's official residence. (Susan Biddle / The Washington Post)

EPILOGUE

■

What If?

The election of 2000 will be scrutinized and debated for generations. Did the right candidate win? Was the election stolen? Many Democrats believe it was. Republicans angrily reject that claim, but many of them were hurling charges of larceny themselves when it seemed possible that the Democrats would prevail in Florida's recount.

The vote was so close in Florida—well within any statistical margin of error, given that more than 6 million votes were cast—that whoever lost could have mustered some convincing evidence that in some measure the result was unfair.

"No matter who won Florida, the loser would have been able to say, 'Yes, but was that a real win or not?'" said Andrew Kohut of the Pew Research Center. "And people accepted that real early. By the second week or so, polls were showing that people thought it would be a flawed outcome no matter who wins." But Kohut said that while the public early on judged that Florida would produce a questionable winner, "They said whoever comes out the winner we will accept as the next president."

Some Democrats see the combination of problems that appeared to hamper African American voters in Florida's polling booths as—at least in part—a deliberate effort to suppress their impact on the election. Some Republicans see the hasty decision by the television networks to call Florida for Gore while polling booths in the state's heavily Republican Panhandle were still open as an act influenced by liberal media bias that had the effect of suppressing Bush votes.

Many of these broad allegations can be difficult to evaluate because there is little hard evidence to definitively support or refute them.

There are still serious questions to be examined about the allegations of disenfranchisement of African American voters in Florida. Computer analysis of the voting suggests that the percentage of spoiled ballots was higher in predominantly African American precincts. The U.S. Commission on Civil Rights held hearings in Florida in January and will issue a report about the state's presidential vote.

Various news organizations, including *The Washington Post*, have also launched projects to examine many of the ballots in Florida— those with more than one vote for president or those with no apparent vote for president. Eventually these investigations will provide more detailed information about what those ballots showed: how many had dimpled chads or hanging chads or obvious votes for Bush or Gore, whatever other markings were included on the ballots.

The descriptions of each ballot, which will be released publicly when completed, will enable news organizations, political scientists, elections officials and the parties to understand in detail what mistakes voters made and how votes slipped through the cracks. It will also attempt to assess the reliability of hand recounts. The findings may provide a much more detailed inventory of Florida's disputed ballots, but this inventory is not intended to "call" the election after the fact.

The role the television networks played on election night remains controversial. Not once but twice the major networks incorrectly called Florida. The networks and Voter News Service, which conducted the exit polls and provided precinct data to the networks, have acknowledged the disaster of election night. The networks face congressional scrutiny over their policies for calling state-by-state results and will undertake internal reviews that likely will affect their decision making in future elections.

Just as some Republicans blame the networks for distorting Florida's outcome, so do Democrats. What if the networks had never projected George W. Bush the winner in Florida and flashed up their graphics naming him the 43rd president of the United States? Some advisers to Al Gore believe the whole dynamic of the battle for Florida would have been different. Their argument is that, from the moment Bush was declared the president-elect, Gore was cast in the position of trying to change the outcome of the election, of trying to take something away from Bush. Had the networks simply shown the state too close to call, with Gore leading in the popular vote nationally and with neither candidate holding an electoral college majority, their task would have been more straightforward and their actions less subject to criticism.

"Had it not been called and it was just 'Dead Heat' headlines and the networks had said, 'We can't call this,' I think our fight in Florida would have been viewed a lot more legitimately," said William Daley, who was Gore's campaign chairman.

A more technical issue concerns the design of the ballots in Florida. The evidence is clear that the infamous butterfly ballot in Palm Beach County confused many voters, at least some of whom believe they voted for Patrick J. Buchanan when they intended to vote for Gore. The former vice president's advisers seriously considered whether to challenge the ballot in court but concluded there was no remedy even if they proved the ballot was illegal. Neither party had objected to the ballot.

Nearly every tactical decision made by the candidates during the last two weeks of the election comes into play as the participants replay the election. For instance, what if Gore had worked harder in his home state of Tennessee, whose 10 electoral votes would have made him president? What if Gore had poured more money into New Hampshire or West Virginia, two small states that nonetheless could have given him enough extra electoral votes to win? In fact, many Gore advisers wrote off Tennessee before the final days. They believed they had a better chance of winning other states of similar size—Wisconsin, for example—but only if they steered extra effort there. In West Virginia, they knew Gore was slipping and debated what to do about it. But to some Gore advisers, the state wasn't large enough to worry about. Florida and Michigan and Pennsylvania and other big states were more important.

Every day the participants were forced to make potentially huge decisions, with little time to think. Gore had to decide in the first days the counties in which to ask for a recount. Bush had to decide at the same time whether to go into federal court, a step that would make him the first candidate in the courts despite public warnings from his lawyers about the dangers of spiraling legal battles.

All these decisions were made with one overriding concern: How would it affect the number of votes on the scoreboard at that time? Out of those decisions have come a series of what-if questions. Lawyers, political operatives and strategists are still debating whether different decisions could have changed the outcome.

These questions include:

What if Gore had never called Bush to concede?

Gore advisers say the networks' projection of Bush as the winner put them permanently on the defensive in Florida. But the evidence shows that almost no one in either campaign monitoring the raw vote totals at that moment believed the networks' projection. Bush strategists closeted in Karl Rove's office in Austin were pleasantly surprised by the projection, but not confident about its reliability. Jeb Bush had the same reservations. Gore's boiler room team did not believe it either. But for a few crucial minutes, the team in the boiler room was not in communication with Gore and his team a few miles away at the Loew's Hotel in Nashville. In those few minutes, Gore concluded that it was unlikely that he could overtake Bush's lead in Florida and that, for the good of the country, he should concede. Gore's phone call to Bush may have done as much to give Bush the upper hand initially as the networks' projection.

Did Gore err in not asking for a statewide recount?

Gore came under heavy criticism from Republicans and some independent analysts for his decision to seek recounts in only four counties that were heavily Democratic. His critics charged that he was trying to win the presidency with selective recounts.

In practical terms, he had no alternative. There was no simple mechanism to trigger a statewide recount. State law required requests in 67 counties, with county canvassing boards given the power to determine whether to grant or reject a recount. Politically, Gore's team believed that such a move, which would have come within 72 hours after the election, would have been a public relations disaster, interpreted by opponents and even neutral observers as an effort to prolong the election unnecessarily. In fact, Gore proposed a statewide recount in his November 15 television appearance, calling on Bush to join him in a request to state officials to order one.

"The only mechanism was for both candidates to ask for a statewide recount," said Ron Klain, who led Gore's legal team in Florida. "Neither could do it alone. You had to go to 67 counties. We would have been turned down in a lot of them."

So then why didn't Bush ask for recounts to counter Gore's recounts?

Throughout the battle, newspaper editorials advocated a statewide recount as a fair—if cumbersome—way to determine the winner in Florida. For Bush, the ideal result might have been a statewide recount in which he came out ahead. That would have put an end to arguments from his opponents that he was trying to frustrate the principle of counting every vote. Had he accepted Gore's proposal and then won, all questions about the legitimacy of the outcome would have been wiped away. Or he could have sought recounts in some heavily Republican counties to offset Gore's requests in South Florida. There were several reasons why Bush's team chose not to do so. First, their own analysis of the vote on Election Day persuaded them that Bush was not likely to pick up many more votes in the most Republican counties. Second, asking for recounts—statewide or selective—would have undermined the Bush legal argument, which is that manual recounts were arbitrary and subjective, in effect creating votes rather than counting them.

"The problem was that we were dealing in a standardless world," Bush said in an interview in January. He added, "There's a difference between recounting and revoting. We survived the recounts. I didn't mind a recount."

Was GOP control of the Florida governor's office and the secretary of state's office decisive?

Gore advisers say this question hardly deserves a response because the answer is so obvious. Had the governor been a Democrat—not Bush's brother Jeb—they argue, the whole process would have unfolded differently. What is clear is that Bush enjoyed an enormous advantage because of the presence of his brother in the governor's office and Katherine Harris as secretary of state.

The role Jeb Bush and his team played in rounding up legal talent, providing political analysis and offering strategic advice is all the more clear from postelection interviews. With Jeb Bush as governor, the Republicans controlled the machinery of state government and with it the power to set deadlines, enforce election laws in ways that were beneficial to the then-Texas governor and put obstacles in Gore's path. Secretary of State Harris also relied on advice from one of the leading strategists in the state—Mac Stipanovich, a well-connected Republican lobbyist who was an ally of Jeb Bush.

Bush strategists counter that at the county level, the advantage went to Gore, that many more counties in Florida were controlled by the Democrats than by the Republicans and that the recounts were in the hands of those county officials.

There are still important questions to be answered about exactly how Jeb Bush and Stipanovich played their hands during the 36-day recount. In an interview, Stipanovich declined to detail his contact with Republican officials while working with Harris. Jeb Bush declined to provide an account of his conversations and actions during the recount, though he did allow his aides to discuss their roles.

Did Gore waste time during the "protest period" rather than moving as quickly as he could to the "contest period"?

The protest period came before Bush was certified as the winner on November 26. It was during this period that Gore sought the recounts in four counties. After certification came the contest proceeding, Gore's legal challenge to the certified results. As this argument goes, Gore allowed the protest phase to run on too long, thereby shortening the time the courts had to deal with the contest. In the end, he ran out of time and the U.S. Supreme Court shut down everything.

Gore advisers argue first that they only extended the protest phase for six days. More important, they say, those were the most productive days of the entire process because they generated so many additional votes for Gore and thereby sharply reduced Bush's margin.

They believe that a shorter period for the first recounts would have left Bush with a more substantial lead heading into the contest proceeding, creating an even greater burden on the Democrats to show they were not trying to undo a Bush victory. They also doubt that the contest proceeding would have moved as quickly through the Leon County Circuit Court of Judge N. Sanders Sauls had it begun any earlier. One way or another, they believe, they would have bumped up against the December 12 deadline for naming Florida's electors.

Bush lawyer Benjamin Ginsberg said the Bush team was surprised by the time Gore invested in the protest period, calling that decision a double-edged sword. The period did produce more votes for Gore, but Ginsberg added, "The more the counts in the counties went on, the more evident it became that it was a process made purposely random by the Gore campaign. The process was looking more and more chaotic."

Klain calls it "the best single decision we made," because of how much the initial recounts shaved from Bush's margin. "If we had gone to the contest on November 19, that certainly would have been much, much more difficult to win," Klain said.

Why didn't Gore's lawyers hold firm in their fight against overseas absentee ballots that had no postmarks?

Gore's running mate, Sen. Joseph I. Lieberman, couldn't take the heat politically when pressed about it on television. Nor could Gore's Florida chairman, Bob Butterworth. Both retreated from the campaign's decision to contest those ballots when confronted with a public relations uproar. Had Gore's team held firm, Bush might not have been awarded the extra 176 votes he ultimately received—and that might have let Gore slip ahead in the count at some point.

Did David Boies commit a major tactical error when he accepted December 12 as the deadline for resolving the dispute?

Deadlines came and went so quickly in Florida it was hard to tell at the time which ones were the most decisive. There is a line from the Florida Supreme Court decision on December 8, for instance, that offhandedly dismisses the significance of one of the deadlines for counting that the justices had set in their earlier decision on November 21. Still, there is a question of what might have happened had Boies, in oral argument before the Florida high court on November 20, not agreed so readily that December 12—the date for naming Florida's electors—was a firm deadline. What if he had held out for December 18, the day the electoral college met in the state capitals? Offered the chance to prolong the dispute until December 12 by Chief Justice Charles Wells, Boies grabbed for it as if it were a lifeline.

In the end, the U.S. Supreme Court used the December 12 deadline to shut down the whole process. By then Boies and other Gore lawyers were arguing that the hard deadline for resolving the dispute was December 18, the day the electoral college met across the country. But it was now too late. Hindsight here is certainly 20–20. At the time Wells offered December 12 as a deadline, the extra 22 days seemed an eternity. That appeared to be plenty of time, Gore advisers say, for the counties to complete their recounts and the courts to deal with any challenges.

Did either candidate out-lawyer the other?

Both candidates had superb legal representation. Almost overnight Bush and Gore assembled what will be remembered as two of the best temporary law firms ever put together. Rarely has so much legal talent pulled so many all-nighters.

Bush, however, may have been shrewder in how he structured his team, a decision to compartmentalize his talent. Bush had one set of lawyers working in the Florida state court system, another tasked to follow the action in the federal courts, including the U.S. Supreme Court. With James A. Baker III overseeing all operations in Florida— legal, political and public relations— the Bush team performed with a discipline and efficiency that impressed even the Democrats.

But the Gore lawyers also performed with great skill. David Boies put on a virtuoso performance, in the judgment of many of his colleagues, demonstrating why he has the reputation as one of the country's most skilled courtroom practitioners. But as Boies raced from county circuit court to the Florida Supreme Court to the U.S. Supreme Court, the advantages of Bush's structure began to show. Bush trusted his team. Gore second-guessed his. At the last moment, he replaced Harvard's Laurence Tribe with Boies for the final oral argument before the U.S. Supreme Court. Maybe the court would have ruled the same in any case, but the decision was an illustration of the difference between the two men seeking the presidency.

Both sides can look back at the 36 days and ask about this decision or that ruling, this legal call or that political judgment. But it is clear, in retrospect, that there were two significant turning points in the final weeks of the battle.

The first came one day after the Florida Supreme Court extended the deadline for certification to November 26 and ordered the counties to keep the recounts going. That decision came late on a Tuesday night, two days before Thanksgiving. The next day, the Miami-Dade canvassing board resumed counting, then at midday abruptly called off the count, declaring there was no way to meet even the extended deadline. The decision represented a huge setback to Gore, whose entire strategy was based on putting points on the board, as his advisers so often put it. If Miami-Dade never represented the numerical linchpin of Gore's recount strategy, the county offered the prospect of providing enough extra votes to put Gore ahead of Bush at some point before the November 26 deadline.

Democrats remain bitter over the Republican protests in Miami-Dade that day, led by a group of congressional staffers. Some of these Democrats also believe the news media underplayed the role of those staffers, arguing that had Clinton administration officials been caught doing the same thing, the coverage—and condemnation—would have been enormous. The decision to stop counting in Miami-Dade forced the Gore team to expend precious energy and resources trying to undo the action. In retrospect, they believe, they might have done better to make sure the Palm Beach canvassing board continued working on Thanksgiving and completed its work before the 5 p.m. deadline on November 26.

Even more significant, Gore advisers believe, was the December 9 decision by the U.S. Supreme Court to stop the statewide recount that had been ordered the previous day by the Florida Supreme Court. That final weekend marked a moment of maximum jeopardy for Bush, and many of his advisers knew it. They feared that at some point that weekend that Gore might pull ahead in the count, largely because they believed there were no rigorous or uniform standards for examining the ballots.

Bush campaign chairman Don Evans told Bush after the recount had been halted that day that he was convinced Bush would win if the counting were later resumed, but he was in the minority in the Bush camp. Gore strategists believe they would have pulled ahead if the counting had proceeded to its conclusion.

"They were always ahead," said Gore strategist Michael Whouley. "If we had once pulled ahead it would have changed the whole dynamic."

"I think we would have stayed ahead," Ginsberg said. "But the more arguing there was over ballots that were standardless, the messier it was and the more chaotic it was. That's really not how you want the presidency of the United States decided."

The Supreme Court's decision to stay the counting prevented that possibility from developing.

Florida exposed how fragile democracy can be—and underscored how much it depends on the faith of ordinary people that the system is fair and equitable. Many will argue that the country survived the battle just fine. There was no constitutional crisis, there were no riots in the streets. Perhaps no state could withstand the scrutiny Florida's voting system has and will continue to receive. But politicians in both major parties believe there is now a clear need to address the problems Florida exposed.

The challenges include what to do about faulty voting machines, how to improve voter education and whether oversight of elections should be lodged in the hands of partisan Republicans and partisan Democrats. And there remains unresolved what once seemed like a simple question: What constitutes a vote? Florida is hardly the only state in the country without a clear answer.

PRESIDENT BUSH ON THE FLORIDA RECOUNT

Excerpts from an interview with George W. Bush, January 11, 2001.

Q: When those first exit polls came back on Election Day and showed what they showed—

Bush: I realized it could be trouble. I heard them around noon. Right before I went [to work out]. A lot of friends were beginning to show up. And a lot of chatter and "hey" and all that. I got the smell. I got the early drifts. . . . I went to work out and went back and told Laura, "I don't know." I went into Election Day—you know, you never know in an election, but I felt great. The national polls were confirming our own polls. We had a voter turnout mechanism I thought was great. The crowds were huge. The intensity was great. But to Al Gore's credit, to his credit, he had the same thing going. Even more so in certain areas than we ever anticipated. He deserves a lot of credit for firing up his troops.

And then I went to dinner over at the Shoreline Grill. Family dinner. I had told Mother and Dad on the way over that it could be a long night. Long night—little did I realize how real that was. I meant long night that their son may not be elected president.

Q: How did they take that?

Bush: Stoically. And so was I. Let me step back and tell you I felt like I had waged the best campaign I could possibly run. I felt like I was facing formidable odds. And Laura and I talked about this that day. I said, "Honey I gave it my best shot, that's all I can do." I might have made a few tactical decisions differently, probably should have responded to some really ugly ads that came out against me, but we never really realized how much money was behind them, if you know what I mean. As a candidate, I felt like, when I was called upon to give the big speech, I gave it my best shot. At the debates, I felt like I held my own. I worked hard, went after the states we thought we had a good chance in.

So at dinner they called the three states [Florida, Pennsylvania and Michigan for Gore]. I whispered to my dad, "I'm not going to stay around, I want to go back to the mansion," and asked him if he wanted to come. And he did. So Laura and me and Mother and Dad went back to the mansion. Jeb was obviously upset, he thought Florida had been lost. . . . We went off in the corner and he said, "I'm sorry, brother," and gave me a hug and off he went. And I went back to the mansion, you know, irritated that the election had been called before the polls had been called in Florida, but realizing yet again that the exit polls tended to be fairly accurate. . . the early reads tended to be fairly accurate. [He laughs.] Like that time [on primary day] in New Hampshire when I told [chief strategist Karl] Rove, "Are you sure it's right? 18 points?" It turned out to be right on the money. . . . So we just sat there [at the mansion]. Karl kept calling with this, "Florida's wrong."

Q: Did you believe that?

Bush: I didn't know. I was, I hope so. You've got to understand my frame of mind at this point. You're like, you're spent, you've run the race, it's out of your hands. It's been in your hands for 18 months, starting with getting on the airplane in Austin, Texas, called Great Expectations or whatever we called it. I could have fumbled, I could have cursed more often, whatever. . . . I wasn't upset. I had seen victory and I had seen defeat, and defeat was settling in. You begin to think, well, gosh, if that happens, we'll spend a lot more time at the ranch. I'm always a person who looks on the sunny side of life. . . .

I wasn't the least bit bitter or angry or anything, I was just reconciled to defeat, and all of a sudden, victory was at hand, Florida's back. And then it was [tight] in all these states. It made the night a lot more interesting, obviously. I was sure we were going to win Wisconsin and Iowa and Oregon. It should have dawned on me that Vice President Gore's turnout mechanism would affect those states just like it did the other states in a very close election. Tennessee and Arkansas came in and Missouri and that obviously made it what it is.

[After the networks projected Bush the winner in Florida, Gore called Bush to concede.]

Bush: He said he was out. I can't remember exactly. It was like you know, you won. I said I know this is hard, thanks, good luck to you. It was a short conversation. And then he called back [to withdraw the concession].

Q: When you got off that call, what did you tell people?

Bush: Well Cheney was there, Mother and Dad were there, Dick and Lynne were there, Alan Simpson and Ann Simpson were there, Laura was there. And I walked in and said, "The vice president's changed. He's withdrawn [the concession]." And they said, what are you going to do? I told Jeb to get up there and find out more about Florida. At this point in time there was no accuracy of what was coming out of there. I felt it best at that point in time not to go out and make any statement. I felt it was good for the country. I did. Don [Evans, campaign chairman] went out. I went to bed. It's over. Go to bed.

The next morning Mother and Dad got up early, like I do. We're early risers. They said, we're going to Houston. We had a cup of coffee and off they went. I said, "I love you, stay in touch, keep us posted," and off they went.

Q: There had been a perception from the beginning of the campaign all the way through that you had kept [former secretary of state James A.] Baker [III] at arm's length. Then the morning when you had this problem in Florida, Baker's right back.

Bush: There was a sense that there was an issue between Baker and, not me, but the Bush family. That's not the case. Look, I was very mindful of the need to be as independent as I can possibly be when I'm asking for the vote. It's an issue that I've dealt with all my life, obviously. It's just so important for people not to assume that . . . it's very dangerous for a candidate to be stuck in the past, let me put it to you that way. Every campaign must talk about the future to be successful. That's one of the real traps of incumbency, by the way. . . .

Jimmy understood. He is a wonderful man. He offered any help any time. . . . This was easy for me to make on Baker. He's a lawyer and he's tough and he's articulate. He's a great strategist, Jimmy Baker is. . . . I'm so thankful he did it. I thought he was masterful. He had a huge influence on how things were run there. I remember watching Jimmy in the '88 campaign. He'd have a room full of operatives, the senior people reporting to him and he was just, man, he was decisive. I've always trusted him and I've always liked him and he did a fabulous job.

Q: That first day, the feeling was, this could be intense and it could be over—

Bush: Quickly. That's right. It settled in when people started focusing in on December 12, that was the date the electors had to be certified. That's when I started going to the ranch. You know, we made some early moves to show people we were engaged [in the transition]. I thought it was important that people know that I was beginning to think about putting a White House staff together. Dick [Cheney] and I were meeting all the time about the Cabinet. . . . I wanted to show movement. I wasn't trying to say I am the president.

Q: You got some criticism for that.

Bush: Yeah, we did, and I thought unfairly. It might have stopped me from talking about what I was doing publicly, but I went doing it anyway. We didn't interview people for the Cabinet, for example. Let me rephrase that. We didn't offer jobs. We talked a lot about potential Cabinet people. But I did not want the word out that Bush was picking a Cabinet while the recount was going on, but nevertheless I had to make some moves.

Q: I take it you were concerned that time was ticking away.

Bush: Absolutely. So we put a system in place. . . . The Florida operation required a huge organization. So we sent [campaign manager

Joe] Allbaugh over there. We had the legal team. It was really like a campaign in many ways. We had a support staff and field operations. Baker was perfect at managing a complex task. What made this more complicated was that there were a series of decision points where I was called upon in consultation with senior folks—Cheney on every call—to make a decision. The most notable of all was to go to the Supreme Court. . . . That was the gamble. If we lose, we're in trouble.

[Bush explained later through an aide that the most difficult decision involving the Supreme Court was whether to continue with his appeal after he had been certified the winner in Florida on November 26.]

Q: [Former Montana] Gov. [Marc] Racicot said he had dinner with you on the night of November 17. . . . He said at that dinner that he had presented his sense of how this whole process was out of control.

Bush: First of all, he is a wonderful man, and he's not one to hyperventilate. He's a pretty steady kind of western person. And he reported to me that what he had been observing just wasn't right. This is how I describe it: I'd survive any recount, I couldn't survive any re-vote, and they were re-voting. And it was political and it was chaotic and it was beyond description. He was appalled and amazed. . . . I told Karen to put him out there. This guy needed exposure.

Q: A couple of days before that Gore had gone out and proposed a statewide recount if you wanted that. You had to drive back from the ranch. Did that cause you any concern?

Bush: I can't even remember what it was about. It was nothing new, really. So long as the Florida Supreme Court was rewriting the law and people were divining intent, we had a battle on our hands. And if he wasn't willing to address that, then all the rest of it was PR. That's why I rushed back: PR.

Q: This is the first crisis of whoever was going to be the next president. What should people take from it about a Bush presidency?

Bush: That I remained very steady. That I was pretty peaceful throughout. That I called upon the very best people I could find to solve the problem and that when called upon I was able to make decisions. There were decision points. The facts were laid out, Baker laid them out, I consulted with the top folks, Cheney and Andy and others, and decided. It was a good exercise for our team.

Q: Why did you not ask for recounts of your own in different places?

Bush: Because there's a difference between recounting and re-voting. We survived the recounts. I didn't mind a recount.

Q: But you could have asked for a manual recount.

Bush: Because there's no standard. The problem was that we were dealing in a standardless world. The only area where we urged and fought hard for to make sure people got their ballots counted was the overseas ballots. That's why all this stuff going on down there in Florida, it's nothingness. They tell me we're actually gaining votes when they use the tough standard.

Q: The night of November 26, deadline hits, Katherine Harris comes out and declares you the winner in Florida. You came out and gave a speech at the Capitol. What were you trying to do with that speech?

Bush: I remember going out there. I remember being concerned that it was a weird setup. I was concerned that we were in the Capitol. I didn't know how it was going to look. I was concerned with the logistics. How's this going to work? I think it was just to draw a marker in public opinion. It was the formality. We had been saying we had won every recount, and this was another recount that we had won.

Q: Two of your advisers said that the day of the Judge Sauls ruling, that before he even finished his ruling you were on the phone with them.

Bush: Yeah, Evans and Karen. I was thrilled. As he [Sauls] was going on, it became apparent that we had won. It was such a strong ruling. Then I called Baker to thank him. Everybody was feeling great and then . . . the next Friday [December 8], Laura and I were sitting in the living room [waiting for the Florida Supreme Court to issue its decision on Gore's appeal of the Sauls decision]. Just Laura and me, and we had two cameramen getting ready to record the great moment. And I'll be damned that they ruled 5–4, no, 4–3, against me, in a ruling that just astounded the legal minds.

Q: Did you think you were possibly cooked at that point?

Bush: I knew that our decision to go to the Supreme Court now had a heck of a lot riding on it.

Q: The next morning two other people said you called them about 6:30 in the morning.

Bush: Yeah, that's right. I'm fully engaged now, that's right. I'm engaged the whole time, but I've got a lot of Lyndon Johnson in me, I guess. I'm on that phone. What does it mean? What are you seeing? What are you hearing? . . . I was on the phone all day chatting with people. Rove and I were on the phone ad nauseam.

Q: Then the Supreme Court stops the counting. Evans calls you. You're out with [*Time* magazine] at the ranch. . . . He called you a second time later in the evening and told you that you will win the recount.

Bush: That's right. We were winning. [Gore lawyer David] Boies had spun this thing that they'd gained 57 votes, which wasn't the truth, according to people down there. We'd actually picked up votes. Donnie [Evans] was very upbeat. He said, let the count go on. [I was] feeling better.

Q: Where were you when the Supreme Court ruled on [December 12]?

Bush: I was in bed with my wife. Not sleeping. Watching. And the court ruling came down and it was one of the more chaotic news moments. No one knew what they had said and networks were all spinning it different ways. A very interesting moment, I felt. It was kind of an interesting end to the campaign because it was hectic and chaotic and it was as much about the news broadcasters getting the story first as it was understanding the story and reporting it.

So I'm on the phone to Evans. I said, "Find Olson [Theodore Olson, who argued the case for Bush before the Supreme Court] and find out if we won." This is how it's unfolding on TV. My dad calls me and says, what does this mean? I said I think we won. I think this is a victory. Neither of us is a lawyer but I said I think it means the election is over. He said, call me back when you get something. I talked to Donnie [Evans]. [Baker's longtime aide Robert] Zoellick and Josh [Bolten, campaign adviser] are back there reading all the fine print. Finally it looked like our strategy had paid off, the Supreme Court had seen the wisdom of our suit.

Q: **Baker went out and gave a two-sentence statement. What was your strategy?**

Bush: I felt, our team felt that it was important for there not to be a rush to judgment, that the process was now working our way and that eventually our opponent would do the right thing. . . . Let me put it another way, it just wasn't the time to pile on. Secondly, it helped set a tone for the ending of a difficult period. I felt like the vice president's speech was very gracious. I tried to be equally as gracious, to set a tone for the country. . . . In my statement I said I believe things happen for a reason.

Q: **Did you have at that point a sense of what that reason might be?**

Bush: Yeah, I do have a sense of what that reason is. . . . The immediate reason is it will give us a chance—us being those of us who have been entrusted with power. . . to rise above the expectations of what a divided house means. And at the same time, to diminish cynicism. I believe it is an opportunity for people who go to Washington for good reasons—both Republicans and Democrats—to come together.

Q: **The last night, after the speech, you went back to the mansion for a little gathering. Others have said it was fairly emotional.**

Bush: Well it was interesting. We'd had no celebrations, no parties. I really had never hugged Karl Rove. I never thanked Joe Allbaugh. I had never thanked Karen Hughes. You never had that moment of time when you said "thanks for fighting the fight" with the soldiers with you. I gave the speech there in the chamber. On the spot, right after the speech, I'm waving and see all these faces of people who had been an incredibly important part of my life and I realized I'd never thanked them in person. They knew I loved them, but I'd never said it.

Q: What happened in the last call from Gore?

Bush: He started off with an icebreaker, something like I promise this is the only time I'll call tonight, which is good. I laughed. I love a good line. Our meeting [later in Washington] was similarly brief. There are only so many ways you can say you fought a good fight and he says you fought the good fight, you ran a good campaign. There was not that much to visit. He was very gracious. People ascribe it [the short meeting] to bitterness and chilliness. I don't feel it that way.

It's a heck of an interesting tale, isn't it?

INDEX

PUBLICAFFAIRS is a new nonfiction publishing house and a tribute to the standards, values, and flair of three persons who have served as mentors to countless reporters, writers, editors, and book people of all kinds, including me.

I.F. STONE, proprietor of *I. F. Stone's Weekly*, combined a commitment to the First Amendment with entrepreneurial zeal and reporting skill and became one of the great independent journalists in American history. At the age of eighty, Izzy published *The Trial of Socrates*, which was a national bestseller. He wrote the book after he taught himself ancient Greek.

BENJAMIN C. BRADLEE was for nearly thirty years the charismatic editorial leader of *The Washington Post*. It was Ben who gave the *Post* the range and courage to pursue such historic issues as Watergate. He supported his reporters with a tenacity that made them fearless, and it is no accident that so many became authors of influential, best-selling books.

ROBERT L. BERNSTEIN, the chief executive of Random House for more than a quarter century, guided one of the nation's premier publishing houses. Bob was personally responsible for many books of political dissent and argument that challenged tyranny around the globe. He is also the founder and was the longtime chair of Human Rights Watch, one of the most respected human rights organizations in the world.

·   ·   ·

For fifty years, the banner of Public Affairs Press was carried by its owner Morris B. Schnapper, who published Gandhi, Nasser, Toynbee, Truman, and about 1,500 other authors. In 1983 Schnapper was described by *The Washington Post* as "a redoubtable gadfly." His legacy will endure in the books to come.

Peter Osnos, *Publisher*